Jannus, An American Flier

JANNUS

UNIVERSITY PRESS OF FLORIDA

Gainesville · Tallahassee · Tampa · Boca Raton · Pensacola · Orlando · Miami · Jacksonville

an American Flier

THOMAS REILLY

02 01 00 99 98 97 6 5 4 3 2 1

LIBRARY OF CONGRESS CATALOGING-IN-PUBLICATION DATA
Reilly, Thomas, 1946–
Jannus, an American Flier / Thomas Reilly.
p. cm.
Includes bibliographical references and index.
ISBN 0-8130-1544-8 (alk. paper)
1. Jannus, Tony. 2. Air pilots—United States—Biography. I. Title.
TL540.J27R45 1997
629.13'092—dc21
[B] 97-23419

The University Press of Florida is the scholarly publishing agency for the State
University System of Florida, comprised of Florida A & M University, Florida
Atlantic University, Florida International University, Florida State University,
University of Central Florida, University of Florida, University of North
Florida, University of South Florida, and University of West Florida.

University Press of Florida
15 Northwest 15th Street
Gainesville, FL 32611

To Charlene Patricia Reilly,
a young woman who possesses wisdom far beyond her years.

Contents

Preface

FOR MOST OF my adult life, I have been involved in aviation, both avocationally and professionally. I was trained initially as a historian and was fascinated by the accounts of aviation's pioneers. As a licensed pilot of both airplanes and hot air balloons, I learned firsthand the joys and fears associated with flying. As the chief financial officer of several airlines, I witnessed the economic side of aviation.

Several years after passage of the Airline Deregulation Act, I had the opportunity to do the financial planning for a new entrant airline. All airlines, great or small, need money, and lots of it; as part of the fund-raising, I attended the Tony Jannus Awards Dinner. Each year since 1964, the coveted Tony Jannus Award has been presented to individuals for their contributions to commercial aviation. The venue for this prestigious ceremony is the Tony Jannus Awards Dinner held in the Tampa Bay area of Florida. Legendary pioneers of aviation such as Juan Trippe, founder of Pan American World Airways, Captain Eddie Rickenbacker, General James Doolittle, and Herbert Kelleher of Southwest Airlines have been past recipients.

That dinner was my introduction to Tony Jannus, and it was cursory at best. By the end of the evening, all I knew about Jannus was that he was an originator and the pilot of the world's first scheduled passenger airline, the St. Petersburg–Tampa Airboat Line. Over the next several years, I often wondered about Jannus's other accomplishments; in 1993 I decided to investigate. What I found was fascinating; Jannus was no one-trick pony. His list of achievements is extraordinary. In his *Wings in the Sun*, William C. Lazarus wrote that there were three seminal events in the early history of aviation in Florida: Robert Fowler's west-to-east transcontinental flight, which concluded in Jacksonville; the development of the Pensacola Naval Air Station; and the establishment of the St. Petersburg–Tampa Airboat Line. He was absolutely correct; all three served to give credibility to a heretofore very dangerous science. Jannus has yet to come into his rightful reputation as one of the most gifted and accomplished early American fliers.

The fliers in early American aviation were practically an extended family. Jannus crossed paths at one time or another with many of the legends of early aviation—Glenn Curtiss, the Wright brothers, Lincoln Beachey, Katherine Stinson, and Glenn Martin. Jannus was one of the American fliers who helped to alter the character of aviation forever.

Manned, powered, heavier-than-air flight began with Orville and Wilbur Wright in 1903. Many people know the story of Charles Lindbergh and his solo nonstop flight across the Atlantic in 1928, but few people know what flying was like during the first decade of flight. Pilots were still flying largely by the seats of their pants, by trial and error; there were no instruments. It was a rare day when an aviation accident resulting in death did not occur, always making front-page news. The first journeys of these men and women were only a few hundred feet at altitudes of no more than a few feet above the field, yet they were every bit as dangerous as a flight to the moon. Most of these pilots went out to a field where they built, borrowed, bought, or stole an airplane and flew it without benefit of any instruction. Once in the air, many did not know how to land and were forced to crash.

There were many excellent transitional fliers between the Wright brothers and Lindbergh. Without the experimentation, the crashes, and even the deaths of these men and women, the world of aviation would never have experienced the rapid progress that it did. Tony Jannus was not only an intrepid transitional aviator, he was one of the most exciting and dynamic fliers of his era. He was a news maker; everywhere he went, he made headlines.

Every American is familiar with the giant wide-bodied airplanes carrying hundreds of passengers, as well as routine NASA space shots.

There is little recollection or appreciation of what it was like to fly in a rickety skeleton-framed airplane constructed of bamboo, piano wire, and cloth. Capable of flying only several hundred yards, these early aircraft had neither seat belts nor licensed pilots.

In June 1995, the Air Transport Association celebrated the ten billionth passenger carried on America's airlines. The Air Transport Association forecasts that it will take only thirteen years to carry another ten billion airline passengers. Tony Jannus began all of this in January 1914 with the St. Petersburg–Tampa Airboat Line.

As I logged two years of research, reviewing thousands of primary documents, just as many newspaper and magazine articles, and hundreds of photographs, and had many conversations with people who were well-versed in early American aviation, I soon realized that the life, accomplishments, people, and tragedies surrounding this young American flier deserved much more than a few words covering his involvement with the St. Petersburg–Tampa Airboat Line. I decided to tell his story in its entirety.

MANY PEOPLE HAVE indirectly assisted in the writing of this book. I am heavily indebted to the early work of Gay Blair White. In 1952, White undertook the herculean job of collecting data to prove that St. Petersburg, Florida, was the home of the world's first scheduled heavier-than-air airline. Through perseverance and extensive research, she collected thousands of documents and written interviews with many of America's premier fliers, who had helped to shape the direction of American aviation during the first two decades of the twentieth century. Along the way, she also proved that the St. Petersburg–Tampa Airboat Line was definitely not only America's but the world's first scheduled passenger airline. Several years after her death, her children donated her collection to the Florida Aviation Historical Society, which graciously allowed me full access to her materials, as well as the rest of its archival collection.

In 1980, the directors and members of the Florida Aviation Historical Society decided to build an exact reproduction of the Benoist Model XIV, Number 43 flying boat, which made history on the world's first scheduled airline flight on January 1, 1914. After thousands of hours of research, design, and construction, this copy was flown on January 1, 1984, re-creating that historic twenty-one-mile flight. Today, this flying boat is on exhibit in the St. Petersburg Museum of History, no more than fifty feet from the spot where the world's first airline began.

This project could never have been completed without the cooperation and assistance of the St. Petersburg Museum of History, the Smithsonian Institution's National Air and Space Museum, the Curtiss Museum, College Park Museum, and the Museum of South Florida. The days I spent with Dr. George Vergara, an expert on the life of Hugh Robinson, a Jannus contemporary, provided valuable background insight into, as well as photographs of, the aviation community in St. Louis and the Midwest. The memorabilia and photographs which Lois Oeming, the daughter-in-law of Roger Jannus, generously gave to me allowed me to feel almost as if I were a part of history, as well as Tony's family, and not simply a chronicler.

The distinguished Edward C. Hoffman Sr., one of the first employees of National Airlines, a founder of the Florida Aviation Historical Society, and well-deserved recipient of the prestigious Percival Fansler Award in 1994, read the entire manuscript. He made many helpful comments but, more important, was a constant source of support throughout the entire research and writing process. *The World's First Airline*, edited by Warren J. Brown, provided a chronology of the St. Petersburg–Tampa Airboat Line and saved several steps in my research.

I am indebted to Andrei Alexandrov of St. Petersburg, Russia, for his research in the Russian State Archives. His efforts uncovered a great deal of information on Tony Jannus's activities and difficulties while working for Glenn Curtiss in Russia. This period of Glenn Curtiss's company and the relationship between the Imperial Russian Navy during the Great War and Tony Jannus has heretofore been ignored.

Thank you Marie for all of your assistance.

Lynn M. Homan graciously agreed to proofread and edit the manuscript. Because of her efforts, the final product is certainly more readable. Without her perseverance, this work would never have been completed.

1 An American Flier

HE HAD THE experience and desire to be the first flier successfully to attempt a transatlantic crossing. As early as 1912, he had started planning for the feat, but the equipment was insufficient. The flight over the Atlantic, though not practical in 1912, became a reality a few years later, when in 1919 John Alcock and Arthur Whitten Brown flew the 1,890 miles from Newfoundland to Ireland.[1] Throughout his short career, Tony Jannus was, either by design or coincidence, constantly building toward that goal.

Had Jannus lived beyond the age of twenty-seven, he would almost certainly have become one of the most famous of American fliers. R. E. G. Davies, curator of air transport at the Smithsonian Institution's National Air and Space Museum, has written, "Of all the early aviators, his career and achievements were possibly the most influential before the outbreak of the first World War. Had Jannus lived, Charles Lindbergh would have had a worthy rival."[2] He was a legitimate legend in his own time because of his exploits as well as avid coverage by the press. The abject worship of people such as his maintenance sidekick James D. Smith, affectionately know as J. D., helped enhance his fame.

A pilot in the dawn of aviation history, Jannus followed pioneers Orville and Wilbur Wright, Samuel P. Langley, and Glenn Curtiss. Without them, Jannus, Lincoln Beachey, Glenn Martin, Katherine Stinson, and other transitional fliers would never have been able to make the contributions to aviation they made. Without them, pilots such as Charles Lindbergh, Amelia Earhart, and Wiley Post would never have been able to realize their own remarkable accomplishments. Fliers of Jannus's era were the second step in the process. Lindbergh and the World War I aviators were the third step.

Jannus was a pragmatist and a dreamer. His vision of flying over the North Pole was unrealistic in 1912, but it was done only a few years later. Tony Jannus was not the only person who believed that such a flight was possible. Captain Robert A. Bartlett of Robert E. Peary's North Pole expedition party also thought it feasible. He outlined his plan to the members of the Aero Club of New England on November 30, 1912.[3] Lieutenant Commander Richard Evelyn Byrd and his pilot Floyd Bennett accomplished the feat in 1926.[4]

Envisioning the airplane as a legitimate weapon of war, Jannus argued that the United States needed to increase its inventory of military aircraft. He and Spencer Heath of the American Propeller Company urged manufacturers, fliers, and the general public to write to their congressmen complaining about the lack of preparedness of the U.S. military in the face of the wartime situation in Europe. The slogan of their unofficial organization was "More Aeroplanes and Less Grape Juice!"[5]

Jannus had the ability to take the difficult, the dangerous, and the historic and make them seem commonplace. He fervently indulged his passion for flying. A renaissance man, he was a pilot, designer, trailblazer, builder, and writer. Not only did he fly, he wrote about the art and joy of flying. Within months after his first flight, he wrote an article for *Aeronautics* in which he exhaustively discussed the merits of four-cylinder, six-cylinder, and eight-cylinder engines for use in flying machines.[6] In April 1911, he coauthored an article with W. Wilson Southard for *Aeronautics* in which they discussed the various airframes and engines on exhibit at the Washington Aeroplane Show.[7] His articles were published in *Scientific American*, one of America's leading scientific journals. He was equally adept at writing about the merits of various types of engines as at describing the miracle of flight or writing a humorous poem. Few active aviators were as prolific with the pen; many early fliers were known to use ghostwriters. Following his flight from New York to Paris, Charles Lindbergh hired *New York Times* reporter Carlisle MacDonald to author his first account of the cross-

Tony Jannus. Courtesy of the Florida
Aviation Historical Society.

ing of the Atlantic Ocean. Not so Jannus. His command of the English language was remarkable.

Jannus held the distinction of being the first American flier in the United States to be awarded a federal license to operate an aircraft. He applied for his license at the port of Tampa while flying for the St. Petersburg–Tampa Airboat Line in 1914. It was not until August 10, 1914, while he was in Ohio, that the license reached him. Jannus always encouraged the control, registration, and licensing of operators by the federal government.[8]

Henry R. Waite, a Boston-based hydroplane pilot, claimed that he had received the first federal license.[9] In February 1914, Waite went to the Steamboat Inspection Office in Boston and requested a license to operate an airplane but was informed that he did not need a license to operate a flying boat. Waite insisted that he did. On February 24, 1914, Henry Waite was issued license number 66198 and thus claimed to have the first license. Technically, Waite may have been the first person to possess a license from the federal government, but he certainly was not the owner of the first license ever issued.[10] That honor unarguably belongs to Tony Jannus.

On January 21, licenses had been requested for the pilots of the St. Petersburg–Tampa Airboat Line. The Department of Commerce had recorded the requests and issued Tony a license with the serial number 54578. Even Roger Jannus's license number 61012 predated Waite's.

Born June 22, 1889, Antony Habersack Jannus was the second son of Frankland and Emeline Carlisle Weightman Jannus. Reginald Woodcock claimed that the name was actually spelled "Janus." Woodcock wrote, "Sometime in their high school and college education period, both boys, by an odd personal fancy changed the spelling of their last name to 'Jannus.' At the death of both Tony and Roger, other surviving relatives—located in the East, acceded to the boys' whim, and inscribed their tombstone with their preferred spelling 'Jannus.' "[11] This was no capricious whim; the spelling was unarguably "Jannus." Their birth certificates, school records, and the obituary of their mother proved that the correct spelling was "Jannus."[12]

Major General Roger Chew Weightman, Tony's maternal great-grandfather, had a long line of accomplishments in his lifetime. Weightman served as a cavalry officer in the War of 1812 against England. He was elected mayor of Washington, D.C., in 1824. During the Civil War, Weightman, by then an old man, was commander of the Union troops quartered in Washington, D.C.

Tony Jannus's maternal grandfather was also an army man. Major Richard Hanson Weightman attended West Point and later served with bravery and distinction under Colonel Alexander Doniphan during the war with Mexico in 1847. Major General Roger Weightman was a staunch defender of the Union; his son Richard was not. Colonel Richard Weightman served the Confederate States of America, assigned to the First Brigade of the Missouri State Guard. Weightman lost his life during the Battle of Wilson's Creek, Missouri, on August 10, 1861, six months before his daughter Emeline Carlisle Weightman was born.[13]

Frankland Jannus, a prominent Washington, D.C., patent attorney,[14] and Emeline Weightman were married on October 25, 1883. Tony's older brother, Roger Weightman Jannus, was born on December 25, 1886. Sometime before 1902, Frankland, Emeline, and their two sons moved to New York City. Upon the death of Frankland, the family returned to Washington, D.C. When Mrs. Jannus died on March 8, 1903, Roger and Tony went to live with their mother's sister, Lillian Spalding. The Spaldings acted as the brothers' guardian, but there is no proof that they ever legally adopted the boys.[15]

Roger graduated from high school in June 1904 and entered New York Polytechnic Institute in Brooklyn, New York. In 1908, he transferred to Lehigh University in Bethlehem, Pennsylvania. Antony Jannus entered the eighth grade at Washington's Hubbard Elementary School in 1903 at the age of fourteen. Under Horton Simpson, he studied penmanship, reading, spelling, arithmetic, geography, and history. Following middle school, Tony entered the McKinley Technical High School. There he learned to play the saxophone and was a member of the school orchestra.[16] While still attending McKinley Technical School, Tony worked at a garage on First Street near V Street in Washington, developing his interest in things mechanical and his strong foundation in engine mechanics. He graduated from McKinley Technical High School on June 12, 1908, with an above-average record.[17]

Following graduation, he was hired as an engine mechanic at the Emerson Marine Engine Company.

Jannus's expertise in the field of aviation has been confirmed by a legion of early aviators. His skill as a mechanic was also highly respected by many, including the mechanics whose job it was to keep the airplanes flying. Walter E. Lees, who worked for Tom Benoist in St. Louis in 1912 and 1913, believed that Jannus was "one of the top pilots of that time, and one of the few men who knew how to get the best out of the Roberts engine."[18]

Despite his skill and safety record, Jannus could be reckless if the mood struck him. Gay Blair White related, "If there is one story, there are a score, of accounts of Tony—sitting back in his seat with arms crossed, or holding them high over his head, to signal to watchers that his plane could 'fly itself.' Men who rode with him here speak of it too; of being petrified with fear and astonishment when Tony would suddenly abandon the controls and crawl back to the engine, or gaze over the side of the airboat, at the scene below, like a spectator at a circus who had nothing to do but watch. Others tell of Tony's saying: 'Here, take the controls while I read the funnies,' or a like ridiculous thing."[19]

Jannus was frequently a jokester and a minor lawbreaker. On one such occasion in November 1913, the Benoist fliers had been working with the Benoist flying boat on the Mississippi River just off Market Street in St. Louis. Wishing a diversion, Jannus organized a duck hunting trip with H. C. Kilmer of New York City. Early on the morning of November 7, Jannus and Kilmer headed up the river to Alton, Illinois. Between the two of them, they shot eight ducks. Learning that the game warden was awaiting their return, Jannus made a short stop in North St. Louis, where he offloaded the ducks and hurriedly cleaned up his flying boat.[20] Without their feathery cargo, Jannus and Kilmer proceeded to Market Street. Met by the game warden, who insisted on searching the flying boat, Jannus acted surprised but made no objection. Not a single feather was found. Jannus and his friends had a good laugh at the game warden's expense while they feasted on their supper of roasted duck that evening.

Once, Jannus's speed found him on the wrong side of the law. The problem was not his speed at five hundred feet in the air but his heavy-footed driving of an automobile. When Tony was arraigned before Judge Henry Kimmel in the St. Louis police court on Clark Avenue, the cherub-faced aviator acted as his own attorney. The charges were exceeding the speed limit in an automobile and disregarding a policeman's signal. When asked by Judge Kimmel how he pled, Jannus responded, "Guilty your honor, but up until recently, I have been doing all of my motoring in an airplane."[21] He explained that he had not yet familiarized himself with the traffic laws. Judge Kimmel discharged Jannus, with the strong recommendation that the young aviator stop at the recorder's office and obtain a copy of the ordinances.

On September 7, 1913, Jannus took a young woman for an airplane ride against her father's wishes. His actions almost resulted in his arrest and bodily harm to the innocent Tom Benoist. Jean Baker, a fresh-faced seventeen-year-old student at the Visitation Convent in St. Louis, had previously crossed Jannus's path. Four months earlier, while in Paducah, Kentucky, she had been a passenger with Jannus on a short flight. When Jannus announced that he intended to fly the 248 miles from Paducah to St. Louis and was looking for a passenger, Jean Baker eagerly volunteered. When her parents adamantly refused to allow her to make the trip, Jannus found another passenger.[22]

It was a pleasant September afternoon when Jean Baker asked her father to accompany her to the foot of Olive Street, abutting the Mississippi River. Jannus was scheduled to fly there that afternoon, and Jean wanted to watch the exhibition. Her father consented, and the pair went off to Olive Street. The levee was crowded with people. Jean Baker, trailed by her father, pushed through the crowd and captured Jannus's attention.

"Papa," she said, "Won't you let me get in the flying boat just to have my picture taken?"[23] Seeing no harm in his daughter simply sitting in Jannus's aircraft, her father quickly gave his permission. Baker's memory must have been short; he had apparently forgotten that only a few months earlier Jean had wanted to fly and had been forbidden to do so. Jannus, Benoist, and several others pulled the flying boat against the riverbank. The smiling Jannus helped the young woman into the passenger compartment.

When Jean was comfortably situated in the flying boat, Tony suggested that the aircraft be pushed several feet into the river. "To make the picture more lifelike," he explained to the elder Baker, who approvingly nodded his head.[24] Twenty feet from the shore, Jannus cranked the engine over, pushed on the throttle, and away they went, Jannus and Jean laughing and waving their hands.

As the aircraft lifted into the air, Baker stood helplessly on the shore, angrily shaking his fists in frustration. Enraged, Baker went after the innocent Tom Benoist. Unaware of what had happened, Benoist could only suffer Baker's verbal barrage, as Baker accused him of having engineered the kidnaping and threatened to beat him to a pulp. Twenty minutes later, Jannus taxied to the foot of Olive Street. When Baker saw that his daughter was safe, his anger dissipated.

Tony Jannus's fondness for women sometimes inconvenienced people other than irate fathers. J. D. Smith told of the night he left Tony in Chicago with Ruth Stonehouse, the actress, while he accompanied the Benoist aircraft to Des Moines, their next engagement.[25] When Tony failed to make the train, Smith, with only a few cents in his pocket, beguiled the conductor with tales of Tony's exploits and persuaded him to let him leave the train at the final stop before Des Moines, then reboard and pay only the fare for the short trip to his final destination. Tony showed up the next day, contrite but confident that Smitty would manage. Because of the liaison with the actress, Jannus had missed one day of contracted flying at the opening of the Keokuk Dam in Keokuk, Iowa, in August 1912. It was something Jannus would not have tolerated from anyone else.

Much has been made of Tony Jannus's attraction to the opposite sex and theirs to him. Women at times seemed an obsession with him. He thrived on adulation. When Jannus arrived in New Orleans after flying nearly two thousand miles, he was supposedly met by a fiancée.[26] His landlady in St. Petersburg reported that when he left Florida, at least half a dozen young women had tears in their eyes; they all thought they were going to marry him. Russell Froelich, the official photographer for the Benoist Aircraft Company, was once asked about Tom Benoist's supposed romance. Froelich replied, "Nuts! This gal must be off her rocker. If Tom had a girl friend, I'd have photographed her like I did Jannus and his sweetie. Jannus had several sweeties, for he was quite a lad."[27] Even after his death, women avowed their love for Tony. Emily Prettyman of Chicago claimed that she had been engaged to be married to Jannus. She told a newspaper, "I won't give up hope . . . I will believe Anthony Jannus alive unless his reported death is confirmed officially."[28] There is no proof that Jannus was ever engaged to Emily Prettyman or that he even knew her. It may have been a case of wishful thinking or hero worship from afar.

Jannus always had faithful supporters, and he frequently traveled with an entourage. J. D. Smith, his mechanic for several years, was always at his side, more than willing to do his bidding. Ever protective of Jannus, Smith cautioned exhibition onlookers at the Detroit State Fair in 1913, "Please don't get away from the fence when he starts to come down . . . you might hurt him." At the same event, Jannus said of Smith, "If I didn't have him, I would have to do all the work myself. It is a matter of life and death with me. But when old Schmitty is on the job, there is no use worrying."[29] Selflessly, Tony never hesitated to give credit to those who deserved it. W. H. Burke, the president of the Roberts company, advised Smith, "Jannus has always expressed the fact that you were the best mechanic that he had ever employed and that when anything was entrusted to you he could be assured that it would be taken care of properly."[30]

Fame followed Jannus from Washington to St. Louis, to New Orleans, to St. Petersburg. Stories of his exploits appeared in hundreds of newspapers and magazines. From his very first flight, he was the center of attention. During the years that Rexford Smith had a flying operation at College Park, several fliers flew his airplanes, but none of his pilots became as well-known as Tony Jannus.

Whether Roger Jannus resented his younger brother's role as primus inter pares is unknown. Tony was highly motivated and dynamic by nature. He was never a follower but always destined to be out in front. Roger, although three years older, often acted as if he were the younger brother. Even Tom Benoist, fifteen years older than Jannus and the owner of his own company, was frequently eclipsed by the supremely confident Tony. Benoist manufactured hundreds of aircraft and just as many aviators flew his equipment. No one from his organization achieved the level of fame Jannus did.

Did Jannus's personality overwhelm others, or were there more complex reasons? How did Jannus garner so much publicity while everyone else was relegated to the shadows of anonymity? The St. Petersburg–Tampa Airboat Line was a prime example. Tony made a contribution to the company, but it was not his company. The airboat was owned by William D. Jones, and the planning had been accomplished by Percival Fansler. Yet, nearly a century later, it is still known as Jannus's airline or Jannus's flight, just as it was in 1914. The names of Fansler, Benoist, Smith, and Roger Jannus are all but forgotten. Why did others allow him to rise to the forefront and capture all the publicity? Martha Benoist Davis pointed out that her brother "needed publicity but had no time to pursue it and Tony was just a natural to furnish it and leave Tom free to do the part that Jannus couldn't do."[31] Tom Benoist was smart enough to realize that Jannus was one of the best young fliers in America. Wisely, he allowed him his lead and the ensuing publicity. After all, airplanes did not sell themselves. All manufacturers, except possibly the Wrights, recognized this as gospel. Glenn Curtiss had his Lincoln Beachey and Charles K. Hamilton. Tom Benoist had Tony Jannus.

Tony Jannus was once asked if flying satisfied his thirst for adventure. "That's one reason I took it up," he said. Then he added, "I always liked a bit of excitement and this sure offers it. The money? Oh yes, that had something to do with it too."[32]

TONY JANNUS STOOD behind the rickety biplane and slowly turned the heavy wooden propeller. Pop, crack! The Emerson engine shook to life with a deafening roar as it belched black and white smoke. The unmuffled exhaust spit stubby fingers of fire. Rex Smith sat forward of the biplane wings. His seat was nothing more than a jury-rigged contraption that would allow him to sit and operate the airplane's controls. A small crowd stood on the edge of the grassy field at College Park, Maryland, watching several people prepare the biplane for its maiden flight.

Smith, the owner of the biplane, claimed first chance at flying the machine. He throttled it to half speed and steered straight down the field. When he thought he had sufficient ground speed, he pulled back on the lever, causing the nose to lift off the ground. Within seconds, he pushed the nose down and made a rough landing. The flight on November 11, 1910, covered a distance of only twenty feet at an altitude of ten feet. Smith had never flown an airplane before.

Frederick Fox, the builder of the airplane, was next to try it out in the air. His flight lasted only slightly longer than Smith's. Tony Jannus then got his turn and took the machine up for his very first flight. Eight months earlier, Jannus's cousin asked if he had "had a chance to fly yet."[1] Now he had had that chance. From that point on, Jannus's passions consisted of airplanes and flying.

In 1909, Rex Smith had built his first aircraft, but it never flew. The machine had been constructed and the engine ordered. Weeks later, the builder of the engine returned his money and told him he could not make delivery. Smith contacted the Emerson Engine Company, located in nearby Alexandria, Virginia. Frederick Fox assured Smith that he could rework an Emerson marine engine to power the biplane. Smith ordered the Emerson and designed his new biplane around the engine which Tony Jannus, a young shop mechanic at Emerson, was sent out to install.

In design, the Smith biplane was similar to the equipment constructed by Glenn Curtiss. It was Jannus's opinion that several aspects of the Smith plane were superior to the Curtiss construction, most notably the wing struts.[2] The machine was rudimentary at best. In appearance it was not far advanced from that which the Wright brothers had constructed in 1903. The engine was elevated approximately two feet above the lower wing and behind the pilot. The skeleton airframe was constructed of lightweight bamboo.

The six-cylinder engine provided 105 horsepower.[3] A six-foot Paragon pusher propeller was mounted on the rear of the engine.[4] The thirty-two-foot-long by six-foot-wide wings provided approximately four hundred square feet of lift surface. With a small fuel tank, the aircraft weighed slightly over one thousand pounds. Engine controls were calibrated to function with a single front lever, with stops for maximum and minimum speeds. The propeller turned at eleven hundred revolutions per minute, with a top flying speed of sixty-two miles per hour.

The three men made eighteen short, straight flights before nightfall that first day. Jannus wrote that Smith "discovered that in order not to rise, depressing the tail (this causing the backs of the skids to drag) was all that was necessary, as the forward speed was therefore greatly retarded." Throughout November, Smith, Fox, and Jannus coaxed more from the plane each day. It took a long time to overcome the difficulty of an aerial turn. Not knowing what to do, Jannus used only his rudder in his first efforts to make a turn. Without banking the aircraft at the same time, the result was an uncontrolled skid in the direction of the outside of the attempted turn. There was an immediate loss of airspeed and the plane stalled. Only after hours of nerve-racking trial and error did Jannus bank the biplane as he put it into a turn. Jannus wrote that they "were three rank amateurs, neither of whom had ever operated glider or a 'motor bird' before."[5] Nonetheless, Tony Jannus's flying career had begun.

Growing up in Washington had been advantageous to a young man interested in the newly emerging field of aviation. The Wright brothers were flying at Fort Myer, Virginia. Professor Samuel P. Langley was conducting his own flying tests on the Potomac River, the site of many of Jannus's own early successes. Many of Langley's tests, like those of the Wright brothers, were held in an almost paranoid shroud of secrecy. The newspapermen resented it; Jannus from the outset courted the press.

Jannus was intrigued by the early French aviator Hubert Latham and his flight over Baltimore during the Second America's Air Meet at Halethorpe, Maryland, November 6 through 10, 1910.[6] Jannus could not have chosen a better role model. At the Halethorpe Meet, which featured nearly $55,000 in prizes, Latham was the big winner. On the first day, Latham earned $6,500 by winning duration and distance contests.[7] In his front-engined, fifty-horsepower Antoinette monoplane, Latham soared high above Baltimore for nearly forty-eight minutes.

College Park, site of Tony's first flight, was the most modern flying field on the East Coast. A War Department order on July 3, 1909, had established the United States Army Signal Corps Aviation School at College Park.[8] An area of three thousand by four thousand feet had been plowed, rolled, and seeded in grass. Because of the absence of fences and the open land, fliers could take a plane up and make a circle of two miles. In case of an engine stall, there was plenty of open land to bring the aircraft down safely. Almost as important, the field was easily accessible to Washington by a forty-five-minute ride on the electric car.

By mid-January 1911, Jannus had flown nearly 140 times with little damage to himself or the airplane. No longer satisfied with short, straight flights, he was practicing figure eights. John W. Mitchell of *Aero* reported, "Jannus told me afterward (following a flight) that he was learning a lot of things about the 'feel of the air.' He says he has found several of the spots that aviators refer to as 'holes in the air.' Sometimes he has been able to crawl out, and sometimes he has been forced to alight. He said also that after he had been a mile down the field he was able to feel his own wake as he crossed it near the start coming back. That just indicates how little we know about what is really going on in the air."[9]

Smith's original plan had been to build the airplane, fly it during the fall, then store it until the spring. Once Jannus started flying with regularity, that plan was changed. Through the winter he flew without interruption, even flying in heavy snowstorms. By the end of his third month as a flier, he had made an uninterrupted cross-country flight of twenty-eight minutes.

Frequently he flew even closer to home, right in the middle of Washington, D.C. It was not unusual for him to take off from Potomac Park, just south of the Mall, in clear sight of the towering 555-foot Washington Monument. Many Washington civic and political leaders knew Jannus, and some dared to fly with him. Washington lawmakers were supportive of amateur aviators, although elsewhere everyone was not as friendly to the infant field of aviation. In January 1911, Representative Charles Warner of St. Louis introduced a bill in the Missouri legislature limiting the altitude of flights to no more than one thousand feet. The crime of exceeding the thousand-foot level was to be classified as an attempted suicide and punishable by a five-year prison sentence. Fortunately for the advancement of early aviation, Warner's bill was defeated.[10]

In Washington, Jannus was as well-known as Glenn Curtiss or the Wright brothers. That he received frequent coverage is easy to understand. Although not large in physical stature, at five feet, seven inches and 155 pounds, Jannus had a commanding presence. His dark eyes blazed with excitement as he talked about flying. A handsome young man of only twenty-three, he possessed an energetic and charming personality. He fit in with the Washington social life and the city's politicians. He came from a respected family with strong social ties to the political and military underpinnings of the nation's capital. Financially, he was well-off. After the death of his father and mother, he and his older brother Roger had inherited both money and property.

Jannus was reserved and unassuming. In his early years as well as later on, he let his flying speak for him; he always had others writing or speaking of his achievements. As a fledgling flier, his successes, failures, crashes, and feats of heroism were recorded by the *Washington Post*. He continued to get publicity from people such as Tom Benoist during Jannus's St. Louis and Midwest flying days, then from Percival Fansler during the history-making time of the St. Petersburg–Tampa Airboat Line. James D. Smith served as Jannus's diarist, much as James Boswell had done for Samuel Johnson.

During the first half of 1911, Jannus continued as the main pilot of Rex Smith's biplane. On March 4, Jannus, Smith, and several other men went out to College Park where Tony was scheduled to make a short cross-country flight. He planned to fly south-southwest to Washington and to land at the Exposition Hall at North Capitol and M Streets. Upon his arrival, he was to be met by workers from the Rex Smith Aeroplane Company who were to display the biplane at the Aero Show scheduled for the following day.

When news of Jannus's flight spread, hundreds of people went out on the streets of Washington hoping to catch a glimpse of the biplane. His takeoff was perfect; the airplane was airborne after only one hundred feet. He slowly circled College Park until he reached an altitude of five hundred feet. After gaining his desired altitude, he began the cross-country flight to Washington. When he had been in the air for only a few minutes, he decided that the winds aloft were too strong for the lightweight biplane and put it down. Following his unplanned landing, he was forced to wait until the Rex Smith crew arrived on the scene. As soon as the workers showed up, the biplane was disassembled, loaded onto a wagon, and trucked to the Exposition Hall.

The Aero Show was a major attraction for Washington in 1911. Nearly every American aircraft manufacturer was represented. There were three Curtiss planes, a Wright biplane, a Hubbard monoplane, a Rooney triplane, Henry Orme's biplane, a Christmas biplane, a Walden-Dyot monoplane, and two Rex Smith biplanes. The show was attended by two thousand people each day; it was also a large draw for government officials of the United States and foreign countries.

One of the main attractions was a Curtiss airplane that had recently been purchased by the War Department for use in Mexican border maneuvers. This aircraft was taken out and flown on two separate occasions. John A. D. McCurdy flew it so close to the War and Navy

Building that the whir of the engine could be clearly heard in the office of the secretary of state.[11] Glenn Curtiss's *June Bug*, the airplane constructed in 1908, was also on exhibit. The *June Bug*, winner of the *Scientific American* trophy in 1908 for completing a flight of one mile in one minute and forty-two seconds, was the aircraft that had galvanized the Wrights into a patent fight with Curtiss.

On the afternoon of March 11, fifteen thousand of Washington's public school children were the invited guests of the aeronautical exhibition at the Exposition Building. The managers of the exposition had provided a hundred miniature airplanes to be used to teach the students about airplanes.

On the morning of March 21, Jannus made several flights at the College Park Airfield. More than a thousand people saw Jannus fly throughout the morning. On Jannus's sixth flight of the day, he carried James O'Hagan and Fred Fox of the Emerson Engine Company as his passengers. That was the first time an aviator had flown with two passengers in the College Park or Washington areas.

Jannus continued to set local aviation records. Dressed in a suit and tie and wearing a small cap, he instilled confidence in those who suffered anxiety about flying. Nearly every day, the newspapers publicized an account of another flier falling out of his machine or having a "crackup," a euphemism for a fatal crash. In 1911, the death of an aviator was front-page news.

Jannus always took several short flights around the field by himself to be sure the aircraft was operating to his satisfaction before he let a passenger come aboard. Such excursions were usually only several minutes in length. His longest flight was a ten-minute ride with Charles D. Walcott, secretary of the Smithsonian Institution. Following his flight, Walcott said, "I have enjoyed rides in many kinds of conveyances in my life, but none could compare with my trip in the aeroplane."[12] Svante A. Arrhenius, director of the Nobel Laboratory in Stockholm, Sweden, and a winner of the Nobel prize for chemistry, also flew with Jannus.

GLADYS HINCKLEY, one of Washington's belles of society, earned a place in history on March 25, 1911, when she became the first woman to fly in an airplane in Washington, D.C.[1] Jannus helped her up onto the small jerry-built seat just forward of the lower wing's leading edge. To prevent her skirt from billowing up over her legs and to ensure that it would not become entangled in the aircraft's control mechanism, he tied a white cloth around her ankles. In 1913, French flier Auguste Bernard and his passenger, Rose Amicel, would meet their deaths when Amicel's skirt became caught in the lever connections and Bernard lost control of his aircraft.[2]

Looking at his mechanic, Jannus called out, "Jannus ready." The mechanic pulled down on the propeller. The Emerson engine caught on the first pull. Mindless of the thousand or more spectators watching his every move, Jannus gave an affirmative signal to his mechanic, who released the airplane, and it lurched forward. Lumbering down the sod field of Potomac Park, the airplane bounced on its bicycle-type wheels, slowly picking up speed. By the time Jannus had traveled one hundred feet, he had ground speed of about thirty miles per hour. He pulled back on the wheel and the biplane lifted its nose off the grass.

Rising to an altitude of fifty feet, Jannus flew over Potomac Park, putting the airplane through a series of long, slow, gliding turns. After they had circled the field several times, Jannus slowly made his descent. Upon landing, Gladys Hinckley adjusted her hat and enthusiastically declared, "I am going to plead for another ride, and just as soon as machines are so perfected I shall be one of the first to adopt the sport of aviation. Really, there is nothing that I know of that can compare to such a ride."[3] Of the day's passengers, John Mitchell recorded that "the freight included two pretty society girls, two of the most distinguished scientists in the world and a man weighing 280 pounds, besides half a dozen common or garden passengers."[4]

Most of the passengers offered rides were either connected with the government or were wealthy. Exhibitions were a means of promoting the sale of aircraft, as well as a lure for potential investors in the Rex Smith Aeroplane Company. Smith hoped to sell as many machines to the United States government as Glenn Curtiss and the Wrights did. The company was trying to float a stock issue that would increase capitalization to $500,000.[5]

The Rex Smith Aeroplane Company announced, "There's Money in Flying." During the preceding year, the Wrights had earned a quarter of a million dollars, and Glenn Curtiss had profited to the tune of $85,000.[6] Prizes in 1911 included a $50,000 purse offered by William Randolph Hearst for a flight from the Atlantic to the Pacific Ocean and $25,000 for a flight from New York to Chicago. The French government was contracting for $240,000 worth of military airplanes, and the English government was reported to be expending $3 million for the advancement of aviation.[7] There was also money to be made by aerial exhibitions.

On the morning of April 5, 1911, Rexford Smith and Jannus took the biplane to Potomac Park. The previous day, Jannus had attached two pontoons to the biplane, converting it into a hydroplane. Jannus and Smith were not the first American aviators to experiment with the hybrid land and water type of aircraft. Earlier in the year, Glenn Curtiss had taken off in his own hydroplane in San Diego.[8]

At the foot of Twenty-Fourth Street, the machine was pushed into the Potomac River. Jannus positioned himself on the aircraft's seat and was ready to go. Normally, on land, the airplane would have had adequate speed to take off after running about one hundred feet. The drag of the pontoons in the water prevented Jannus from developing his desired speed. As the hydroplane slowly moved down the river, the pontoons dipped below the surface. By the time the machine had gone two hundred feet, the pontoons were completely submerged. Jannus chopped the ignition. Momentum kept the airplane going forward for another few seconds. Then the nose of the biplane pitched downward and the tail raised up, cartwheeling the airplane. As Jannus and the airplane sank under the waters of the Potomac River, Smith and thousands of onlookers feared the worst. For half a minute, there was no sign of Jannus.

Finally, Jannus's head bobbed to the surface; he wiped the muddy water from his eyes and swam toward the shore and the relieved crowd. Jannus quipped, "The water was too murky for sightseeing, and that was one of two reasons I came back."[9] Jannus was taken to the U.S. Navy hospital located just north of Potomac Park where he was treated for a slight bruise on his head, given dry clothes, and sent home. The *Maple*, a government buoy tender, went out to the submerged biplane, and the crew attached a block and tackle and towed it to shore. The airplane was then loaded onto the back of a truck and returned to College Park. Already showing his propensity for design, Jannus knew what the problem had been. The pontoons were too short.

A day later he was back in the air. On the afternoon of April 7, he gave a ride to two new members of the aero club of the society girls of Washington. At 4 P.M., Laura Merriam and Dorothy Williams arrived at Potomac Park in their chauffeur-driven car. The young women had to wait while Jannus tinkered with the engine.

Finally Jannus was ready, and the women were called over to the machine. When they asked Rex Smith which one was going to get the first ride, his answer surprised everyone. Smith announced that both women would fly with Jannus at the same time. Neither woman realized that anything extraordinary was happening. Laura Merriam sat to Jannus's right and Dorothy Williams to his left. The engine was cranked up, Jannus added power, and off they went. Rolling down the field, it took slightly longer than usual for him to lift the nose of the biplane off the ground. At an altitude of about thirty feet, Jannus slowly turned the aircraft and again flew the full length of the field gaining both airspeed and altitude.

One minute after their flight began, Jannus was ready to land and began his approach. Just as Jannus was about to land the airplane, one of his passengers changed her position. The sudden weight shift caused the aircraft to hit the ground at a sharper angle than desired. The tail section bounced against the ground, breaking several pieces. Their flight had lasted one minute and twenty-nine seconds and had covered a distance of about two miles. It was the first time in the history of aviation that two women had been carried as passengers simultaneously. It was only the second time that two passengers, in addition to the operator, had gone up at the same time in the United States. Laura Merriam said, "I was not a bit scared when I made the flight and saw no reason to be."[10]

Not to be outdone by the women of Washington, the upper crust society men were also forming an exclusive aero club of their own. One of the early members claimed to have witnessed each and every flight of Tony Jannus at Potomac Park.[11]

Earlier on the morning of April 7, Jannus had given two short flights to the actor Nat Wills. Alice Roosevelt Longworth, daughter of Theodore Roosevelt and wife of Speaker of the House Nicholas Longworth, was also at the airfield. At least one source claims that Alice Roosevelt Longworth flew with Jannus, but it is doubtful. The *Washington Post* reported that she had been invited to fly with Jannus and had expressed her interest in flying but had declined the invitation. If a woman of Alice Longworth's fame had flown, it would have been a front-page story. Three biographies of her fail to mention any early airplane rides.[12] Authors of two biographies have stated that Mrs. Longworth made no mention of Tony Jannus.[13] For years, it was believed that a photograph existed of Alice Longworth sitting with Jannus in his airplane. In fact, the woman in question was Leonora Martin Rivera, daughter of Antonio Martin Rivera, the Cuban minister to Washington.[14]

Rex Smith's plans for the day were dashed, however; he had also intended to attempt to set additional aviation records. Earlier in the day, Smith had claimed "that flights with four and five passengers, in addition to the operator, will be attempted."[15]

Each day, a squad of officers from the Army Engineer and Signal Corps was detailed to Potomac Park to watch Jannus's flights and report to the War Department.[16] Now the minor damage to the aircraft forced the postponement of planned testing of wireless air-to-ground

Jannus at the controls of the Rex Smith biplane, Potomac Park, Washington, D.C., 1911. The passenger, Leonora Martin Rivera, was erroneously believed to be Alice Roosevelt Longworth. Her skirt is tied around her ankles to prevent it from becoming tangled in the controls. Courtesy of the Florida Aviation Historical Society.

transmittals. Neither the disappointed R. R. Bermann of the Signal Corps nor Jannus had long to wait, though.

On April 8, Jannus and Bermann made three flights in which they struggled to put the wireless to a test. Earlier attempts with wireless had used batteries. The wireless installed in the Rex Smith biplane used a generator geared to the main shaft of the engine. The first flight of the day ended with poor results. F. W. Popp, the man on the ground, determined that his machine needed adjustment. As soon as the proper calibration had been made, Jannus and Bermann were back in the air. While Jannus circled at an altitude of two hundred feet, Bermann transmitted messages. Several more flights had been planned, but the day's activities had to be aborted. While taxiing the biplane, Jannus smashed it into a tree, damaging one of the wings. A representative of the Signal Corps announced that the "flights had proven that before the quality of the air-to-ground wireless messages was satisfactory, the sending apparatus would require some changes."[17]

One month earlier, J. A. D. McCurdy, the Curtiss flier, had claimed to have sent the first air-to-ground wireless message.[18] At an altitude of five hundred feet, McCurdy tapped out his message, "Another chapter in aerial achievement is recorded in the sending of this wireless message from an aeroplane in flight."[19] The man on the ground receiving McCurdy's message was P. G. B. "Bud" Morriss, assistant engineer of the Marconi Wireless Telegraph Company of America. Jannus would one day work with both McCurdy and Morriss.

Smith and Jannus were doing everything they could to promote aviation in the nation's capital. There were free rides at Potomac Park, sorties with the society belles, and the project with the army. In mid-April, Smith planned a unique promotion. The *Washington Post* reported, "Never before in the history of aviation has such a novel method of giving away rides been inaugurated."[20] There was to be a contest in Potomac Park during which Jannus would drop three pennants bearing the inscription of the *Washington Post* from the airplane. Finders of the pennants would be awarded a ride with Jannus. Smith hoped to create a demand for paid rides in his airplane and to generate interest in the purchase of stock in his company. The *Washington Post* wanted to increase its daily circulation.

Jannus promised the pennant holders big thrills, saying he "would take his passengers to a reasonable height."[21] The atmosphere on the afternoon of the pennant drop was like that at a small county fair. The crowd was estimated as the largest ever to have attended a flying exhibition at Potomac Park. At approximately 4 P.M., Jannus was ready. Smith's biplane sat in the shadow of the Washington Monument. The Emerson engine cranked over without hesitation. Seconds later, Jannus was in the air. Thousands of people scrambled across the field in an attempt to follow Jannus as he flew.

Jannus flew circles around the field, gradually gaining altitude. He headed south across the park, with the Potomac River to his right. Finally, he tossed a tiny pennant overboard. As it fluttered toward the ground, hundreds of people frantically ran to where they hoped it would land. As the pennant settled into the group of eager men and women, hands greedily grabbed and elbows collided. It took nearly a minute for one person to emerge from the crowd with the pennant safely grasped in his hands. Elsewhere on the field, the result was the same.

By the end of the day, three prize winners had been rewarded with short flights above Potomac Park.

Throughout the month of April, Jannus continued his herculean flying pace. Day after day he flew, each time pushing himself and his airplane a little farther, constantly setting new personal records. Early on the morning of April 17, he made his longest flight yet—a total of nineteen and one-half minutes.

By April, the United States government was finally starting to take aviation seriously. Lieutenant Roy C. Kirtland, one of the first members of the new flying squadron of the army, was ordered to Washington with the Signal Corps. Kirtland was assigned to College Park, where the army was in the process of establishing its aviation training camp but was unable to learn to fly because the aircraft ordered from Curtiss had not yet arrived. Rexford Smith offered to train Signal Service officers using his biplane because it was similar to the Curtiss aircraft in construction.[22] Both types of aircraft used ailerons, and their control mechanisms were similar. The army availed itself of Smith's services periodically but never on a large scale. Tony Jannus served as one of the United States Army's earliest flight instructors, albeit unofficially.

His flying never failed to excite the crowds that gathered at local airfields. The hometown Washington boy had developed a tremendous following. Jannus was exceedingly popular, but by no means did he hold a monopoly on the thrills. Jannus was a young man, still learning, while many of the others were older, more experienced, and far more willing to take chances.

An article in the *Washington Post* of May 4 offers a clear picture of just how much flying the young, unlicensed, and relatively inexperienced Jannus was doing. The paper reported that "improvements upon the REX SMITH AEROPLANE are unparalleled in the history of aviation. The first day of operation saw eighteen flights made without damage to any part of the machine. . . . Since that time SEVERAL HUNDRED flights have been made."

On May 5, 6, 7, and 8, Glenn Curtiss brought his aerial road show to Washington. J. A. D. McCurdy, Hugh A. Robinson, and the redoubtable Lincoln Beachey were featured in a fantastic aerial circus. For fifty cents, the viewer could go out to the Benning Race Track and observe a real spectacle. On May 8, those who went to the Aeroplane Racing and Aerial Contests saw McCurdy and Beachey at their best.

Jannus also participated in the flying at the Benning Race Track.[23] Undoubtedly he enjoyed the trick flying of the Curtiss fliers; he learned by observing and talking to them. He was a scientist in the world of early aviation. When Jannus was questioned about whether he feared death, he said, "Part of my measure of success has been due to my study of the deaths of other flyers."[24] This air show gave Jannus the opportunity to meet Robinson, McCurdy, and Curtiss. Years later, he would work with all three of these men.

That same month, Jannus also became involved with Edward R. Brown, Donovan Swann, and Clyde Loose testing the newest product of the Baltimore-based Brown Aeroplane Company. As a tick of the minute hand showed the time to be 5:20 P.M. on May 17, 1911, the biplane was pulled out of the temporary hangar abutting the ball field of Yockel's Park, a small Baltimore enclave. Jannus settled into the seat and pulled the goggles over his eyes. The rear-mounted Paragon propeller was soon spinning at eleven hundred revolutions per minute. Jannus pushed the throttle to the maximum stop and waved to Edward Brown, the biplane's owner. The aircraft moved down the length of the field, gradually increasing its speed. At thirty-five miles per hour, the aircraft lifted into the air.

Jannus had agreed to go only a short distance over the Patapsco River before returning. Instead, he flew three-quarters of a mile beyond the river. Waggling his wings, he slowly turned the airplane and headed in the direction of the field. Three hundred yards off the shore of the Patapsco River, Jannus dipped the biplane's nose and headed straight toward the water. Just as the wheels submerged, he pulled back on the controls and the nose headed toward clear blue sky. Rising from the river, Jannus flew over the crowd, then landed the plane almost exactly on his starting point.

The biplane with which Jannus shocked the crowd was named the *Lord Baltimore*. It had been designed and constructed by Edward R. Brown of Baltimore, who had sought Jannus as a test pilot because of his growing reputation and experience. The *Lord Baltimore* had a movable front elevator and a fixed tail. The wings were made of tin and had a span of thirty-two feet. An Emerson four-cylinder, two-cycle, sixty-five-horsepower engine powered the aircraft. Its landing gear was Curtiss-style with three wheels. With the 155-pound Jannus flying, takeoff weight of the hydroplane was about 900 pounds.

Brown had built the *Lord Baltimore* but had never previously flown an airplane. Once Jannus pronounced it perfect in construction and capable of sustained flight, Brown wanted to take it up himself. On the day following Jannus's test flight, Brown made a takeoff and took his airplane up to an altitude of fifty feet. Quickly realizing that he was out of his element, he attempted to turn the biplane and return to the ground. In the middle of his turn, he was struck by a gust of wind and spun out of control into Curtis Bay. Pulled from five feet of water, Brown was carried to the shore. He sustained a broken wrist, two sprained ankles, and lacerations on his body and head.[25] Brown never flew the plane again; his wife refused to allow him to take further aerial risks.[26] Donovan Swann, secretary and treasurer of the Brown Aeroplane Company, also wanted to fly the plane on May 18. After one successful flight, Swann's wife also forbade him to fly, and he never did again. Many years later, Swann recalled that first flight, saying, "After having flown to an altitude of fifty feet, I couldn't, for the life of me, think how to turn the darn thing."[27]

Jannus soon had an opportunity for heroism. Unlike the stunts that Beachey and McCurdy had performed at the Curtiss air show, Jannus's were not scripted. On May 23, Jannus and Rex Smith took the well-used biplane to Bristol, Virginia, where they had contracted to perform exhibitions at the Bristol Aviation Meet.

After flying the biplane around the old race track at the Bristol fairgrounds, Jannus prepared to land. Having already shut off his ignition, he had begun to lose airspeed; there was no possibility of regaining altitude. Suddenly he was faced with a split-second decision. A crowd of people had gathered on his landing place. Had Jannus continued on his course, he would have plowed the airplane head-first into a crush of people. A similar accident in France had ended with the death of the French war minister and injuries to several bystanders.[28] Steering the biplane away from the crowd, Jannus smashed into an embankment.

On impact, Jannus was ejected from the airplane and thrown nearly one hundred feet, landing on his shoulder and neck.[29] As soon as he struck the ground, he was back on his feet. In shock, he failed to realize that he was hurt and walked to a nearby automobile. En route to the hospital, Jannus passed out. Doctors ordered X-rays, which disclosed a dislocated shoulder and a fractured collarbone.

In a bedside interview from the hospital, Jannus told a reporter from the *Washington Post*, "I am not the least unnerved by my experience, and I fully expect to be flying again within a month."[30] While Jannus recuperated from his injuries, he put his leisure time to good use composing a manuscript for *Scientific American* entitled "Learning How to Fly." The article began: "Common sense, mechanical ability, patience, good nerves and good eyesight are indispensable personal attributes of the man who wants to fly."[31] It was a well-written, intelligent primer on flying, engineering, and navigation.

During Jannus's recuperation, Rex Smith worked on several projects. He constructed a new shop at College Park and opened a flying school. Jannus became the flight instructor for Smith's flying school, starting with a class of five pupils.

As Rex Smith worked on production of a second aircraft that summer, Jannus's activity with the company decreased. As late as July 1911, Jannus was still associated with Emerson and flying for Edward Brown, as evidenced by a letter that he wrote to the Adjustable and Detachable Propeller Company on Emerson Engine Company stationery. Jannus complained of having experienced "four months of unfruitful experimenting for the Emerson Engine Company."[32] By August 1911, Paul Peck, whom Jannus had trained, had become the workhorse flier for Smith, and Jannus was doing little flying. Jannus then headed to Mineola, New York, where he flew headless Curtiss biplanes.[33]

4 New Faces, New Places

WHILE JANNUS WAS titillating the crowds in Washington, the Missourian Tom Benoist was building his own flying operation at Kinloch Field, just outside of St. Louis. Thomas Wesley Benoist was born on December 29, 1874, in Irondale, Missouri.[1] His first meeting with the American balloonist John Berry introduced him to the world of aviation. While employed at the McNish Auto Company, he invested in the Berry Aerial Navigation Company, and in 1904, Benoist and Berry set up a booth at the aviation field of the Louisiana Purchase Exposition held in St. Louis.

In 1907, Benoist invented an improved storage battery called the "Black Jack."[2] During that same year, Benoist and his brother Charles opened an automobile parts supply store in St. Louis. The partnership did not last long, nor did the automobile supply store. Charles Benoist left his brother for a better-paying job as a salesman.

Tom Benoist sold the automobile parts store and opened the Aeronautic Supply Company, known also as Aerosco. In addition to the new venture, Benoist took on a partner, E. Percy Noel. The business carried an inventory of aircraft parts and kits for the construction of airplanes. The team of Benoist and Noel sold their first kit, a copy of the Blériot monoplane, at the Aviation Exhibit in the St. Louis Coliseum on November 10, 1910.

When Benoist's original Aeronautic Supply Company outgrew its floor space, he prepared to move into a new facility at 6664 Delmar Avenue in University City, abutting the western part of St. Louis. To avoid transporting excess inventory from one facility to another, Benoist

Tom Benoist's Aeronautic Supply Company, which opened in St. Louis in 1909. It was the first business in the United States dedicated entirely to the sale of aviation parts and supplies. Courtesy of the Florida Aviation Historical Society.

held a removal sale. A buyer interested in aviation parts could purchase a six-foot laminated propeller, beautifully finished with a five-and-one-half-foot pitch, for only $27.50. Two complete Curtiss control gears, consisting of seat, shoulder control, and steering wheel, were offered for immediate sale and removal.

In September 1910, Kinloch Field, one of the largest airfields in the United States, was completed. No longer just a cow pasture but a real airfield, Kinloch Field attracted droves of aviators. In the spring when heavy rains made the field impossible for flying, a wooden plank runway was constructed. Kinloch fliers used this one-hundred-yard "Promenade" for takeoffs and landings. It was here that Benoist made his first solo flight in his overhauled Howard Gill biplane.

In October 1910, Benoist traveled to Amarillo, Texas, to participate in an exhibition. He was flying a biplane purchased from Howard Gill the previous March. After flying for a few minutes, he landed but neglected to shut off the engine. The machine lurched, throwing him from the biplane and running over him. The propeller hit his right foot, cutting through his boot and severing his big toe.[3] In another version of the incident, while Benoist was working on the engine, a would-be passenger climbed into the seat and began fooling with the controls. The engine started, and the airplane moved across the field. Benoist leaped to shut off the engine and was hit by the whirling propeller.[4] Benoist's accident may have led him to be more cautious, but it did not deter him from further flying.

Benoist began teaching students to fly while working on his own designs. In January 1911, he opened the Benoist School of Aviation at Kinloch Field. As the enrollment grew, he was able to make a living. In addition to the principles of flight, he taught airframe and engine mechanics and hands-on flying, using the Gill biplane to train his students. The enrollment of flight students became a lucrative business for aircraft manufacturers, generating a stable income. Once students learned to fly, they wanted to buy their own airplanes. Tom Benoist's flying school offered a sound curriculum with both ground and air instruction. His instructors were experienced, at least for the era.

According to Reginald Woodcock, Benoist "won his Aero Club of America license at Kinloch Field on December 22, 1910."[5] A roster of licensed pilots through 1911, however, does not include Benoist's name.[6]

Exactly how to pronounce Tom Benoist's name has been the subject of nearly as much debate as the spelling of Jannus's name. John C. Henning, former vice president of sales for the Benoist company, said that it rhymed with "wah."[7] In 1913, A. C. Beech wrote a limerick about Tom Benoist and his name:

> There is a plane builder—Benoist,
> Whose feelings have grown very raw,
> Because his name's spoken
> In French very broken.
> When it always should rhyme with "wah-wah."[8]

Buoyed by the success of the sales of aircraft kits, Benoist made the decision to design and manufacture his own aircraft. By early 1911, Benoist had completed his own biplane. Blue lettering on the side spelled out *Benoist*, with a red arrow superimposed over the name.

Specifically designed and constructed to teach students, the machine had been built with a new type of tail and a double elevator control. Special passenger accommodations and control systems allowed dual flight instruction. This feature alone was a novel approach. Aircraft previously held only the pilot. Most early flying instruction involved nothing more than rudimentary flight instruction, after which the pilot-trainee would solo.

Fliers liked Benoist's creation. By March 1911, Benoist had completed two of his biplanes and had orders for three more. As advanced as Benoist's biplane may have been, it was still lacking an element that would become very important in aviation: it had no ailerons, though neither did most aircraft at that time. Benoist later used ailerons in violation of a Wright brothers' injunction, as did nearly every other manufacturer. First used by Benoist as an addition to the wing tip, ailerons were later incorporated into the trailing edge of the wing.

Benoist's company never came close to reaching the production capabilities of Glenn Curtiss, Glenn Martin, or even the Wright brothers, but he did produce a substantial number of aircraft and was a major presence in the midwestern market. Tom Benoist, as well as Glenn Curtiss, was in violation of infringement of the Wright brothers' U.S. Patent Number 821,393.[9] Benoist, unlike Glenn Curtiss, was never sued by the Wrights. He was more reserved in his approach and never sold enough aircraft to be viewed as competition by either Orville or Wilbur Wright.

On October 20, 1911, Benoist's factory was destroyed by fire. He lost five planes and two automobiles, a loss estimated at $20,000.[10] Authorities claimed that the fire had started as a result of gasoline stored in the factory. Benoist asserted that the cause was arson.[11] Whatever the reason, the fire was undoubtedly accelerated by the paraffin and alcohol used to treat the wings and other cloth-covered surfaces. Ten days later, Benoist opened another facility. At the time, Benoist hinted to local officials that several other cities had offered him cash bonuses to relocate his business. He refused to name the cities, preferring to keep his options open.[12] Benoist did not want to leave St. Louis but was attempting to get the city to offer him an incentive to remain. That incentive was never provided.

Tom Benoist in one of his early headless biplanes, 1910. Author's collection.

At this time, Benoist changed the name of his company to the Benoist Aircraft Company, incorporated under the laws of Missouri. Shares cost $10 each; the total capitalization of the company was $50,000. Much has been made about Benoist's general lack of financial well-being. Was he ever prosperous as a manufacturer of airplanes? He may have done well in 1910 and 1911. Before Jannus joined Benoist, at least thirty-one students had gone through his flying school, which should have yielded close to $8,000. His airplane manufacturing business was doing equally well. According to Benoist, "In 1910 and 1911 the Benoist Aeroplane Company built and sold or used for experimental purposes more than forty airplanes."[13] He claimed to have turned out twenty-eight successful machines during the summer of 1911.[14] If that statement was true and he sold all the aircraft, his company would have realized in excess of $100,000.

After the fire and the company's name change, Benoist began to build his management team. Tony Jannus joined the company in November 1911. While in a cafe near Kinloch Field, Jannus met another young aviator named P. G. B. "Bud" Morriss. The two men discussed the best way to approach Benoist and interest him in their services. They were successful; Benoist hired them both, Morriss as vice president and safety engineer, Tony as chief pilot.[15] Shortly after, Morriss left the Benoist company to become publisher of *Aero and Hydro*, the best-known aeronautical journal of the day. Over the years, Jannus wrote numerous articles for Morriss, developing at length his ideas on airframes, engines, safety, and other contemporary aviation issues. *Aero and Hydro* played a major part in building the early legend of Tony Jannus.

John C. Henning, a graduate of the Wright School, joined the company as vice president of sales and promotion. Edward Korn, also hired by the Benoist company in 1911, said, "Benoist formed a company with Tom Benoist as president, Tony Jannus chief pilot with pilots, Dr. Frank Bell, Clifford C. Vandwort, Hugh Robinson, Walter Lees and Edward Korn. Perhaps others." He remembered Jannus as "an expert with 2 cycle-engines."[16] In fact, Hugh Robinson did not come into the Benoist fold until late in 1912.

J. D. Smith, the mechanic from Johnstown, Pennsylvania, was also hired by Benoist in November. For the next few years, Jannus relied heavily on Smith's talents as an engine mechanic and frequently referred to him as "Smitty the Infallible."[17] In 1911, Benoist and Kinloch Field held a magnetic attraction for young men interested in aviation. Smith, having read and heard about Tom Benoist, went to St. Louis hoping to land a job with the entrepreneur. As the story goes, Smith was at Kinloch Field during a snowstorm. When the storm ended, the airplanes were covered with snow. Smith sought out Benoist's airplane and swept it clean, earning himself a job offer.[18] Benoist called Smith into the factory and introduced him to Jannus. Tony wasted no time in assessing Smith's skills, asking, "Jay Dee, how would you like to be my head mechanic?"

"Outside of the fact that I'm no mechanic," Smith replied, "the idea's all right with me."

"You're too modest," retorted Jannus. "I know the work you've been doing on planes and engines, and you're all the mechanic I want."[19] The two young men hit it off from their first meeting. Both had an overwhelming interest in flying and airplanes. They were also the same age. Smith was born in May 1889, one month before Tony. There was a marked resemblance; a quick glance at a photograph of the two might give the impression that the men were brothers. One thing was never in doubt: Tony was definitely the boss.

When Jannus arrived at Kinloch Field, it was an aviation boom town. Its population included eleven fliers and as many airplanes. There were three Benoists, a Curtiss, two Wrights, and several home-builts. Spectators were admitted to Kinloch Field for a charge of twenty-five cents. The proceeds were divided among the aviators flying. At that time, Kinloch Field may have been the largest flying field in the United States west of the Mississippi River. Situated on a former cornfield of many acres, Kinloch housed five hangars arranged in an "L" shape.

Before their arrival at Kinloch Field, most of the Benoist fliers would have had experiences similar to that described by Edward Korn, Jannus's assistant. Korn related: "My brother Milton and I became interested and began the study of birds in flight. We used geese from mother's flock, taking them to the top of the wind mill. When they were pushed off the platform they would go into a dive then straighten out and sail across the barn yard. We began making models in 1908, finally, my brother made one with two propellers turned by rubber strands. This model would fly 350 feet in still air."[20]

There was no learning curve for Jannus at Kinloch Field. He immediately assumed almost all of the exhibition flying for Benoist. Jannus had a strong work ethic. He was a hands-on flight instructor and made certain that his pupils were ready for anything. *Aero* reported, "The Benoist students are now doing practically all the flying for themselves and rather resent Jannus' intrusion, but he insists upon making things interesting for them by playing such tricks as switching off the motor at unexpected times and watching the fun. The fun is the student's utter consternation at the dreadful silence that follows, and this practice is calculated to keep the most heedless pupil on the jump thereafter."[21]

The early relationship between Jannus and Tom Benoist was symbiotic, each man feeding off the other's personality. Jannus was young, talkative, outgoing, and sometimes cocky. Benoist was the opposite in every way; he was reserved, shy, and frequently reclusive. There were

NEW FACES, NEW PLACES

Benoist with his students and mechanics, Kinloch Field, Missouri, 1911. Tony Jannus is seated second from right; Benoist is standing third from right. Author's collection.

many reasons why a young flier like Jannus would want to work for him. Benoist had a reputation as a builder of well-made airplanes. His *1912 Flying Boats and Hydro-Aeroplanes* catalog clearly defined his attitude about the construction of his airplanes. He claimed, "His planes were designed down to the last nut and wood members and cloth examined, tried and tested before being placed in his planes." [22]

Jannus also wanted to become associated with the Benoist company because of the readily available source of airplanes and the opportunity to fly on a full-time basis. With the well-known Tony Jannus as his chief pilot, Benoist was able to curtail his own flying and teaching. He could now devote all of his time to the design, construction, and sale of Benoist airplanes.

Barely a week had passed since Jannus had gone to work for Benoist, and his influence was already being felt. During the week of November 20, he flew six out of seven days. He logged several hours of flying time each day.[23] Edward Korn recalled, "Tony took the Benoist Curtiss type plane out for a flight. He wasn't in the air but a few minutes until we all recognized him as an exceptional flyer. Tony was really a good pilot." Korn's skill at the controls of his Wright Model B and later in a Benoist school airplane impressed Jannus. Korn made only four flights with Jannus so he could learn the Benoist controls, after which he was on his own.[24]

During the afternoon of November 19, on his third flight of the day, Jannus set an aviation record for biplanes of the Curtiss type. While giving a lesson to Alfred Boulette, a Benoist student, Jannus set the record for flying thirty minutes with a passenger.[25]

One of the goals Jannus set for the last week of November was to acquire his Aero Club of America license. A license was necessary only to establish official records or to participate in Aero Club of America meets. Jannus became an Aero Club of America certified pilot on December 2, 1911.[26]

Late that day, as sunset approached, Tony took the Benoist airplane up in an attempt to earn his license. The judges, A. B. Lambert, G. L. Holton, and Tom Benoist, were unconcerned about possible charges of conflict of interest. Five figure eights were required; he had already completed two of them. All that remained were three figure eights and the accurate landing test in which he had to land within 150 feet of a spot chosen before his takeoff. It was nearly impossible to see the ground in the darkness. A. B. Lambert turned on the acetylene lamps of his automobile and pointed the lights in the direction of Jannus's assigned landing spot. From his altitude of 400 feet, Jannus slowly spiraled toward the spot. Swooping out of the darkness, like a moth attracted to light, Jannus hit the ground and chopped his ignition. His aircraft rested only six inches from the goal. After landing, he immediately took off again into the darkness. Lambert drove his automobile to one of the points on the ground. With the headlights as a ground reference point, Jannus flew the final three figure eights in the dark and earned the eightieth license issued by the Aero Club of America.[27]

Jannus loved competition. When he won at something, he never boasted or bragged about his success. When he lost, he took it without complaint. On March 26, 1912, Jannus signed a contract for a match race with Jimmie Ward, a former student of the Glenn Curtiss flying school. The race was to take place on March 31, north of Kinloch Field over a ten-mile triangular course laid out by the technical committee of the Aero Club of St. Louis.

Jannus was able to complete only one lap before he had to quit the race. His Roberts engine stopped while he was in midair, forcing him to glide to earth. Benoist, ever the apologist for the Roberts engine, claimed that "the motor would not have stopped if he or one of his men had taken the time to look over the engine before the race." There were two inconsistencies in Benoist's argument. Jannus seldom flew without at least a cursory check of the aircraft and engine, and J. D. Smith always carefully examined the engine thoroughly before Jannus flew. Benoist also related that the Roberts engine had been recalled by the factory but had not yet been sent back. Jannus made no excuses. He believed that he "could not have won the race even if his engine hadn't stopped because Ward's airplane was simply faster."[28]

Jannus had no reason to be embarrassed at having lost a race to Jimmie Ward. Ward was a formidable competitor with a great deal of flying experience. Two years earlier, in September 1910, Ward had attempted to fly from the east to the west coast of America in hope of collecting the $50,000 prize offered by William Randolph Hearst for the first person to fly from coast to coast in thirty days or less. Ward made a gallant effort, suffered through several crashes, and quit only after Chicago bookmakers set odds of five to one on his demise.

5   Like a Crazy Arrow

JANUARY 7, 1912, was bitterly cold in St. Louis. During the morning it started to snow; the wind blew heavily and the temperature fell. By the night of January 8, the temperature had plummeted to fourteen degrees below zero. Ignoring the bad weather, Benoist and his crew worked steadily for two weeks straight. They had been building a new machine, an airplane markedly different from any they had produced before.

The new aircraft was a complete redesign, adding features that would boost speed, increase safety, and allow easier shipping. With a top speed of sixty-eight miles per hour, the two-seater was capable of three hours of sustained flight. Frequently the wings were damaged when an airplane landed hard. Therefore, Jannus and Benoist designed a landing gear that would prevent the shock of landing from being absorbed directly by the flimsy wings. The two-wheeled landing gear, mounted on steel springs, permitted the flier to taxi the aircraft under power and avoided the necessity of a team of helpers to maneuver the machine to its starting point.

Goodyear Model 10 rubberized fabric covered the fuselage and wings of the Benoist Model XII. The aircraft could easily be dismantled and towed behind an automobile. The triangular horizontal stabilizer became an easily recognizable design and trademark of all future Benoist aircraft. Tony Jannus was given equal credit with Benoist for the design and construction of the 1912 headless Benoist.[1]

Although the airplane was finished, the inclement weather prevented its being flown. The snow was still falling, and the wind continued heavy gusting. Official weather bureau temperature readings were ten degrees above zero with a twenty-mile-per-hour wind. But despite the poor weather conditions, it was necessary to test the plane's new system of control levers and newly designed landing gear.

As it emerged from Benoist's hangar, the airplane was a strange sight. A man was hanging from each wing, as well as from the tail. Although powered only by a Roberts seventy-five-horsepower engine, the airplane felt very strong to Jannus. He had to reserve power, even with the human ballast tagging along for the ride. The cold air had a positive effect on the engine's performance.

Jannus planned to run the airplane straight across the field. With the three men still hanging onto the airplane, he headed back toward the hangar. Three things happened nearly at once. The wind blew from behind the airplane, the three men let go, and Jannus applied power. As the airplane left the ground, Jannus pushed down on the wheel, intending to put the airplane back on the field. Just then, the wind lessened and he found himself heading for the ground much too fast. Instinctively, he pulled back on the wheel to avert a crash. Another violent gust of wind nearly blinded him with ice and snow as it threw the machine almost forty feet into the air.

Jannus pulled back on the controls and flew over the rapidly approaching hangars. Having safely cleared them, he made a slow turn and came back toward the hangars, intending to land. He overshot his mark and found himself above a field of dead cornstalks. Running out of open space, he was forced to gain altitude and circle back toward Kinloch Field, heading again toward the safety of the hangars. Now he had to deal not only with his own airspeed but with the force of a very strong tailwind. When he tried to land, he leapfrogged across the field, again overshooting his mark. Once more, Jannus circled. Flying level and low to the ground, he pressed his body into the seat as securely as possible. The bucking of the airplane and the gusty wind threatened to blow him loose, as the snow continued to swirl around the airplane and the field. When the wind diminished just enough, Jannus dropped the airplane to the ground.

Only when Jannus was safely on the ground did he allow himself to feel any fear. He wrote, "My eyes were shrieking distress, my hands were numb, and my face stiff, but good fortune had been mine and the gratification of knowing that the machine was a perfect success soon overcame my physical sufferings and the mental strain consequent to circling about unwilling in a young blizzard in a new and strange machine."[2]

Following the flight, Jannus critiqued his performance. He had been fortunate to escape disaster, and he knew it. Looking to the future, he said, "Next winter, it will be reasonable to fly under such weather conditions. My accident did show, however, that it is possible to handle very unfavorable conditions with the average type of aeroplane as made today, and more experience and preparation will make it reasonably easy."[3] He realized that he should not have flown and used the frightening episode as a learning experience.

Shortly after the flight in the snowstorm, Jannus had a much more pleasant flight in the new Benoist airplane. In cold but clear weather, Jannus put in a long day of flying on January 21, carrying a total of sixteen passengers. With the exception of the five Benoist pupils, each was flying for the first time. Most of the passengers were residents of St. Louis, but two, Katherine Stinson and Major Frank R. Lang, had traveled some distance to fly with Jannus.

Jannus gave Katherine Stinson her first airplane ride that day at Kinloch Field.[4] Stinson had come there to enter the Benoist flying school, and she was determined to learn to fly. For Stinson's first flight, Jannus quickly ascended to an altitude of one thousand feet. When she begged Jannus to land, he ignored her pleas and flew even higher. He banked the headless biplane until it stood nearly perpendicular to the ground. As the coup de grace, he cut his engine off and glided without power for two hundred feet before gently setting the aircraft on the ground. Immediately after her flight, Stinson begged for another ride and then signed up at a flying school. But Katherine Stinson did not enter Tom Benoist's flying school. Jannus believed that women should be passengers only and were not capable of becoming pilots. Judy Lomax, author of *Women of the Air*, wrote of Stinson's first experience with flight: "During her first lesson she was convinced that the aircraft was out of control when the pilot banked, but she wanted to go up again immediately. . . . Although her instructor was convinced that she would ei-

Katherine Stinson received her first flying lesson from Jannus on January 21, 1912. She eventually earned the 196th license awarded by the Aero Club of America. Author's collection.

ther be killed or catch pneumonia, and refused to continue her lessons."[5] Stinson eventually persuaded a reluctant Max Lillie to allow her admission to his flying school. She earned the 196th license given to certified pilots by the Aero Club of America.

Tony Jannus was not the only man reluctant or unwilling to teach women to fly. The Wright brothers refused even to consider the idea. Although Glenn Curtiss had taught at least one woman to fly, it had been with great reluctance. In an interview for the Columbia University Oral History Project, Matilde Moisant, sister of the American aviator and airplane builder John Moisant, summed up the prevailing attitude toward women learning to fly: "In those days, well, to put it this way, it was man's work, and they didn't think it was woman's work or that a nice girl should be in it. There were a few fliers that thought we had as much right as they, but most of them didn't. 'Why don't they leave it to us?' was the attitude."[6]

In February 1912, Benoist and Jannus began working on a new type of airplane. After long discussion, they decided on a tractor biplane with a covered fuselage. An airplane with its engine mounted in front of the wings, with the propeller placed in front of the engine, was called a tractor. It had a fuselage similar to those being built by the Europeans. Until then, most of the American pusher airplanes were of the skeleton type. A pusher aircraft had its engine mounted behind the wings, with the propeller behind the engine. The fuselages of the first three Benoist tractors consisted of a wooden framework covered with Goodyear rubberized cloth. The wings were also covered with this rubberized material. The Benoist plane was not the first tractor airplane to be constructed, but it was the first practical and successful tractor to be built in the United States.

Over the years, many of Tom Benoist's accomplishments were greatly overshadowed by those of Glenn Curtiss. Design and construction of a tractor aircraft with a front-mounted engine was, however, not one such instance. It was not until 1913 that Curtiss produced a tractor aircraft of his own. When he did, Curtiss benefited from the experience of men such as B. Douglas Thomas, the English engineer, Alfred Zahm of the Smithsonian Institution, and Alfred Verville.[7] Yet, in the

Jannus at the controls of a Benoist Model XII tractor, Kinloch Field, Missouri, early 1912. The Benoist tractor was the first practical and successful tractor to be built in the United States. Author's collection.

LIKE A CRAZY ARROW

end, Curtiss received the credit for the tractor airplane because of the Jenny that was mass-produced in large numbers. The aircraft being built in 1912 were rudimentary in design. In 1962, J. D. Smith recalled: "The only instruments the little plane had were the pilot's watch, an 'on' and 'off' ignition switch, and a piece of string tied on a wing strut. If it was trailing straight back you had plenty of speed; if it started flopping and dropping you were getting too slow."[8]

Three of these biplanes were produced in the spring of 1912. The first aircraft, a small box-type with an enclosed fuselage, was constructed entirely of wood. The pilot sat on top of the fuselage on a specially constructed seat. This aircraft was purchased by Frank Bell. The second plane was used by Tony Jannus for exhibition work. The third biplane was purchased by Edward Korn and his brother Milton.[9]

On March 1, 1912, Jannus and Albert Berry set out to prove that a parachutist could safely jump from a moving airplane. Taking off to the cheers of the students at the Benoist School of Aviation, they left Kinloch Field at 2:30 P.M., heading in a south-southeasterly direction. Their destination was Jefferson Barracks, thirty minutes away. Meanwhile, Benoist was waiting anxiously at the factory for word that Jannus had departed the field. When he received the affirmative telephone

The Benoist Model XII tractor biplane featuring wing-tip ailerons. Jannus was given equal credit with Benoist for the design of this aircraft. Three of these tractors were manufactured in 1912. Author's collection.

Frank Merrill Bell in front
of his Benoist Model XII
tractor at Kinloch Field,
Missouri, February 1912.
Author's collection.

call from Frank Bell, he climbed into his automobile and headed for Jefferson Barracks.

Twenty minutes after leaving Kinloch Field, Jannus was almost to his destination. Nearing the drop area over Jefferson Barracks, he went into a series of long, slow circles descending from his altitude of thirty-five hundred feet. At approximately fifteen hundred feet above the ground, they were over the field. Jefferson Barracks was bordered on three sides by large stands of dense woodland; to the east was the Mississippi River. There was little room for error.

Berry carefully climbed from his seat and slowly maneuvered himself to the front of the biplane. Hanging from the undercarriage of the airplane, Berry climbed onto the trapeze-like contraption attached to the aircraft. Reaching forward, he pulled the cone-shaped container toward his body, while Jannus leveled the Benoist as straight as possible. Holding the parachute with one hand, Berry used his other hand to cut the cord attaching the trapeze to the bottom of the biplane.[10] Then he dropped. Jannus's airplane immediately shot upward in a steep climb, threatening a stall. Jannus pushed the lever forward, dropping the biplane's nose.

Berry dropped one hundred feet and nothing happened. After he fell another hundred feet, the parachute began to open, finally billowing out as expected. Before the flight, J. D. Smith and Berry had packed and checked the conical parachute. Between each fold of the parachute's fabric they had placed a layer of paper, hoping to ensure against a tangle.[11]

According to Jannus, "Mr. Berry gauged his landing with perfect authority and landed in back of the Mess Hall."[12] The parachute drop had been perfect. It had been a hard but safe landing. Almost before Berry touched the ground, a crowd of soldiers rushed toward him, lifted him up, and hoisted the fearless Berry up on their shoulders.

Jannus circled twice above the parade grounds before losing enough altitude to land directly in front of Colonel William T. Wood's quarters. Hopping from his airplane, he received the same tumultuous greeting that Berry had. The day was cold, and both Jannus and Berry found it necessary to warm themselves in Colonel Wood's office. After Jannus refueled his airplane, he headed back toward Kinloch Field. Benoist drove Berry and his parachute back to Kinloch in the automobile. On the return flight to Kinloch Field, Jannus got lost. Flying at an altitude of four thousand feet, he mistook the St. Charles River for the Natural Bridge Road and flew almost to the Missouri River before realizing his navigational error.[13]

When asked if he would ever perform the dangerous stunt again, Berry quickly responded: "Never again! No, I don't mean that, for I intend to do the same thing again Sunday afternoon at Kinloch Field, if we don't have the same sort of weather we had the last two Sundays. But I had the never-again feeling when I landed. . . . Honestly, I believe I turned five somersaults on my way down. Maybe more—I just lost count. My course downward from the time I left the biplane was like the course of a crazy arrow."[14]

After the successful jump, officers and cadets alike debated the experiment's usefulness. Some thought it was nothing more than a stunt, good only for excitement. Others predicted that the day would come when airplanes would transport thousands of parachutists hundreds of miles and unload them. One farsighted officer even had the boldness to envision jumps by "more than 5,000 to 10,000 men" that could "alter the whole aspect of a campaign."[15]

Less than a week and a half had passed since the successful jump when a Benoist advertisement appeared in *Aero* magazine. It read, "Anthony Jannus and Capt. Berry in the new Benoist School Machine, carrying 100 pounds extra equipment flew from Kinloch to Jefferson Barracks, over twenty miles in twenty minutes. Jannus dropped Berry with a parachute into the Barracks and returned to Kinloch without a hitch. Benoist Planes do not have to go south to fly."[16] Benoist was smart to advertise the event. It had been an aviation first and would help him sell airplanes. This was the first mention of Jannus's accomplishments in any Benoist advertising literature.

When the history-making feat was concluded, Jannus readily admitted that he was not anxious to repeat the ordeal. He said, "As far as I am concerned, Sunday will be the last time for this stunt. We are duty bound to the people who paid admission to see the jump a week ago Sunday, to do it once more. We hope to get through with it next Sunday. After that, never again."[17]

On March 10, Jannus and Berry gave an encore performance. The proper military authorities had not been at Jefferson Barracks on March 1. This time, the jump was made over Kinloch Field from an altitude of only eight hundred feet. The weather was less than perfect and very misty. If the plane had been at a higher altitude, the spectators' and photographers' views of Berry jumping would have been obscured.

Before the month was out, the biggest question about parachute jumping from an airplane was no longer the safety of the pilot and the parachutist but what price to charge for an exhibition. In a letter to the editor of *Aero*, Tom Benoist made it clear that "we beg to say that under no condition will a parachute jump be put in with a regular flying exhibition at anywhere near the same prices. It is absolutely necessary, because of the great risk of an exhibition of this kind, to get at least twice as much for it as we would obtain in straight flying."[18]

Did Jannus simply fly out to Jefferson Barracks and drop Berry from an airplane as a circus stunt? Of course not. The flights were conducted as scientific tests. Before their initial jump, Jannus and Berry experimented. The first step included carrying a fifty-three-pound blacksmith's anvil with a parachute attached.[19] At four hundred feet above the ground, Jannus cut the rope allowing the weight to fall freely. Nothing happened to the equilibrium of the airplane, but the parachute failed to open. The heavy anvil with its unopened parachute buried itself several inches into the rocky ground of Kinloch Field. J. D. Smith raised several blisters on his hands after wielding a shovel to dig the sunken anvil from the hard winter ground.[20] Gradually they added more weight, trying to approximate the actual two hundred pounds which Berry weighed.

Wilbur Wright and Glenn Curtiss believed the shifting of heavy weight or the sudden loss of weight would violently disturb an aircraft's equilibrium, causing it to go into a spin and an uncontrolled dive. Each time Jannus and Berry experimented with parachuting, they were placing their lives in jeopardy. In a subsequent test with the anvil, the parachute opened at fifty feet above the ground. The deadweight fall stopped and the anvil floated to the ground. These first experiments with the parachute proved difficult because the packed parachute blew loose as soon as the jumper balanced himself on the trapeze below the airplane. Each time that happened, Jannus faced the risk of the billowing cotton sheets catching in the airplane's control mechanisms or obscuring his vision. The problem needed to be remedied quickly. Several contraptions were tried, but the most effective solution was to stuff the parachute into a hammered tin cone-shaped tube resembling a megaphone. A year after Berry's successful parachute jump in Jannus's airplane and a subsequent unsuccessful attempt of his own, Frank Merrill Bell wrote a full-page story about parachuting. Bell discussed their difficulties before finally hitting on the right answer.[21]

That phase of testing behind them, Berry had been ready to go; Jannus was not. They compromised. Before Berry could make the jump, they would undertake one more test. Jannus would fly at altitude while Berry shifted his weight. Before the test flight, the men tied a rope to the middle of the axle attached to the aircraft's undercarriage, the biplane's center of gravity. Climbing onto the flat board seats arranged just forward of the lower wing, Jannus and Berry prepared for their flight. When they reached fourteen hundred feet, Jannus leveled his aircraft. Berry clambered from his seat and made his way to the biplane's

Albert Berry, Jannus, and Tom Benoist shortly before Berry became the first person to parachute out of an airplane. Jannus served as pilot. Jefferson Barracks, Missouri, March 1, 1912. Courtesy of the Florida Aviation Historical Society.

LIKE A CRAZY ARROW

undercarriage and the twisting rope. He grabbed it and began going through a series of acrobatic twists and turns. Before he was through, the intrepid parachutist was hanging by his heels at an altitude of a thousand feet.

As Berry hung upside down, Jannus put the machine through a series of prearranged turns. Banking left, then right, he dropped the nose and headed toward the ground. Berry, still hanging upside down, was approaching the ground at an alarming rate of speed. As Jannus pulled back on the controls, the aircraft came out of its dive, but not before Berry's head bounced repeatedly on the ground. He was pulled headfirst across the muddy field for nearly three hundred feet.[22] When Jannus realized that he could not gain any more altitude, he put the nose down and landed. As he did, Berry's body plowed into the thick mud.

Fearing that Berry had been killed, the spectators rushed to the aircraft to pull out his body. Berry climbed out unassisted from beneath the airplane, scraping mud from his face and head. Berry escaped with only minor scrapes and contusions. With that final step behind them, Jannus and Berry announced that they would attempt the world's first parachute jump from an airplane on Sunday, February 18.

The exhibition, intended as the opening of the 1912 flying season at Kinloch Field, was to begin at 3 P.M. Early spring winds forced cancellation of the program. Two days later, St. Louis was buried under sixteen inches of snow. Not for another two weeks would Jannus and Berry be able to make their historic feat a reality.

Fortunately for history, William Trefts, Jr., had been at Jefferson Barracks to photograph Berry's parachute jump on March 1. Russell Froelich, who usually photographed Jannus's accomplishments, opted not to go out to Jefferson Barracks that morning, telling Benoist that it was too cold.[23]

Spurred by Jannus's and Berry's feat, Frank Bell was ready for his turn. In mid-May, Bell and his passenger, Wood Lineback, climbed into Bell's Benoist Model XII in hope of duplicating Jannus's success. Throttling down, Bell took off from the west end of Kinloch Field. The biplane took several hundred feet to get off the ground, never attaining great speed. Normally, Bell would have made a left turn before reaching the end of the grassy field. Instead he found himself head-

A shot of Berry's dramatic parachute jump. Courtesy of the Florida Aviation Historical Society.

Berry and his parachute just after landing safely. Courtesy of the Florida Aviation Historical Society.

ing for the trees without adequate clearance. The biplane spiraled and roared headfirst into the ground. Smashed into a heap, the aircraft was nearly destroyed. Spectators believed that both men had been killed.[24] When the crowds arrived at the scene, they were surprised to find Bell attending to the bloodied Lineback.[25]

Lineback and Bell were not put off by their accident and made several later jumps. For his jumping, Wood Lineback received fifteen dollars a week, fifteen dollars for each jump that he made, and traveling expenses for himself and his wife.[26]

As a result of their work with the parachute and its apparatus, Jannus and Tom Benoist applied for a patent on March 9. The application stated that they "have invented certain new and useful Improvements in Parachute Carrying and Dispensing Means Carried by an Aeroplane and Attached Thereto." They were granted United States patent number 1,053,182 on February 18, 1913.[27]

The jump by Berry opened a Pandora's box. Less than two months following the historic performance, a parachute jump from an airplane into water was accomplished.[28] On April 13, 1912, F. Rodman Law, known as the "Human Fly," jumped from a Burgess hydroplane. Thirty-five thousand spectators saw Law free fall for 150 feet before his parachute opened. On April 28, William M. Morton leaped from an airplane piloted by Phil Parmalee at an altitude of nearly three thousand feet over Los Angeles. Morton's homemade parachute snagged in electric wires as he made his descent.[29] Morton freed himself and dropped ten feet to the ground, walking away with only a few minor cuts and bruises.

Benoist's oldest pilot at this time was Frank Merrill Bell, a flier plagued by frequent accidents. On May 8, Frank Bell took his new Benoist Model XII tractor biplane out in high winds. Shortly after taking off, he was forced to land only one-half mile from Kinloch Field. Jannus and Korn went in search of him. Within minutes of their takeoff, they sighted Bell's disabled biplane. With Jannus at the controls, the biplane went in for a landing. The soggy ground, softened by spring rains, caused the aircraft to lose its forward momentum. Jannus prematurely shut off the engine. With the lack of power and the bogging down of the landing gear, the airplane nosed down. Jannus was thrown clear of the machine; Korn bounced against the aircraft's control surfaces. Korn suffered superficial bruises on his left leg; Jannus was unhurt. Instead of one grounded Benoist machine, now there were two. The three men set about making repairs to the airplanes but shortly gave up because of the heavy winds. They tied the machines down to prevent further damage and walked back to Kinloch Field.

Less than a week later, the black crepe of death hung on the doors of the Benoist Aircraft Company. On May 13, Peter S. Glasser and Raymond Wheeler took one of the Benoists out for a training flight. Glasser, a twenty-seven-year-old Benoist student, was at the controls. Wheeler, also a student, was riding as a passenger. While approaching Kinloch Field for a landing, their aircraft was hit by a violent updraft. The thousand-pound machine immediately shot twenty feet upward. Just as quickly, the airplane dropped. Struggling to control his airplane, Glasser barely managed to clear a tree. Those watching breathed a collective sigh of relief, but it was short-lived. Glasser misjudged the distance, cut his landing short, and sheared the top off a telegraph pole. Diving headfirst to the ground, the aircraft crashed on the steel tracks of the railroad bed. The attempted landing was described as like "a pigeon dropping to the ground."[30]

The airplane caught fire on impact; the unconscious bodies of both fliers were dragged from the flames by spectators. The thirty-year-old Wheeler died in the United Railway car that transported the injured men to Welleston where an ambulance awaited. Glasser was taken to St. Luke's Hospital, Wheeler to the city morgue. The prognosis was guarded but optimistic for Glasser; doctors had decided to amputate his right leg just above the knee. Suddenly, Glasser took a turn for the worse and died two days later. The deaths of Glasser and Wheeler were the first flying fatalities at Kinloch Field and the only fatalities while the Benoist school was located there.[31] Glasser had been deemed qualified to try for his license.[32] The accident was blamed on pilot error.[33]

With the deaths of Glasser and Wheeler behind them, Benoist and Jannus needed to get on with the business at hand. Despite the trag-

Students of the Benoist Flying School, Kinloch Field, Missouri, April 6, 1912. Tom Benoist is on the extreme left. Jannus is fourth from left. Author's collection.

edy, there were still students to be taught and airplanes to be built. At least half a dozen students were still enrolled at the flying school and needed attention.

Accidents in aviation were a way of life to young fliers. Hubert Latham, Jannus's early role model, was pragmatic about aerial accidents and death. Latham said, "The death of one of our comrades does not frighten us."[34] Ironically, the Anglo-French Latham did not meet his end in an airplane crash; he died on the ground, gored by a wild buffalo during a hunt in the French Congo.[35]

The early airmen had good reason to be uneasy. A lot could go wrong while flying, and it often did. In the early years of the 1900s, it was generally accepted that there were only four men in the entire world who could fly an airplane—Wilbur and Orville Wright, Henry Farman, and Alberto Santos-Dumont.[36] By the end of the first decade of the twentieth century, it was believed that there were two thousand to six thousand aviators. Some of them were experienced, some were not. Because of so many unknowns in the world of aviation, all aviators were experimenters.

THE NEXT MONTH saw Benoist and Jannus involved in several new projects. On June 4, 1912, Major Frank R. Lang of the United States Army's Signal Corps conducted air-to-ground firing tests of a weapon while flying with Jannus. Colonel J. J. Dooley, a reserve ordnance officer, had the weapon especially built for Lang by the Savage Arms Corporation of New York. A pistol with a skeleton attachment, the gun could be used from the shoulder if desired.[1] The size of the weapon without the shoulder piece was the same as a Savage automatic or a Luger pistol, about nine inches in length and weighing only a couple of pounds. The addition of the shoulder piece made the weapon approximately the size of a light rifle. It used a .32 caliber cartridge fired from a clip with the cartridges carried in a single line. With the cartridges loaded one above the other, the weapon could be fired in a machine gun–like fashion as long as the trigger was pressed. In the classic definition of a machine gun, however, it was an automatic pistol.

Early on the morning of June 4, Jannus, Lang, and Dooley went to Kinloch to prepare for rapid-fire air-to-ground tests. The men staked several four-foot square sheets of white muslin as targets in various sections of the field. While Lang and Dooley alternated as passengers, all three men took turns firing the Savage automatic from as high as five hundred feet above the field. The *St. Louis Post-Dispatch* reported that it was "the first test ever made of aeroplane marksmanship with an automatic pistol."[2]

Jannus was reported to be an excellent shot and seldom flew without some kind of firearm on board. Later, Jannus and Lang conducted further tests at Creve Coeur Lake in one of the Benoist flying boats. Unfortunately, and unusual for a Jannus-Benoist project, there were neither cameramen nor newspaper reporters on hand to record these tests.

The first firing of an actual machine gun from an airplane had occurred at College Park on June 7, 1912.[3] Captain Charles Chandler operated the gun, while Lieutenant Thomas D. Milling flew the airplane. Jannus and Chandler were latecomers when it came to firing weapons from airplanes. Lieutenant T. E. Fickel of the United States Army's Signal Corps had first performed this feat in August 1910.[4]

Later that same month, Benoist and Jannus decided to become heavily involved in the hydroplane business. Jannus began scouting out waterways near St. Louis, deciding upon Creve Coeur Lake in St. Louis County about twelve miles west of Kinloch Field. On July 20, the hydroplane was taken there. One large pontoon measuring fifteen feet long and five feet wide was fitted beneath the body of the airplane. A small pontoon was attached to the bottom of each wing tip.

Jannus and J. D. Smith spent most of the day making adjustments to their plane. Finally, both men were satisfied that the new creation was ready to go. At five o'clock, wearing only a bathing suit, Jannus climbed behind the controls to test the capabilities of the newest Benoist in the fleet. Standing in a small skiff, Smith turned over the propeller by hand. The six-cylinder engine purred like a large, noisy cat. Smith hung onto a wing tip as Jannus towed the boat and its passenger back to shore.

After effortlessly gliding across the calm waters of the lake for five hundred feet, Jannus tipped the elevator. Almost immediately the plane reached an elevation of 150 feet. In several minutes he had pushed it to an altitude of 1,000 feet. Nearly all activity on the lake had ceased; all eyes were on Jannus. The maiden flight of the hydroplane was short. Jannus stayed in the air only long enough to reach altitude and then spiraled back down. His return to the water was every bit as graceful as his liftoff. While taxiing to his landing place, however, Jannus struck a submerged buoy, damaging the large pontoon.[5] Fearing that there might be danger to his aircraft, he hurried toward his mooring, still a mile away. He opened the throttle, picking up speed and lifting the nose to keep the head of the smashed pontoon from taking on water.

Once safely moored, Jannus and Benoist excitedly patted each other on the back with congratulatory gestures. The hydroplane had fulfilled their expectations. It had easily taken to the air the first time it was tested. Equally important, it had not sunk when it sustained minor damage to a pontoon. This first flight taught them to divide the large middle pontoon into several smaller chambers. If damage occurred to one part of the pontoon, the entire float would not take on water. A celebration was in order. After a hard day of flying, the group frequently drove to the Hesperian Rowing Club located on the west shore of Creve Coeur Lake. The Hesperian offered a floating pavilion where the men could sit, discuss the flights, and unwind with a glass of cold beer.

In mid-July, St. Louis and the surrounding area was hit hard by a series of severe thunderstorms, resulting in heavy flooding of the Missouri and Mississippi Rivers. Streets and sewers overflowed with the runoff. Electric tramway lines were quickly knocked out of commission. Concrete levees that lined the rivers were destroyed, bridges were torn up, and thousands of houses were washed from their foundations.

When the weather finally cleared enough to fly, Jannus and William Trefts, Jr., the *St. Louis Post-Dispatch* photographer, set out to conduct an aerial survey of the damage. They flew over the Florissant Valley, Creve Coeur Lake, and the St. Charles territories bordering the Missouri side of the Mississippi River.[6] When the two men returned to Kinloch Field, they alerted the authorities to what they had witnessed. Several boats were dispatched to remote farmhouses to rescue people who had been forced to the tops of their roofs by the flood.

During the week of August 1, the Aero Club of Illinois announced details of the Second International Air Meet, including $24,000 in cash prizes. In September 1912, Jannus shipped the hydroplane to Chicago, where he planned to participate in the contest. Chicago's Grant Park and Cicero Aviation Field, the dual sites of the meet, featured new hangars, fences, concessions, and grandstands.

The events strongly favored Jannus's style of flying. Few fliers in the United States were more skilled in hydroplane piloting than Jannus. The most difficult of all the events for Jannus would be the speed races. Certainly flying skill would be necessary; just as important would be engine size. Jannus's Benoist was equipped with the seventy-five-horsepower Roberts engine. Several entrants had aircraft powered with Hall-Scott eighty-horsepower engines. There were also entrants running Gnome fifty-horsepower engines and even a Wright thirty-two. A system of handicapping had been developed to even up the odds and give everyone a fair chance.

Tom Benoist in his advertising circular described the Chicago meet of 1912 as "the most ambitious venture into the field of aeroplane exhibitions attempted in the country this season."[7] Benoist's assessment was correct. At times during the event, the crowd was estimated at just under one hundred thousand people.

Before the meet opened, catastrophe struck when Paul Peck crashed while flying at Cicero Field. Peck had gone up in his new Columbia-Gyro biplane for a short test flight just before twilight. At an altitude of one thousand feet, he put the biplane into a dive. The aircraft moved into a gentle spiral. Coming out of his second spiral, his nose and left wing were at too severe an angle. The airplane sideslipped. At one hundred miles per hour, Peck was unable to pull out of the steep dive. Before he could recover control, the nose of the airplane smashed straight into the field. So severe was the head-on impact that Peck's glasses and goggles were ground into his head.[8] He died of a fractured skull and internal injuries. Jannus had taught Peck to fly in the spring of 1911.

The first full day of the meet featured the 124.8-mile Gordon Bennett race. Everyone expected it to easily be won by the overconfident French aviator Jules Védrines. That was exactly what happened. Védrines won with a time of 70 minutes 56.8 seconds as only a few hundred people watched him fly his Armand Deperdussin monoplane to a world's record.[9] Much larger crowds would turn out for later events. Perhaps the speed races around the closed course were of little interest to Americans; Védrines was of little interest to Chicagoans.

The Wright brothers were always parsimonious when it came to recognizing the efforts of anyone but themselves. In 1903, Roy Knabenshue had won a $100,000 prize for piloting the dirigible *California Arrow* three and one-half miles in twenty-eight minutes. When Wilbur Wright heard of the success of the *California Arrow*, he managed only the caustic comment, "The performance of the Baldwin machine is creditable though not remarkable."[10] A spectator at Clearing when Védrines won the $10,000 Gordon Bennett trophy, Wright was unimpressed and said, "It was a pretty exhibition of speed, very pretty; and the fliers did well. It was to be expected that the French machine would win. The French have made a specialty of perfecting speed machines. American sportsmen call rather for a utility machine. So far as we are concerned we will continue to try to develop the aeroplane in that direction. I expect to see the time when we will have perfectly safe passenger carrying machines in America."[11]

With the Gordon Bennett race accomplished, the Aero Club of Illinois began the international aviation meet. Held at the Cicero Aviation Field, this part of the twelve-day event had drawn twenty-four well-known aviators from all over the world. The entrants were as varied a group of fliers as could be assembled. Maurice Prévost, the Frenchman, was known for speed. Max Lillie had been the only American pilot to enter the Gordon Bennett event. Farnum T. Fish was the first person to pilot an airplane from Chicago to Milwaukee. Giuseppe Callucci, a former Italian military pilot, had an excellent record in Europe.

Jannus's first day at the races was a wonderful success. In a head-to-head duel with Glenn Martin, Jannus proved his mettle. With a time of twelve minutes and forty-eight seconds, he placed first in the biplane speed race and earned himself $275.[12] Martin was second with a time of thirteen minutes and four seconds. The duration flying event, which carried a total prize of $500, saw Martin prevail with eighty-seven minutes in the air. Jannus was not even close with only thirty-seven minutes.[13] Scoring of the event was simple. Each aviator received $1.35 for each minute flown. Martin won the landing contest; Jannus did not place. Dropping a mailbag into the net went to Jannus. His bag was only forty-nine and one-half feet away from the net. Jannus was top money winner with $475 while Martin finished a close second with $463.

Day two was marred by a light drizzle. Martin won the accurate landing contest with a distance of only nine feet. Jannus managed a second-place finish in the twenty-kilometer biplane speed race. The big nonflying event was the firing of Giuseppe Callucci by his sponsor because of his second crackup of the day.[14] Other than second place in the speed race, Jannus was shut out. Martin was now the leading money winner.

On the third day of the races, Jannus's hopes began to fade. He failed to finish the twenty-kilometer biplane handicap race. Fortunately for Jannus, Martin had been disqualified at the outset for crowding at the pylons. Jannus earned less than $30 for his efforts at duration flying.

Jannus's day had been bad, but at least he was still alive. The twenty-kilometer race had ended in tragedy. Late on the afternoon of September 14, Howard Gill took to the air above the Cicero Aviation Field in his Wright biplane. Only minutes before, George Mestach of France had taken off in his Borel monoplane when race officials decided to run the biplane and monoplane races at the same time. Mestach later claimed that it had been too dark to fly, but he had been forced to race because of the nearly five thousand spectators at Cicero Aviation Field.[15]

When Mestach arrived at the far turn of the twenty-kilometer course, panic hit when he heard the whirring of Gill's engine. Mestach pulled back on the controls hoping to avoid Gill's airplane, but his monoplane was struck by the biplane at an altitude of two hundred feet. Both aircraft uncontrollably plummeted to the ground. Gill was killed; Mestach eventually recovered.

Following his near shutout of the previous day, September 15 saw Jannus emerge with substantial prize winnings. Thanks to Jannus, crowds at Cicero Aviation Field were treated to an aviation first when he became the holder of a new American record for duration flying. In a flight lasting no more than a minute, Jannus flew around the Cicero race course. Once he touched the ground briefly but bounced back into the air. In his one minute of flying time, Jannus earned $450. More important, he won two events and set the American duration flight record for carrying three passengers in addition to the pilot.[16] At the same time, he won $250 for carrying three passengers more than five hundred feet.

Max Lillie was awarded the $250 prize for having achieved the greatest duration in the single-flight-with-a-pilot-and-two-passengers event. Rightfully, it belonged to Jannus. A joint statement signed by Jannus and Lillie explained what had happened: "It was really won by Antony Jannus in a Benoist. Max Lillie picked up two newspaper men and flew 5:30 [minutes] with them. Jannus who wasted a great deal of time, having passengers officially weighed and certified, carried his 4:35 [minutes], and finding that on Saturday and Sunday that no one else had weighed in for the two and three passenger events, considered the decision his. When the error was discovered protest was too late, according to the rules. Lillie, who himself suffered from a technicality in the accurate landing event, offered to split the $250 with Jannus and admit officially that the event should have been awarded Jannus in the event of protest."[17] The two men, if not friends, were more than passing acquaintances; both operated flying schools at Kinloch Field.[18] Lillie had not meant to cheat Jannus of prize money or recognition. The situation had developed only because of the poor management and officiating which had been rife at the Chicago meet.

The final day of the event Jannus excelled. He took a first and second prize in two crib races which allowed the racer to pilot his hydroplane either in the air as an airplane or on the water as a motor boat. A third place in the steeplechase netted Jannus $50.

So proficient was Jannus in the figure eight event that he won first prize every day during the meet. His secret in making the required five figure eights was to stall his engine. Then he would tilt the wing tips toward the ground and make his Benoist biplane swing around on one wing.

When the events concluded, Jannus was second in total earnings with $4,003. Only Glenn Martin with $4,854 had outdistanced him. Only two records had been set throughout the entire twelve-day event, and one belonged to Jannus.[19] The other was the speed record set by

Jules Védrines during the Gordon Bennett race.[20] Following Chicago, Jannus was recognized as the premier hydroplane pilot in the United States.

Benoist claimed that Jannus's hydroplane was the only machine to fly through the entire event without repairs. The *New York Times*, however, reported that Jannus suffered from a punctured pontoon and on one occasion his machine had to be towed in.[21] An advertising circular bragged, "During the four days of flying with hydro's at Grant Park, Jannus' Benoist machine was the only one that went through the whole meet without repairs. One of the competing machines was found to be damaged after each days flying and required from two to ten hours work to keep it in condition for flying each following day."[22] Years later, Glenn Martin recalled, "Tony Jannus was an excellent flier and a good competitor." [23]

The "bad boy" flier, Lincoln Beachey, made several appearances. His flying stunts amazed as well as frightened the crowds and event officials. In his Curtiss biplane, Beachey did everything he could to aggravate the race officials. He used light posts and cars lining Michigan Avenue for an aerial steeple chase. When he dived his biplane toward busy city streets, spectators ran for safety. The *Chicago Daily Tribune* claimed, "He did a 'Texas Tommy dance' up Michigan avenue in the late afternoon, jigging his wheels on the pavement, rocking sideways so that Miss Alice Walsh, the cigar clerk in the Auditorium hotel, thought he was going to fly through the window and grasped her purse and ran."[24]

Politics and disagreement had been prevalent around the hangars and airfields at the meet. As races and aerial meets were taking place, an inquest was being held. Testimony about the Howard Gill crash charged officials of the Aero Club of Illinois with malfeasance.[25] When the hearings concluded, Mestach had been cleared of any wrongdoing in the death of Gill. Blame for the midair collision was laid at the feet of race officials. The accident and responsibility for it were not the only problems. Competitors claimed that Lincoln Beachey was involved in the meet contrary to the rules of sanction. Winners of some races were stripped of their prizes.[26] A minor flap developed when several aviators, including Jannus, were refused admittance to the hangars at the Clearing aviation races before the Gordon Bennett race. The fliers claimed that they had been promised admittance to any aviation field, hangar, or aero meet in the state of Illinois. Matters were made worse when the legendary Jack Johnson, the African-American heavyweight boxer, was allowed to visit the hangar.[27] Unrest became so pervasive among the fliers that on the night of September 20 they had held a meeting to decide whether to strike.[28]

After two weeks of grueling flying in Chicago, the Benoist team returned to St. Louis. They took a short breather and prepared their aircraft for Jannus's next event, the New St. Louis State Fair. While performing there, Jannus carried the first air freight in St. Louis and proved that the airplane was faster than the automobile.[29]

At 3:30 on the afternoon of September 24, workers loaded a case of Lemp Brewery Falstaff beer onto Jannus's airplane. Shortly after, he took off from the grounds of Lemp Brewery. Twenty minutes later, he was sure that he must be close to his destination, the St. Louis Fairgrounds. Smoke belching from the smokestacks of the factories in the west end of St. Louis had obscured his vision. Jannus was lost, enveloped in smoke. When he increased altitude, he saw only a thick dirty blanket of smoke below him. Blindly descending through the thick smoke, Jannus landed in a farmer's tomato patch, still at least four miles away from the fairgrounds. Unable to take off from the tomato patch, Jannus had to push and drag the nearly one-thousand-pound airplane to an adjacent hay field. Armed with directions, he took off and headed toward the fairgrounds.

Jannus arrived at the fair at 5 P.M., nearly an hour late. Spiraling down, he made a dramatic landing in the infield of the fair's race track. In his three-passenger Benoist, Jannus had become the first aviator to carry a consignment of air freight in St. Louis.[30]

That Benoist, a strict Methodist and nondrinker, would use beer as a way to support his endeavors was an irony not lost on his friends. The Benoist tractor was christened the *Falstaff Flyer*. Undoubtedly Benoist accepted the inevitable ribbing with his usual dry humor as he pocketed the $500 from Lemp Brewery.

The afternoon of September 26, known as "Big Thursday," saw Jannus participate in what was described as "the most thrilling race on

Jannus, in the *Falstaff Flyer;* racing Dude Iseminger at the New St. Louis Fair, September 26, 1912. Courtesy of the Florida Aviation Historical Society.

the programme." Jannus in his Benoist biplane was competing with Dan "Dude" Iseminger, a Warren, Missouri, automobile racer. The grandstands were tightly packed. A thick crowd had collected for over one-half mile along the quarter and back stretch of the track. The long-anticipated contest between the two early twentieth-century marvels, the airplane and the automobile, was delayed while Iseminger performed last-minute repairs to the automobile's clutch. Once the repairs were out of the way, the race was postponed again because a mule race was scheduled for the track. While Iseminger worked on his clutch and the mules raced, Jannus kept busy flying two exhibitions over the fairgrounds.

Finally at 5:30 P.M., everyone was ready for the three-mile race. Jannus left Iseminger in his prop wash. He flew as close to the surface of the oval track as possible. Iseminger pushed his Warren Racing Car as fast as it could go. It was nip and tuck for the first two miles. By the third mile, Jannus had a clear advantage. He crossed the finish line one hundred feet ahead of Iseminger. Paid attendance exceeded 127,000 people.

On October 5, Jannus flew from Hardin, Illinois, located on the Illinois River, to St. Louis, a distance by river of nearly seventy-five miles. Accompanied by Benoist mechanic Elmer Straub, Jannus had recently concluded several days of exhibition flying at Hardin. Loading his toolbox and trademark suitcase into the airplane, Jannus was ready to go. Halfway down the Mississippi River, Jannus crossed paths with the northbound steamer *Spread Eagle* of the Eagle Packet Line. Wildly and repeatedly, the captain of the *Spread Eagle* yanked on his whistle. Later the captain claimed to be the first steamboat captain on the Mississippi River to have exchanged signals with an airplane.[31] One hour and eighteen minutes after leaving Hardin, Jannus and Straub landed in St. Louis just off Market Street. As he flew low under the steel trestles of St. Louis's McKinley Bridge, Jannus's flight unceremoniously came to an abrupt halt. He ran out of gasoline and was forced to land in the middle of the Mississippi River at the foot of Carr Street. Jannus and Straub sat in the fuselage of the hydroplane talking and smoking Fatima cigarettes until a river tug towed them back to Market Street. Jannus's

Jannus was rumored to have been romantically involved with many women. One was the actress Ruth Stonehouse, shown here with Tony in August 1912. Author's collection.

trip from Hardin to St. Louis was extraordinary not because it was the first time a hydroplane had been seen on that part of the river but because Jannus's seventy-eight-minute trip would normally have taken half a day and all night on a Mississippi River steamboat, there being no railroad connections between Hardin and St. Louis.

On October 10, heavy winds, at times gusting to thirty-five miles per hour, swept up the Mississippi River. Thousands of people lined the riverfront in anticipation of Jannus's afternoon exhibition. The wind was so fierce and cold that many of the crowd had already given up, certain that the exhibition would be canceled. After much deliberation, Jannus decided to fly. At 1:15 P.M. he taxied the hydroplane from the foot of Market Street into the middle of the river. Giving it full throttle, he headed into the wind and was quickly airborne. Flying south, skimming along the water at no more than fifteen feet above the surface, he flew under the steel spans of the partially completed Free Bridge. Still headed south, he was soon out of sight. Turning over the river, he headed toward his starting point and his objective—an aerial bombing attack on the United States Navy cruiser *Isla de Luzon*. Jannus made a low scouting pass over the *Luzon* and continued north to the Eads Bridge. He flew under the middle span of the bridge and continued north for another three hundred yards. Turning around, he flew south, flying and skipping on the water's surface until he returned to the foot of Market Street. The *Luzon* was safe for another day. The wind was too strong; Jannus had been unable to drop even one tomato bomb onto the deck of the ship.

Two days later, Jannus went after the *Luzon* in earnest. After takeoff, Jannus took the hydroplane up to an altitude of 250 feet. Headed north along the Mississippi River, Jannus flew over the Eads Bridge. The crowd watched in anticipation as he banked over the river and prepared to return and begin his attack on the *Luzon*. Instead of flying over the bridge, he piloted the aircraft under the bridge, emerging from inside the middle span.

Unknown to the watching crowd, Jannus had nearly crashed into the Mississippi. After the flight, he said, "When I circled and started back south, I ran into a thick bank of smoke from the Union Electric Light plant at the foot of Biddle Street. Instantly the aeroplane went dead. The cloud of smoke was filled with gas too light to support the planes [wings] and I fell a couple of hundred feet as sharply as if I had been hit by a real shell from the one pound guns that had kept firing at me from the *Luzon*. The gas nearly overcame me and I was very sick when I regained control of the plane just a few feet above the water. That was why I came back under the bridge, instead of sailing over it."[32]

Flying at low altitude, sometimes leapfrogging across the surface of the water, he continued south until he passed under the Free Bridge. Eventually he disappeared from sight. The waiting crowd heard Jannus's engine before they saw him. He sped over the Free Bridge at sixty-five miles per hour. Swooping down, he banked the aircraft and circled the *Luzon*. Flying over the ship's deck, Jannus drew a bead on the target below. Releasing a bomb constructed of plaster of paris filled with flour, he pulled back on the elevator stick and quickly regained altitude. In his wake he left puffs of smoke from the blanks fired by rifles and the ship's one-pound cannons. Three times Jannus attacked the ship with bombs while its crew attempted to rebuff his aerial assault. Jannus's bombs fell short of their targets; flying the airplane and dropping bombs by himself was more than one man could reasonably be expected to achieve with any degree of accuracy. Forward airspeed, altitude, wind velocity, and weight of the bombs all had to be taken into account.

In 1909, St. Louis had celebrated its centennial as a city. As part of the celebration, city leaders had hired Glenn Curtiss to come from Hammondsport and fly for a guaranteed $6,000. On October 9, Curtiss's flight had been short in both duration and altitude. The exhibition lasted no more than two minutes and was nothing more than a few short hops. On October 19, three years later, in front of a crowd that numbered fewer than three thousand people, Jannus took off from Forest Park headed for Kinloch Field, a distance of thirteen miles. Taking off from Skinker Road directly in front of Washington University, he gained altitude and circled over the Jefferson Memorial. Jannus then climbed to an altitude of one thousand feet and made the thirteen-mile flight in only thirteen minutes.[33] After landing, Jannus said, "Curtiss was not to blame for his failure to fly over Art Hill. With the aeroplanes of two years ago, he would not have been able to accomplish the feat. The park is deficient in adequate starting and landing places."[34]

By the end of October, Jannus was doing most of his flying in the hydroplane at Creve Coeur Lake. Since they had started building the hydros, Benoist's method of student instruction had undergone a change. The flying curriculum now began with a preliminary course of instruction in the hydroplane at Creve Coeur.[35] Only when Jannus was confident of the students' ability to master the hydroplane in overwater flying were they advanced to the more dangerous level of instruction in the land machine. Benoist had produced two hydros in a short period of time; both were now seeing action at Creve Coeur Lake.

✈ *The Great Rivers Flight*

IN THE FALL OF 1912, Jannus was energized by his success at the Second International Air Meet in Chicago. He was about to embark on a new adventure, a 1,973-mile over-water flight. Lasting forty days, Jannus's flying trek would take him from Omaha, Nebraska, to New Orleans, a trip of epic dimensions. Jannus would follow the two longest rivers in the United States, the Missouri and Mississippi.

While Jannus prepared for the flight, Benoist firmed up the finances and management of his company. He traveled to Hammondsport, New York, where he met with Glenn Curtiss, visited the Curtiss factory, and inspected Curtiss's flying boat. While at Hammondsport, Benoist convinced his old friend Hugh A. Robinson to return to St. Louis to work for him. By November, Robinson had arrived in St. Louis. He had also bought a small financial interest in the company.[1] Robinson's affiliation with the company seemed to make great sense. He was an experienced exhibition flier and had been credited with several aeronautical inventions.[2] More important, Robinson was intimately familiar with hydroplaning. He had set a record with an airmail flight of 375 miles along the Mississippi from Minneapolis, Minnesota, to Rock Island, Illinois.

Dour-faced and eight years older than Jannus, he did not possess the magnetism and outgoing personality of the younger man. Brought on board as Benoist's chief engineer and plant superintendent, Robinson did some flying but not as much as Jannus. His entry into the tight-knit company proved to be a source of friction. Jannus had been the unchallenged star of the company and bristled at the suggestions

Robinson made. Benoist was equally unhappy with his recruitment of Robinson.

Jannus regarded the proposed river trip as no more dangerous than a Sunday picnic.[3] His black suitcase was stuffed with his leather coat, three sets of heavy woolen underwear, and a full dress suit. Accompanying Jannus, as always, was the mechanic J. D. Smith. He did not have the luxury of flying with Jannus; instead, Smith traveled overland from city to city to meet him. Smith routinely checked the green-topped Splitdorph spark plugs and listened to the sound of the engine to determine if it was properly tuned. Carburetors had to be adjusted before each flight. When time permitted, tears and holes in the fabric of the wings and fuselage were repaired.

Jannus's aircraft for the trip was a Benoist tractor biplane with the engine mounted in the front. Powered by a six-cylinder, two-cycle, seventy-five-horsepower Roberts engine, the biplane had a nonstop range of 120 miles. The Type XII Cross Country model was the most current of Benoist's fleet, at a cost of $3,950 equipped for land, or $4,150 with pontoons. For $4,350, Benoist would outfit the airplane for both land and water use. Capable of a sixty-mile-per-hour speed, the 925-pound airplane had room for the pilot and two passengers. The biplane was rigged to use either pontoons or wheels, giving Jannus an extra margin of safety.[4]

There was no airspeed indicator, tachometer, or fuel gauge. When the pilot wanted to know how much gasoline remained, he tapped on the tank. An echoing "thunk" would tell him approximately how much fuel was left. The pilot sat in back, while the passenger sat forward, right behind the engine. The noise of the unmuffled engine was deafening.

The Lemp Beer Company agreed to pay $2,500 for Jannus to carry a case of Falstaff beer from the mayor of St. Louis to the mayor of New Orleans.[5] John Henning, who had recently joined Benoist's company, was responsible for this early marketing promotion. As advance man, he drummed up publicity and set up exhibitions in towns along the way. Henning recalled, "Once, when there was no quick way to reach the next town, I had to ride astride a 50-gallon fuel tank in the plane. The tank and our precious case of beer had to be carried in the only seat we had for a passenger, so there was no other place to park me."[6] When Jannus gave exhibitions and rides, the case of beer had to be offloaded. While Jannus was in the air giving passengers five-minute rides, Henning was on the ground sitting on the beer to protect it. In a letter to the St. Petersburg, Florida, Chamber of Commerce, Henning took complete credit for initiating and managing the 1,973-mile trip. In this same letter, he reminisced about his working relationship with Jannus and Benoist: "My connections with Tom Benoist and Tony Jannus are one of the happiest relations of my 55 years of business life: it was like a well-oiled, smooth geared machine: each one knew his part and we all worked, never taking ourselves or the work seriously but rather in a joyous vein."[7] Although never licensed by the Aero Club of America, Henning had been a member of the first civilian pilot class held by Orville Wright.[8]

While flying from Omaha to St. Louis, Jannus planned to take part in a five-hundred-mile race with A. M. Carlson. Driving his high-powered automobile, Carlson was expected to follow the roads along the Missouri River. The automobile's top speed was seventy-eight miles per hour.[9] Jannus could maintain an average airspeed of sixty miles per hour. Jannus told the *St. Louis Times* that "he was confident of winning a race with an automobile."[10] Other than the original story appearing in the *St. Louis Times* on October 24 to promote the race, there is no further mention of it.

Jannus's aircraft had been trucked to Carter Lake on the outskirts of Omaha. He and Smith spent the morning of November 5 assembling the aircraft. That afternoon, Jannus took a practice flight around the Omaha area; Smith labored through the night overhauling the engine. Jannus made six flights on the morning of November 6. The main flight was scheduled to begin that afternoon. Newspapers along the Mississippi River heralded the upcoming event.[11]

While flying an exhibition less than two hours before the scheduled takeoff, Jannus had an accident. When he came in too low over an anchored boat, he sheared off its mast. The aircraft sustained a badly smashed pontoon. By 3:15 P.M., the damaged pontoon had been replaced. Jannus took off at 4:00 to the sounds of a gunfire salute. He carried a letter of greeting from George E. Haverstick, president of the Omaha Commercial Club, to John Wilde, his Kansas City counterpart. This letter carried by Jannus was the first to leave Omaha by air.[12]

Almost immediately, he experienced spark plug trouble. Jannus put the craft down in the water and made minor adjustments to the carburetor which temporarily eliminated the missing of the engine. He was unable to pull the spark plugs because he had opted not to bring a tool kit so as to save weight.[13] With the wind at his back, Jannus took to the air again. As the aircraft lifted from the water, three cylinders cut out. Coaxing what he could from the engine, he nursed the machine the remaining twenty miles to Nebraska City.

The next day, Jannus left Nebraska City at 3:15 P.M., headed for Forest City, Missouri, eighty-seven miles south. Slightly over halfway into the flight, Jannus experienced trouble. He landed in the river and maneuvered onto a sandbar. This time he had a tool kit on board and was able to replace the fouled plugs. He then climbed back into the aircraft and cranked up the engine, but attempts to pull off the sandbar

Jannus in the Benoist Number 35 receiving final instructions from Tom Benoist before starting on his record-setting 1,973-mile trip from Omaha to New Orleans. The trip started on November 6, not November 7 as the photograph indicates. Courtesy of the Florida Aviation Historical Society.

The Benoist Number 35 before Jannus's departure from Omaha on November 6, 1912. Courtesy of the Florida Aviation Historical Society.

The Benoist Number 35 in flames on the Mississippi River, November 21, 1912. Jannus was forced to delay resumption of the flight from Omaha to New Orleans until a replacement aircraft was brought to the river. Author's collection.

THE GREAT RIVERS FLIGHT

Workers load cases of Lemp beer onto Jannus's aircraft on the afternoon of September 24, 1912. The beer was the first air freight to be carried in St. Louis. Courtesy of the Florida Aviation Historical Society.

were fruitless. He climbed out of the craft and began pushing the machine free. Almost immediately, he was in quicksand up to his knees. Jannus recalled, "This did not seem serious until I tried to get out. But by many struggles and a stop of about forty minutes, during all of which time I left the motor running in the hope of attracting human assistance, I was able to extricate myself."[14] Taking no chances after he pulled himself from the gritty trap, he applied full throttle and plowed through the sandbar. He complained of sore legs and limped for a week afterward. With sunset approaching, he ran the machine to the small village of Brown's Landing. When discussing the quicksand episode he quipped that "it was necessary to extricate himself from this difficulty at once or the first death would be charged against hydroaeroplaning when the plane would be found in the morning without the driver."[15]

Jannus left Brown's Landing a little after 6:00 A.M. on November 8. His destination was St. Joseph, Missouri, approximately one hundred miles away. When his gas supply ran out, he was forced to land at

White Cloud. He telegraphed Smith, who had gone by train to Forest City; Smith backtracked to White Cloud. According to Smith's diary, he "hired an automobile to get there, bad place to get to Jannus, had to wade out to him, no boots or tool box."[16]

With a thirty-mile wind at his back, Jannus flew off to St. Joseph, where Smith again had to come to his assistance. According to Smith, Jannus "landed there at 11a.m., landed on Lovers' Island. No way to get there, but to have the Captain of *Dorothy*, a sand boat row us over, everything in fine shape."[17] Most of the people encountered were friendly and willing to help, but not always. Jannus recalled, "One farmer, who, was trying to be the main assistant, and whose sons were standing by, let go and told me I couldn't boss him around in his sons' presence. I had to promise the old fellow a case of beer—that was in a dry Missouri county, opposite Kansas—to pacify him."[18]

Early on the morning of November 9, Jannus gave an exhibition at St. Joseph. At 7:30 a.m., he headed for Kansas City, one hundred miles due south. En route Jannus encountered strong head winds, causing the plane to run out of gas at Parkville, Missouri. During landing, a pontoon was smashed. Jannus called into Kansas City for gasoline. Benoist made the trip by automobile, carrying a load of oil and gas with him.

While waiting for the gasoline, Jannus repaired the pontoon. At Parkville, curiosity nearly wrecked the hydroplane. Jannus related, "I had to go away and leave my machine for a short time, and some college boys climbed on it and tipped it over in the water, so that one of the planes was struck by the current."[19] As soon as the gasoline arrived, he filled the tank and took off. Twelve minutes later he was in Kansas City, floating at the foot of Mulberry Street.

Jannus had been scheduled to make several exhibition flights in Kansas City. When it became necessary to cancel them because of strong gusty winds, Smith took advantage of the downtime to do needed repair work on the aircraft. He installed a new pontoon on the machine and soldered the El Arco radiator. In flight, the leaky radiator had frequently sprayed Jannus with hot water. Jannus ordered a fifty-gallon gasoline tank shipped from St. Louis. The tank arrived on November 14.

For some reason, Jannus had not been communicating with Tom Benoist while he was laid up in Kansas City. Smith received a telegram from Benoist on November 13, asking, "What is the matter with Tony, does not seem to get my wires, see that he gets this, tell him we are working on river tours and give orders to leave K.C. as soon as possible. Jack (Henning) will call from Alton and make arrangements."[20] On November 14, Jannus left Kansas City at 2:00 P.M. After flying for slightly less than two hours, Tony had gone 110 miles. He landed at Waverly, Missouri, flew an exhibition, and left at 4:30 P.M. Half frozen from sitting in the open plane, he was forced to land at Glasgow, Missouri, an hour later.

Arriving in St. Charles, Missouri, during the afternoon of the sixteenth, Jannus turned the hydroplane over to his mechanic, who made sure that it was safely moored along the banks of the Missouri River. Jannus took the electric car into St. Louis where he spent the night. The flier told a reporter from the *St. Louis Post-Dispatch*, "Forty-five miles out of Jefferson City things got so bad that I had to land on a sandbar. When I had fixed the machine, having no one to help me, I had to wade into the water to get the machine off. So I had to go the rest of the way with wet feet and legs. But for that, I wouldn't have felt the cold."[21]

The next morning, Jannus returned to St. Charles by electric car. He then flew south by southeast until the Missouri River merged with the Mississippi. When he landed at the foot of Olive Street on the St. Louis levee shortly before sunset, thirty thousand people witnessed his arrival.[22] It had taken eleven days to cover the 728 miles from Omaha to St. Louis.[23] Jannus had demonstrated the "practicability and safety of the hydro-aeroplanes in sport and cruising."[24]

On November 21, Jannus was ready to leave St. Louis with William Trefts as a passenger. Trefts was carrying a motion picture camera to record the trip's progress through the South, but difficulties with his camera forced a delay in Jannus's departure. Local St. Louis politicians further delayed the departure by rushing up to the airplane to shake hands with Jannus. Finally Jannus became impatient to depart. As Smith recalled in his diary, "Tony said we are ready to start Smitty so I pointed up Smith ready. Tony started so I cranked it and the fire shot out all over the cockpit and set the machine on fire."[25]

Gasoline that had leaked into the cockpit during the engine start caught fire with a flashing roar. Jannus and Trefts jumped out of the plane. Smith tried to beat out the flames, but it was too late. The flimsy doped fabric of the wings had gone up like dry tinder in a forest fire. Within minutes the biplane was a charred wreck. Too much priming of the engine cylinder and Jannus's impatience had caused the fire. The carburetor had been flooded and the gasoline fumes hung heavily in the air. The printed "Instructions for Installing and Operating the Roberts Motors" stated, "When leaving the motor for any time, even for half an hour, it is a good plan to shut the gasoline off at the tank."[26] The burned aircraft was not salvageable; only the engine could be re-used. Trefts had lost one camera but had saved his expensive moving picture machine. When Jannus was asked about the accident, his answer was short: "Too many goodbyes."[27]

The incident could not have occurred in a better place. The Benoist factory, located on the outskirts of St. Louis, quickly provided another airplane. Benoist No. 31 was carried on a flatcar to the riverbank only twenty-four hours after Jannus's first aircraft had been destroyed. Years later, Benoist would claim that Jannus's carelessness led to the fire and destruction of the aircraft, but fire was a characteristic and constant threat with the two-cycle engine.

While waiting in St. Louis for his new machine, Jannus took a newly completed Benoist tractor for a test flight at Kinloch Field. Andrew Drew and DeLloyd Thompson were on the field with their students from Max Lillie's school. When Jannus arrived at the field, Drew and Thompson abandoned their pupils while the three pilots put on an impromptu exhibition. Both Benoist and Hugh Robinson were present at the field and were overheard complimenting Jannus on his skill.[28]

On November 25, Jannus and the photographer were on their way again. The day's flight was quiet and uneventful. After flying a total of 106 miles, Jannus spent the night in Grand Tower, Illinois. He left early on the morning of November 26, made Cape Girardeau, Missouri, in thirty minutes, and gave an exhibition. At 2 P.M. they headed for Cairo, Illinois, taking off in a smothering fog and heavy downpour. Several times he mistook river inlets for the river but realized his error and backtracked.

Narrowly missing crashing into the Thiebes bridge while flying in the fog, Jannus made a stopover in the small town of Thiebes, Illinois, to put on another exhibition. After leaving there, he flew only a few miles before stopping at Commerce, Missouri, for lunch. Departing Commerce, he again ran into navigational problems. In the fog, he mistook the Ohio River for the Mississippi River and flew several miles out of his way.[29] Jannus reached Cairo at 5 P.M. after having logged 181 miles. The large crowd was so anxious to meet Jannus and look at the airplane that an area had to be roped off to keep the surging crowd at bay.

Smith met Jannus and Trefts in Cairo. He fixed a broken oil pump and the still leaking radiator. When darkness made it impossible to continue working on the aircraft on the open banks of the Mississippi River, Smith smuggled parts of the engine, including the pistons, into his hotel room. He worked all night making the necessary repairs.

November 27 and 28 were spent in Cairo. Several exhibitions had been booked for the Cairo Merchants' Association. Jannus and Trefts made a late departure from Cairo at 5 P.M. on November 29, flying less than thirty miles before stopping at Columbus, Kentucky.

Caruthersville, Missouri, was their next destination. After taking off at 8:00 A.M., their first stop was Hickman, Kentucky, only eighteen miles out of Columbus. They landed at Hickman at 8:23 A.M. Because of high winds, Jannus decided to wait until afternoon when the winds would normally abate. He gave a thirty-minute exhibition at 2 P.M., then headed for New Madrid, Missouri. Their flight took them south, then northwest, then southwest, then almost due north. Seventy minutes after departing Hickman, Jannus landed in New Madrid. After a short exhibition, he was back in the air by 4 o'clock, reaching their next stopover at Caruthersville, Missouri, at 5:07 P.M. Because of the windy, rainy weather and the impending darkness, Jannus decided to spend the night at Caruthersville.

Caruthersville ended up being more than a one-night stopover because rain kept Jannus on the ground. In his journal, he wrote, "Dec. 1.—Rained all day. Decided not to leave until next day for Memphis."[30] Smith claimed that Jannus flew. In his diary, Smith wrote, "Broke bottom of boat but flew on to Memphis—where there was another boat for him to fly."[31] Did the second airplane, No. 31, end up crashed on the bank of the river? Because of safety concerns, would Benoist and Jannus purposely avoid making this particular episode public? Eugene F. Provenzo, Jr., wrote, "Several planes were used to make the trip."[32] There is no record of a third airplane being used, however; Smith almost certainly meant a pontoon, not another airplane.

After Jannus left Caruthersville, he made several stops on his way to Helena. He landed at Memphis early that morning while the city was still asleep and there were few people on the wharf to welcome him. E. J. McCormack, a staffer for the *Commercial Appeal* of Memphis recalled, "Jannus is a pleasant youngster, ruddy faced, with coal black hair, black eyes and a smile that spreads all over his face."[33] While in Memphis, Jannus gave several exhibitions and handily won a race with a powerboat.

Jannus left Memphis at 4 P.M. on December 5. Between December 5 and 12, he flew a total of 705 miles and gave several exhibitions. Jannus landed at Fairview, Louisiana, on December 12. Although Jannus suffered an attack of appendicitis, he and Trefts left Fairview at 8:30 A.M. the next day.[34] With a good tail wind, Jannus flew fifty-five miles in fifty minutes and landed at Wilhelm, Louisiana. At the time Smith did not know Jannus's whereabouts or about his illness. Finally, on December 13, Smith received word from Trefts that Jannus was ill.[35]

After an overnight at Wilhelm, Jannus stopped in Baton Rouge. After refueling, he took off for Plaquemine. Headed into heavy winds from the south, Jannus flew a total of ninety-eight miles in 110 minutes. On December 14, Smith was finally reunited with Jannus in Plaquemine. Smith's diary entry for that date reads: "Got up at 8:30 A.M. stayed around hotel all day till 3–30 when I took a walk up town not looking for Jannus to leave after hearing of him being sick, so after I got several blocks away to my surprise I saw the people run for dear life so it struck me it was Tony, and sure enough it was. So I went down to the river and Tony came up the bank and he said it's my fault Smitty for not calling up me."[36]

On December 15, Jannus gave an exhibition in Plaquemine at 1:40 P.M. Fifty miles later, he reached Donaldson, Louisiana, and then headed for the last stop. He arrived on the outskirts of New Orleans at about 4:45 P.M. With sunset approaching, he decided not to land in New Orleans. He turned the airplane around and went back up the river a few miles.

After landing, he and Trefts took a train into New Orleans. Monday morning, December 16, Jannus made his way back up the Mississippi River to his airplane. About the events of December 16, Smith wrote, "Got up at 5–30 am went to start Tony. Had him started at 9–30 am. I got train to Orleans at 10 a.m. Tony landed in Orleans at 9–30 a.m."[37]

Tom Benoist was the first to greet Jannus as he climbed out of his airplane. Pete Cassidy, the general agent for Lemp Beer, next welcomed Jannus to New Orleans. Final delivery of the case of beer represented $2,500 cash money to Benoist.[38] The men then boarded the riverboat *Sidney.* Automobiles waited for the group at the Canal Street landing, and soon they were headed down St. Charles Street. At City Hall, Jannus presented the letters he brought from the mayor of St. Louis.[39] The letter from Lemp Brewery to Martin Behrman, New Orleans's mayor, claimed, "The trip of Mr. Jannus from this city to yours is the longest freight-carrying run ever attempted by an aviator."[40]

By the time Jannus presented Mayor Behrman with the letter from Lemp, he had changed into a clean suit of clothes. He wore a dandy-ish-looking black homburg hat rakishly tilted on his head. Smith wrote, "They took him on the first auto in the parade. They put a captains hat on him and they took him to a big dinner."[41]

As a parting gesture to the Crescent City, Jannus treated more than fifty thousand spectators to a flying exhibition on December 18. While Jannus was in New Orleans, it was rumored that he was ready to end his carefree bachelor days and marry Blanche Flatch of St. Louis. When Jannus could have found the time to court a young woman defies imagination.

Several days later, the plane was crated and transported to St. Louis by railroad. Benoist sold it for $5,000 to a former Benoist flying school student and pupil of Tony Jannus, Cecil Raymond Benedict.[42] With the airplane on its way to St. Louis, the Benoist group split up and went their separate ways.[43] Jannus headed home to Washington for the Christmas holidays, without a bride.

The trip was a much needed financial success for Benoist. One airplane had been sold and there had been a great deal of publicity. He had realized a net profit of approximately $17,500. Following the completion of Jannus's flight, the Benoist flying school was temporarily closed. The big push was on at the factory to complete a new type of aircraft—the Benoist flying boat—in celebration of the success of Jannus's flight. With the pupils at home for the holidays, all efforts were focused on the new aircraft.

What was the motivation behind the forty-day trip? It was obviously intended to generate publicity and promote the sale of aircraft. It was also there to be done. No one had ever flown an over-water trip of such magnitude. It was a test of the pilot, the Benoist aircraft, and the Roberts engine. One of the most frequently asked questions of Tom Benoist was, "Why was Jannus's trip planned for so late in the season, when the weather was apt to be less than pleasant?" He responded, "The company wants to show the possibilities of hydro-aeroplaning under the very worst conditions, and in that way, prove the possibility of this mode of travel during the regular touring season."[44]

Jannus gained a tremendous sense of accomplishment from flying the 1,973 miles. He had set an aviation record for an over-water flight.[45] Jannus flew the first long-distance freight when he carried the case of Lemp Falstaff beer from St. Louis to New Orleans. The number of people Jannus and Benoist introduced to aviation in 1912 cannot be estimated. In some of the smaller towns, Jannus was the first aviator ever to be seen. In St. Louis alone, thirty thousand people turned out to meet him. In New Orleans, the newspapers reported that more than fifty thousand people witnessed his arrival. Thousands were treated to his forty-two aerial exhibitions.

Jannus carried a letter from the Lemp Brewery in St. Louis to an agent in Memphis, thus carrying the first airmail delivery letter into Memphis.[46] Jannus's 1,973-mile trip showed Americans that longer distance flights, including the crossing of the Atlantic, were possible.

Although Jannus received all of the glory, adulation, and hero worship, the trip was a classic example of a team effort. As superb a pilot as Jannus may have been, he could not have done it by himself. His mechanic, J. D. Smith, was every bit as important to the successful completion of the long and grueling trip. They were equally dedicated and motivated to making the flight from Omaha to New Orleans a safe one.

Why was the flight made over water and not over land? Jannus wrote, "A hydroaviator, with a normal appetite for pleasure, can satiate his desires without incurring the dangers attendant upon land flying. I shall not harp on this point, but simply give my word for it, that hydro-aviation is pleasant at worst, while land flying is risky at best."[47] The biggest cities in the Midwest were located on the river, making the exhibitions more effective.

Many sources have credited Tom Benoist as the first person to record financial operating statistics of an airplane company. He kept track of the cost per ton-mile for the 1,973-mile trip. In *Aero and Hydro*, Benoist stated, "Assuming a useful load of only 500 pounds, over and above the weight of the pilot and necessary supplies, the cost per ton-mile, with gasoline at 10 cents per gallon, works out at a fraction more than 5 cents, an amount that is not much greater than current express rates and tends to show that the commercial application of the aeroplane is not so far in the future as the average person assumes."[48]

Jannus and Benoist proved that a flight of such length and duration was not only possible but economically viable. For the entire trip, his aircraft consumed 249 gallons of gasoline, 21 gallons of oil, and about $20 worth of parts needed because of the normal wear and tear of flying.[49] As the 1912 "great rivers" flight ended, Jannus and Benoist were already talking about a flight across the Atlantic.

THE BENOIST FLIERS performed thousands of exhibitions through-out 1912 and 1913. Jannus and Benoist's goal was to give flying a good reputation. They wanted to sell airplanes, not perform Lincoln Beachey–style death-defying aerial circus tricks. The promise of death and mangled airplanes at exhibitions sold tickets to the morbid few who hoped for the worst, but it was definitely not the message either man wished to convey.

During the years 1910–13, opportunities for barnstorming airmen were abundant, although there were difficulties as well. Fields were usually too small and obstructed by fences and rocks. Spectators crowded the fields just as a pilot was attempting to land. Still other crowds grew hostile when a pilot refused to fly. The flights were simple, usually no more than three times around the field, sometimes with a couple of aerial figure eights. As the fliers gained experience and the crowds began to expect more, the exhibitions became increasingly so-phisticated; quick starts, accurate landings, and rapid ascents were added to the acts.

County fairs were willing to spend thousands of dollars for a flying performance, and the barnstormer was the fair's main attraction. Percy Noel, editor of *Aero*, explained the situation: "The aviator who will devote his time to exhibition work during the coming season and who is in a position to guarantee flights in winds up to 25 miles an hour will be able to retire next fall with something like a small fortune in hand."[1] The demand was great. A man of Jannus's ability and reputa-tion could fly exhibitions all year long. On August 21, 1913, the Benoist company answered a fair manager's inquiry by writing, "Exhibitors this year are generally charging from $800.00 to $900.00 for three days, that is $500.00 for the first day and $200.00 for each additional day." For conducting exhibitions, the company required that "an aeroplane must have a clear run of not less than 300 feet, probably 500 to 600, on comparatively smooth ground to get in the air." So few people had ever seen an airplane and so little was known about them that Benoist advised, "Quite a number of Fair Associations believe that an aeroplane goes up vertically like a balloon and cannot understand why an aviator is not able to get off the ground in the infield of a half mile tract with a number of trees."[2]

Airplane exhibitions guaranteed large crowds. Occasionally, the contract between the flier and the fair called for a flat rate for the duration of the event. Others called for a rate for each flight. At some fairs, the fliers were asked to share the financial risk by contracting for a percentage of the gate receipts. The only constant was that the fliers had to guarantee that they would fly.

A. G. Rigby, secretary of the Buchanan County Fair and Racing Association, said of an exhibition he held: "It proved to be a splendid drawing card . . . it increased our receipts more than 70 percent over last year. Many people came every day to see the aeroplane and some of them had not been here before in 20 years."[3] Nearly every state in the Union and several Canadian provinces wanted to host the aerial acts. One town in Mississippi was so eager that it raised $40,000 to bring in several aviators.[4]

As the dog days of summer approached, the Benoist fliers were as busy as ever. In July, flying at Kinloch Field was beginning to wind down as Benoist's troupe prepared to take its show on the road. At the time, more than a dozen aviators were flying out of Kinloch, over half of them associated with Benoist's company. John Woodlief, a Benoist student, had recently signed a contract for a series of exhibitions, opening at Taylorville, Illinois. Ed Korn's first exhibition was set for Anna, a small southern Illinois town. After Anna, Korn was scheduled to spend the rest of the summer crisscrossing Ohio and New York. Ray Benedict, recently back from three weeks of flying in western New York, was

Jannus at the controls of a Benoist
in 1913. Courtesy of the Florida
Aviation Historical Society.

Of the Benoist Air Craft Co. of St. Louis

IS HERE

HE WILL MAKE A SERIES OF FLIGHTS

at Cheney Park west of town between 5 P. M. and sunset

Wednesday Aug. 7th

Under the auspices of the RETAIL MERCHANTS ASSOCIATION. The Fire Whistle will blow 3 times 10 minutes before he flies to give all an opportunity to witness the flights.

Any one desiring a trip to the clouds at $25.00 will apply to Mr. Jannus or the members of the aviation committee.

EDW H. BACH,
F. B. MARTIN,
ROY CHESTNUT.

Courier Print, Taylorville, Ill.

Flying exhibitions almost guaranteed large crowds at county fairs. Promotion for a Jannus appearance, August 7, 1912. Author's collection.

The Benoist exhibition team performed at hundreds of shows in 1912 and 1913. Here Jannus is at the controls in Taylorville, Illinois, August 7, 1912. Courtesy of the Florida Aviation Historical Society.

preparing to return to the exhibition circuit at Unionville, Missouri, on the Fourth of July.

Jannus had his sights set on a $600 purse. All he had to do was fly forty miles from Kinloch to Belleville, Illinois, on July 3. For July 4, he was scheduled to perform a series of aerial exhibitions. For five hours of flying on July 3–4, Jannus would be paid $120 per flight hour.

Ed Korn, Ray Benedict, and the other fliers with Benoist were using the older, time-tested airplanes. Jannus was using an airplane completed only several days earlier.[5] The new Roberts engine had been delivered to the Benoist factory on July 2 and had been hastily hung on the airframe. Jannus left Kinloch Field early on the morning of July 3 and headed south-southeast for the short flight to Belleville. After less than twenty minutes in the air, one of the cylinders in the newly installed engine seized. Realizing that he could not make it to Belleville, he searched for a suitable place to land. Circling in lazy spirals, he began his slow descent from two thousand feet. Jannus made a perfect landing with the disabled Benoist in the alfalfa fields of Kasemire Valentine's farm.

J. D. Smith was sent out with a replacement cylinder. Several hours after his unscheduled landing, Jannus was back in the air and headed for Belleville. He arrived at the fairground too late in the afternoon to fly an exhibition but made up for his tardiness the next day. On Independence Day, he treated the citizens of Belleville to three exhibition flights. So impressed was the Retail Dealers Association with his magical performance that it hired the Benoist fliers for a fair to be held in the fall. On July 8, Jannus returned to St. Louis, where he landed his biplane in a vacant lot next to the Benoist shop on Delmar Avenue. Before he could continue the exhibition circuit, the airplane needed a new engine.

As Ray Benedict had several weeks earlier, Jannus then headed to the western part of New York to put on a few exhibitions. John Woodlief, who had been set to fulfill his engagement at Taylorville, Illinois, on July 4, very nearly never made it. While flying at Kinloch Field, he cracked up his biplane but suffered only minor damage to himself and to the valuable aircraft. The damaged biplane was carted to the Benoist shop and underwent a round-the-clock overhaul until it was as good as new.

As Benoist had earlier copied the designs of Curtiss, Wright, and Farman in the construction of his own aircraft, a St. Louis pair, Alfred Boulette and Fred Hart, were now building copies of Benoist's aircraft.[6] Boulette, twenty-one years old, had traveled from France to learn to fly at Benoist's school. Shortly after noon on June 22, Boulette and Hart assembled their aircraft and prepared it for flight. For several minutes, Boulette taxied through the grass, never leaving the ground. A strong wind behind him provided more ground speed than he had expected. He was soon airborne at an altitude of twenty feet. Immediately he went into an uncontrolled bank and a wing tip struck the ground. The biplane turned over, ejecting Boulette, who spent nearly two weeks in a local hospital for his attempt to fly the cloned version of a Benoist Model XII. Frank Bell had warned Hart and Boulette that their airplane should not be flown because it was tail heavy.[7] Only days later, Bell himself suffered a minor accident while flying at Devils Lake in Minnesota.[8]

By mid-July, Jannus had returned from western New York. On one of his frequent local flights, Edward Korn happened upon the Sunset Inn, a roadhouse twenty-two miles south of Kinloch. Korn flew circles around the restaurant for nearly twenty minutes, encouraged by the patrons. He stopped only after realizing that his fuel supply was getting low. Arriving back at Kinloch, Korn was met by Jannus and Benoist and informed them of the great reception he had received. Jannus and Benoist decided to go to the Sunset Inn for dinner—by airplane.

The hungry duo started at 7:10 P.M. in approaching darkness. They flew for forty minutes but did not find the restaurant. They landed at a farm near Grantwood, a well-known landmark owned by Ulysses S. Grant in the 1850s following his first retirement from the United States Army. Delighted to find that they were only five miles from the inn, the two men took to the air in the darkness. The well-lighted Sunset Inn proved easy to locate from an altitude of five hundred feet. Jannus landed on the front lawn. The commotion of the second airplane visit of the day drove both the diners and the restaurant staff outdoors. Jannus shut down the engine, climbed to the ground, and accepted handshakes and slaps on the back while Benoist stood off to the side observing. Edward Benish, the inn's manager, personally greeted the duo with open arms. Their meal was on the house that night.

On August 4, Jannus performed a short aerial matinee for the large Sunday crowd at Kinloch Field. His passengers were nearly all women. As the crowd thinned, Jannus announced that he would make one last flight to the old Delmar race track. He asked whether anyone would like to fly with him, and several people immediately volunteered. Helen Hudson of Chicago, the prettiest young woman on the airfield, was chosen as his passenger. They climbed into the Benoist tractor and flew into the dusk. When Jannus carried beautiful young women as passengers, the incidences of spark plug troubles always seemed to increase, delaying their return. Jannus made the flight from Kinloch to the race grounds in nine minutes. It is not known how long his return flight took.

Late summer and early fall of 1912 witnessed the Benoist aviators performing from as far north as Minnesota to the southern state of

Tennessee. Between August 7 and October 4, the aviators flew approximately one hundred exhibition dates, performing three or four times a day. They easily dominated the midwestern exhibition circuit. Scheduling pilots and equipment was a nightmare. Frequent crashes did not help. Frank Bell was especially troubled by bad luck. On August 10, while carrying a passenger at Grand Forks, North Dakota, Bell's airplane went out of control at an altitude of two hundred feet and crashed to the ground.[9] Neither Bell nor his passenger, George Sheppard, were badly hurt, but Bell's Model XII Benoist tractor was nearly destroyed. Jannus spent a week flying at Montgomery, Missouri, while Ed Korn was covering northern Missouri.

On August 7, 1912, Jannus was at Cheney Park, Minnesota. "Anthony Jannus" in large bold type screamed from the top of a poster. The St. Cloud Retail Merchants Association promised, "The Fire Whistle will blow 3 times 10 minutes before he flies to give all an opportunity to witness the flights."[10] Those brave enough could fly with Jannus for $25.

The grind of flying went on. August 20, they were at Mystic, Iowa; the next day, Malcolm, Iowa. A day later, exhibitions took place in Newton, Iowa. On August 23 and 24, the citizens of Vienna, Illinois, were treated to the excitement of Jannus and the other Benoist fliers. The aviators also performed two shows at Durant, Iowa, on August 23 and 24 for the Farmer's Festival. Ed Korn spent five days flying at Fulton, Kentucky, between August 27 and 31. Ray Benedict was in Spickard, Missouri, between August 28 and 30. On August 29, he flew at the Farmers Store picnic before nine thousand people. Seymour, Iowa, was the site of another single show on August 31.

Late August also featured the Benoist fliers in Memphis, Tennessee. For twenty-five cents, adults were admitted to the Memphis Fair. The program for Wednesday, August 28, featured a great aerial exhibition. Jannus received top billing over a running race and livestock show. A handbill for the Memphis Fair promised, "The same Biplane and aviator for Wednesday also have been secured for the Great St. Louis Fair Sept 23."[11]

Although they originally booked Jannus for only one day of flying, the fair's managers retained him for an additional four days after he proved his popularity. From the air, he looked down at the crowds watching him and waved. His waves were answered by enthusiastic salutes from the crowds. The *Memphis Reveille* said, "It can truly be said that the flights of Mr. Jannis could not be excelled. Many present who had witnessed flights in other makes of machines say for smooth sailing the Benoist machine has all others beaten." Jannus was always an outgoing and ambitious representative for aviation. The *Reveille* reported, "Mr. Jannis is a very courteous young man and took pleasure in showing his machine to the visitors and answered thousands of questions from day to day."[12]

Following Memphis, Benoist and several of his fliers headed 112 miles northeast to Union City, Tennessee. The Union City Fair, advertised as the biggest county fair in the South, was held September 4 through 7, 1912. Two or more flights at altitudes of a thousand feet were promised for each day. A handbill proclaimed, "This is a $1,500 feature attraction, not an experiment, not a cheap advertising fake, but a contract made with a well known patentee and inventor, Mr. Benoist, of St. Louis, who will give Union City one of the biggest demonstrations ever held in the larger cities in aerial navigation, a sight worth coming hundreds of miles to see."[13]

September brought no respite for any of the harried Benoist Aerial Exhibition Company fliers. Jannus flew at Murphysboro, Illinois, between September 3 and 6. On Tuesday, September 3, the previous attendance records at the Egypt's Big Fair were broken when thousands of people came to the fairgrounds. When Jannus flew over the city of Murphysboro, thousands more were treated to a free show. September 4 through 6 saw Benoist's team flying at Marquette, Michigan. Flora, Illinois, was treated to a Benoist exhibition from September 10 through 13. Ray Benedict was in the air over Armstrong, Missouri, on September 11, 12, and 13. Breeze, Illinois, was the site of another exhibition from September 18 through 21. Benedict was at Scottsbluff, Nebraska, on September 26, 27, and 28.

Frank Bell headed north to fly a two-day exhibition at St. Cloud; meanwhile, Jannus was back in Tennessee for the Weakley County Fair. The clarion call for the fair stated, "This Famous aviator and licensed air pilot will make his ascensions on Thursday, Friday and Saturday,

October 10–11–12, in charge of that great Aerial Monster, the—BENOIST AIRSHIP—."[14]

Benoist, Jannus, and the rest of the Benoist fliers would go anywhere to fly. Benoist advertised, "High-class Aeroplanes with daring and competent BENOIST AVIATORS, for Fairs, Picnics, Barbecues, Homecomings, Carnivals, Political Rallies. By the single flight, week or season. Cross Country, Endurance, Passenger Carrying, Bomb Dropping and Altitude Flights. Complete Meets Pulled off with any number of Machines."[15]

So pleased with Jannus and Benoist was the Montgomery County Agricultural and Mechanical Society of Montgomery City, Missouri, that it passed an official resolution praising the two men. In August 1912, the resolution proclaimed Jannus "a skilled and successful aviator."[16]

Following Jannus's performances in Montgomery, Missouri, the *Montgomery Standard* reported, "What lifts the machine, which weighs about 1,000 pounds is as much a mystery as ever." All anyone knew was that it worked because "the ship certainly went up and sailed all around the grounds, and over town, and away out in the country." The reporter wrote, "This machine went about so easy and was so well handled that people began to speculate at once about traveling on regular schedule time by airship."[17]

Not everyone was happy with the aerial shows put on by the barnstormers. Cortlandt Bishop, president of the Aero Club of America, strongly opposed exhibition flying for money. He thought that "soon we shall have the best people in the world interested in flying machines." To Bishop, the men and women who flew for money were not the "best people." He hoped that appropriate actions would be taken to prevent "the ruthless destruction of a great enterprise and a delightful sport" by an excess of exhibition flying.[18] Bishop, a wealthy man, wanted to preserve aviation for wealthy sportsmen.

Although the Wright brothers had their own exhibition teams, they were also not positively inclined toward exhibition flying.[19] Both Bishop and the Wrights were wrong. Earth-bound scientists made improvements in aviation, but the real advances and discoveries were brought about by the men and women who flew on the exhibition circuits. They were America's early test pilots. Exhibition flying sold airplanes; therefore, manufacturers needed to field teams of exhibition fliers.

In May 1913, Jannus thrilled thousands of spectators at Paducah, Kentucky, where he was described as a man who made friends with everyone he met and always had time for questions about flying. He had been hired to give four shows during the week and ended up giving ten. With his love of flying and carnival-like huckstering, he seldom failed to please. The spectators who congregated on the banks of the Ohio River in Paducah got their money's worth. On the last day of Jannus's visit to Paducah, the crowds were described as the biggest ever.

In the morning flight on May 24 Jannus pushed his Benoist Model XIII hydroplane to an altitude of twelve hundred feet above the Ohio River. He flattened out and floated the airplane through the air, performing a twenty-minute program of diving, spiraling, and volplaning (gliding without power). Near the conclusion of the flight, he flew over Paducah, delighting the few people who still remained in the city. Finally, he spiraled through his descent to the Ohio River. Jannus sped up and down the river's surface, then ran the hydroplane up a planked skidway and beached the machine.

By midafternoon a celebratory parade had just ended. Heavy crowds congregated on the riverbanks in anticipation of the 6 P.M. flight, his last in Paducah. The weather was perfect. A light, steady wind blew from the northeast. Jannus slowly ascended to an altitude of two thousand feet. He flew parallel to the Ohio River, then turned and flew over the city of Paducah. After ten minutes of gentle soaring, Jannus began a spiral downward toward the river and the collected crowds. A couple of hundred feet above the heads of the spectators, he performed several series of figure eights. Effortlessly, Jannus pointed the nose of his airplane toward the middle of the river. Just as the pontoons touched the water, he pulled the Benoist's nose up and shot skyward, rocking the airplane back and forth as he gained altitude. Uncharacteristically reckless, he buffeted the ferryboat *Robertson* with a flyby at eighty miles an hour as he flew with his arms folded across his chest.

After flying for thirty-five minutes and thrilling the crowds, Jannus landed and taxied to the riverbank. The crowd was disappointed to think that the show was over. But it wasn't. A. D. Paschal climbed onto the airplane and Jannus was off again. While Jannus repeated the same stunts that he had performed earlier, Paschal took aerial photographs of Paducah, becoming the first photographer to take pictures of Kentucky from an airplane. Perhaps it was not a true aviation record, but it was definitely a first for Kentucky.

Not long afterward, Jannus cracked a cylinder while flying an exhibition and was forced to land. The only person capable of making the engine repair was a young man named A. B. Chalk. Foreman of a local garage and machine shop but, more important for Jannus, Chalk owned a boat with a two-cycle Roberts engine. Chalk agreed to take on the repair job and quickly had the engine running like new.[20] He later learned to fly "under the tutelage of the famous Jannus."[21] Because of his experiences with Tony Jannus, Chalk's lifelong interest in aviation was born. Eventually, Chalk would start his own seaplane airline, operating from Miami throughout the Caribbean.

In-air emergencies and fires were a definite possibility and obvious concern. Early one morning, Jannus and Dude Iseminger, the race car driver, set out for Chicago. After a quick climb, Jannus leveled at two thousand feet. Only five miles from St. Louis, a wing support came loose. Iseminger instinctively caught the dangling strut, intending to hold it taut until they reached the nearest town. There was no real cause for concern; Alton, Illinois, was only fifteen minutes away. To keep the broken strut from wobbling, Iseminger was forced to stand in the aircraft so his coattails hung directly over the hot exhaust pipes of the engine. Sparks set his coat on fire. If Iseminger released the support, control of the aircraft could be lost. If Jannus attempted to help, they could crash. Jannus let go of the controls and removed Iseminger's coat. Holding onto the strut as tightly as possible with only one hand, Iseminger stuck out his free arm while Jannus struggled to pull off the burning jacket. They then repeated the process until the jacket was off and thrown overboard. Jannus landed near the *Eagle Packet* wharf boat at the Alton Levee as if nothing had happened. The broken strut was fixed and they were shortly on their way.

While flying at the Fair Grounds Aviation Meet in Carmi, Illinois, from September 9 through 11, Jannus did something in an airplane that he may have done only once in his life. Designated as the official mail pilot for the meet and carrying mail under route number 635,003 on September 10 and 11, he circled the local post office and dropped the mail bag almost dead center on target.[22] Jannus frequently carried mail while flying, but this may have been the one and only occasion when it was officially sanctioned.

By contemporary standards, many early barnstormers earned a substantial wage—substantial, that is, until one realizes that it was a dangerous way to make a living. Aviators worldwide were dying in airplanes at the rate of about two hundred a year. On an almost daily basis, major American newspapers such as the *New York Times* and the *Chicago Daily Tribune* reported fatalities. According to Roger Bilsteen, "Fliers got a base pay of $20 per week, plus $50 per day when they flew."[23] That wage is consistent with what Benoist offered J. D. Smith to fly in March 1915. Benoist offered to pay "a straight salary of $75 a month for services, furnish you a machine for school and exhibition purposes and pay you twenty-five percent of the net receipts on exhibitions and passenger carrying, and twenty percent on students."[24]

Jannus may have realized a great deal of money for his exhibition flying with Benoist. Exhibition fliers, if they hooked up with the right management, could earn a very substantial income. Charles K. Hamilton, one of the stable of Curtiss fliers, was believed to have earned $107,000 during his first exhibition season. Lincoln Beachey, the undisputed king of reckless breakneck exhibition fliers, once claimed to have earned $100,000 in three years of exhibition flying. On the other side of the spectrum, many fliers were cheated out of their promised rewards by unscrupulous promoters. Jannus's earnings probably fell somewhere between the two extremes.

The money Jannus earned was irrelevant. He was motivated not by money but by his love of flight. Contemporary wisdom held that "anyone who thinks exhibition aviators fly only for money or glory should have been around the Curtiss factory the first few days in April [1913], and heard those men begging for machines and motors to be hustled over to the field, so they could get out and fly for the fun of the thing. What's more, they got the machines and motors, even though it was a couple of weeks before the time scheduled for the training camp to open up for the season; and they flew around Lake Keuka and over the hills, morning and night, without anyone but themselves to admire or applaud their exploits."[25]

Like the Curtiss fliers and hundreds of others flying in the United States during 1912 and 1913, Jannus flew for one reason and one reason only. He loved to fly. For Benoist, however, flying had become a pure dollars and cents proposition. It had to be. Undoubtedly the Benoist company stayed financially afloat in 1912, 1913, and 1914 because of the exhibition flying. It soon dried up.

During the week of October 6, Jannus flew as much as possible. Benoist, Jannus, and J. D. Smith were preparing for the Columbus Day aerial meet in New York City on October 14. Jannus alternated his daily flying between the Mississippi River and St. Louis's Forrest Park. From noon to one o'clock, Jannus flew the flying boat over the river. From four to five in the afternoon, he flew exhibitions and carried passengers in the Benoist tractor. At the end of the week, they crated the tractor and shipped it by railroad to New York City.

9 A Fall from Grace

IN JANUARY 1913, Kinloch Field was abandoned in favor of an airfield closer to St. Louis.[1] Kinloch was seventeen miles away. The new facility was ominously opposite the Bellefontaine Cemetery. Located on the Broadway electric car line, it could be reached within fifteen minutes. The Aero Club of St. Louis had long considered St. Louis to be the midwestern hub of aviation, but now its importance was on the wane. Many of the fliers who had helped establish the reputation of Kinloch Field had moved on or died. Hugh Robinson, DeLloyd Thompson, Katherine Stinson, Horace Kearney, Lincoln Beachey, and Walter Brookins had all cut their aviation teeth at St. Louis before going elsewhere.

Ralph Johnston and Arch Hoxey, the Wright fliers nicknamed the "Star Dust Twins," had been early St. Louis fliers. Hoxey had carried former president Theodore Roosevelt as his passenger at Kinloch Field.[2] Hoxey crashed and died in Los Angeles; Johnston met a similar fate in Denver. Howard Gill died in a midair collision. Max Lillie moved his flying school to Chicago. Andrew Drew was serving as a war correspondent for the *St. Louis Post-Dispatch* in Mexico. Virtually the only aviators remaining in St. Louis in 1913 were the Benoist fliers, who continued to use Kinloch Field long after the Aero Club of St. Louis opened its new facility. A shift in land fields hardly mattered to them. They were now flying almost exclusively from the water.

Jannus was in Washington, D.C., resting and regaining his health after his triumphant and historic conquest of the rivers. Benoist, Hugh Robinson, and the rest of the crew were busy in St. Louis.[3] The Benoist

Aircraft Company had only recently rolled its latest product out of the factory—the Benoist flying boat.[4] Hugh Robinson deserved much of the credit for the design and ultimate construction of this craft.[5]

Benoist was not the originator of the flying boat. According to Russell Froelich, a photographer for Benoist, "Tom had the flying boat idea in mind in 1909 but it was two years before he started his boat with wings."[6] But Benoist was never just a follower who would grab on to the latest aviation fad and slavishly copy it. He sought out the best inventions and ideas available in the neophyte world of aviation and did everything he could to improve them. Glenn Curtiss had beaten Benoist to the punch by at least a year with the development of the flying boat. In recognition of his accomplishment, Curtiss was the recipient of the Aero Club of America's 1912 Collier Trophy, awarded annually for the greatest achievement in American aviation during the preceding year.[7] The idea had been considered long before Jannus, Benoist, or even Curtiss had gotten around to working with an aircraft capable of taking off from the water. In 1899, Hugo Matullath of New York had filed a patent application for a pontoon-rigged aircraft.[8]

In 1916, Glenn Curtiss received the flying boat patent for which he had applied several years earlier. The Curtiss Aeroplane and Motor Corporation then notified all manufacturers that they would be required to obtain a license from the company before building their own flying boats. Whether Tom Benoist ever received such a letter from Curtiss or whether he ever applied for such a license is not known. Despite all of Benoist's work with both the hydroplane and flying boat, it was Glenn Curtiss who became known as "the father of naval aviation."

Attaching pontoons to the landing gear of an aircraft had proven adequate for over-water operation, as shown by Jannus's 1,973-mile flight, but the rickety pontoon mechanism would be a less than ideal solution for a transatlantic flight. Benoist's 1913 flying boat was advertised as capable of landing on water as well as land when specially equipped with wheels that could be raised and lowered. That feature can be almost definitely attributed to Robinson. In 1911, while working for Glenn Curtiss, Robinson had suggested a mechanism to raise or lower the wheels which was remarkably similar to a retractable landing gear. A flying boat with a large hull would greatly enhance the comfort and perceived, if not real, safety of a passenger-carrying operation. What really mattered was stimulation of the market to sell airplanes.

The Benoist products were finally beginning to take on an appearance of aeronautical sleekness. Hull length was slightly over twenty-six feet. The Curtiss-type controls were abandoned in favor of the Deperdussin, which were virtually the same as previous Benoist controls. A wheel was used to work the ailerons, which were nothing more than a five-foot extension out from and between the top and bottom wings. A turn of the wheel to the right and the ailerons went down; a left turn and the ailerons moved upward. A push or pull of the same wheel operated the elevator. Steering was accomplished by use of a foot bar. The wings used in construction of the flying boat were standard Benoist issue. With a total span of thirty-six feet, the wings were constructed in sections, which were easier to replace than an entire wing assembly. There were six five-foot sections and two three-foot sections.[9] The rear of the hull came equipped with a small wooden rudder for steering through the water. A step, usually located behind the flying boat's center of gravity, served to disrupt the hull's drag. Without a step, a flying boat would skim across the water unable to take off. The engine was a six-cylinder, seventy-five-horsepower Roberts two-cycle.[10] A specially forged ½ x ⅜ x 1 inch diamond roller chain was used to transfer power from the engine to the eight-foot, six-inch-long propeller mounted approximately six feet above the engine and immediately behind the aircraft's double wings. Benoist's philosophy of status quo regarding the Roberts engine was very shortsighted. Perhaps he retained it because of friendship, loyalty, or his poor financial situation, but it ultimately proved to be one of the factors leading to the demise of the Benoist Aircraft Company.

Benoist and Jannus were unique in their placement of the engine in the bottom of the flying boat's hull, thus creating a low center of gravity. Glenn Curtiss believed that the engine should be installed almost level with the wings.[11] Engine mounts in the Benoist were two spruce beams running parallel to each other. Seventeen feet in length, nearly as long as the hull, the beams tapered inward to follow the lines of the

Hugh Robinson cranking up the Roberts engine in a Benoist flying boat in January 1913. Benoist, Jannus, and Robinson were probably equally responsible for the design and development of the first Benoist flying boat. Courtesy of the Florida Aviation Historical Society.

hull. The spruce timbers gave additional strength to the flying boat's frame.

Passenger comfort was an important inducement for people to fly. The passengers sat directly behind the pilot and immediately in front of the unmuffled engine. With a carrying capacity of three passengers besides the pilot, Benoist hoped that his new flying boat would prove to be a popular seller.

Hugh Robinson took the flying boat for its maiden voyage on January 2, 1913. The wind was blowing across Creve Coeur Lake at thirty miles per hour. The first flight of any untested aircraft is frightening enough, but with such heavy winds, Benoist must have wondered if the flight should proceed. After much deliberation, Benoist and Robinson decided to go ahead as planned. Lining up with the wind at his back, Robinson applied the throttle and soon was skimming across the rough waters of the lake. According to an account in *Aero and Hydro*, the heavy tail wind proved to be of great assistance and Robinson was able to nose the thousand-pound flying boat cleanly out of the water in only three hundred feet. This early account is suspect. If Robinson had taken off downwind in a thirty-mile-per-hour wind, his speed over the water would have been approximately sixty-five miles per hour. The flat-bottomed hull would have been pounded out in short order. Robinson made several short flights and everything seemed in fine shape. Robinson was satisfied with the way the flying boat handled. Benoist then flew it himself and was apparently very disappointed with the results.

By mid-January, Jannus left Washington, D.C., and returned to St. Louis. The weather cooperated, temperatures seldom falling below the freezing point, with little snow. Jannus and Robinson flew many hours together and seemed to have gotten along fairly well. Exactly when the tide turned and insurmountable difficulties arose is unknown.

Shortly after the first flights, the crew had decided that all further testing would be conducted on the Mississippi River.[12] The crew loaded the flying boat onto the back of a three-ton Pope Hartford truck. With the tail assembly hanging out ten to twelve feet, they made the fifteen-mile trip to St. Louis. Once they got the aircraft into the river, it sat

Last-minute repairs performed by J. D. Smith, "mechanician" on the Benoist flying boat, St. Louis, 1913. Courtesy of the Florida Aviation Historical Society.

A FALL FROM GRACE

Posing in front of a Benoist flying boat on the Mississippi River, St. Louis, Missouri, 1913. *Left to right:* Hillery Beachey, Tony Jannus, and Fred Essen, the 255-pound St. Louis County Republican politician. Courtesy of the Florida Aviation Historical Society.

there for several weeks. The weather had taken a turn for the worse and conditions for testing the flying boat were unsafe. No sooner did the weather improve than Jannus became ill.

A recurrence of his attack of appendicitis made life extremely unpleasant. In Jannus's absence, Benoist was thankful that Hugh Robinson was still around to pilot the flying boat. In late February, Jannus became seriously ill and was taken to St. John's Hospital. He had earlier diagnosed his illness as a case of tonsillitis and had attempted to treat himself with salves and warm drinks. Once he arrived at the hospital, doctors quickly diagnosed appendicitis and operated.[13] Following several days of recuperation, Jannus was again ready to fly.

Jannus's illness nearly kept Robinson from flying as well. When Jannus had returned from Washington, the flying boat's original controls were replaced with Benoist controls. With Jannus hospitalized, Robinson had to resume the role of test pilot, necessitating the rerigging of the aircraft with Curtiss controls. Robinson was unfamiliar with Benoist controls; he wisely refused to learn them while testing the flying boat. Curtiss controls featured a yokelike device that was strapped around the pilot's shoulders and was used to make the aircraft bank in a turn. All the pilot had to do to bank was to lean his body in the direction he wished to turn. With each right or left movement of the body, ailerons on the trailing edge of the wings moved up and down.[14]

Robinson's first test flight on the Mississippi drew thousands of spectators between the Eads and McKinley Bridges. By the end of the day, Robinson had four flights under his belt. On his first flight of the day, he taxied north from the foot of North Market Street up the river. Heading toward the Eads Bridge, he skipped and leapfrogged the flying boat along the water before becoming airborne. Before Robinson prematurely shortened his flying because of cold and wind, he had made one flight of twenty-five minutes' duration, pushed the craft through the waters of the Mississippi at fifty miles per hour, and, with a heavy tail wind, reached an airborne speed of eighty-five miles per hour.[15]

Of major importance to Jannus in early 1913 was the arrival in St. Louis of his brother, Roger, fresh from his duties as a civil engineer on the Panama Canal. Roger's first job with the Benoist Aircraft Company was as a shop mechanic. William H. Bleakley, the inimitable Irishman who had been a student of the Benoist school and had only recently received his pilot's license, was now the instructor at the school assigned the task of teaching Roger to fly. Before turning to aviation, Bleakley had briefly earned a living as a professional boxer and was not at all averse to occasionally giving a thickheaded student a less than gentle tap on the noggin. It is doubtful that Roger ever needed such prodding.

According to R. D. Woodcock, William Bleakley did the unthinkable with the flying boat—he looped-the-loop. If it actually happened, it was probably the last loop in a Benoist flying boat. Woodcock said, "While coming in for a landing on the Mississippi River, atmospheric conditions caused a sort of mirage—thought he saw one of the large bridges in front of him, so he pulled completely back on the elevator, then after straightening out, again he saw the bridge, so again he repeated—hence another loop."[16]

Benoist and Jannus soon set their sights on the prestigious Great Lakes Reliability Cruise to be held in July 1913. The contest featured an over-water race course from Chicago to Detroit along the shoreline of the Great Lakes. The race was sponsored by Benoist's former business partner, E. Percy Noel, publisher of *Aero and Hydro* magazine.

The cruise had been the brainchild of promoter Bill Pickens, personal manager of the legendary automobile racer Barney Oldfield. Pickens originally suggested to Glenn Curtiss that a race from Chicago to Detroit would be an ideal way to publicize his new flying boats. Reluctant at first, Curtiss finally agreed that if such an event were to be held, he might consider entering one of his machines. With that somewhat firm commitment, Pickens convinced Percy Noel to sponsor the race.[17]

By mid-May, there were ten entrants, with Benoist, Jannus, and Hugh Robinson heading the list. It is doubtful that Benoist ever intended actually to pilot an aircraft in the competition. Benoist said, "We will enter three machines, Robinson and Jannus flying two of them. I was planning to fly the other myself, but as a young sportsman who has just placed an order for a machine is anxious to compete, we will probably enter him."[18] By race day, only Jannus remained to represent Benoist. Robinson had been injured and was unable to compete. The unnamed entrant was probably William D. Jones of Duluth, Minnesota. In May, he had ordered a Benoist Model XIV flying boat with an expected delivery date of mid-June,[19] but his flying skills had not reached competition level by the beginning of the event.

In early June, Robinson brought the recently completed flying boat named the *Lark of Duluth* from St. Louis to Duluth. While flying the first flight following delivery, Robinson and his mechanic Wells Ingalls had a serious accident. Ingalls was unhurt and received only minor bruises; Robinson was not as fortunate. A wing brace snapped upon impact, cutting him badly across the face and eyes and nearly blinding him. Robinson was forced to drop out of the upcoming race in Chicago. The accident effectively ended his flying career. The flying boat was quickly repaired. *Lark of Duluth* had been painted on the underside of the upper wing. Following the repair work, all that remained of the wording was "*of Du.*"

On June 24, Jannus arrived in Duluth, where he gave a series of exhibitions in the repaired flying boat as part of the Lark of the Lake celebration. At the same time, he taught Bill Jones to fly the *Lark of Duluth* in only a couple of days. In an article for *Aero and Hydro*, Jannus discussed the method used to teach Jones and Julius Barnes, who probably was the owner of the flying boat, to fly.[20] He wrote, "With Jones at the levers, I handled the throttle with one hand and directed with the other."[21] Jannus's exhibitions over Lake Superior were the first ever in a flying boat.[22] Once the aircraft had been delivered and Bill Jones had been taught to fly, Jannus headed for Chicago.

The participation of Benoist, Jannus, and Robinson in the event had been an important factor in Noel's decision to hold the *Aero and Hydro* race. Noel had traveled from Chicago to St. Louis to meet with the Benoist team to discuss their participation. After receiving an assurance that they would take part, he told the newspapers, "The contest is now assured."

Benoist strongly believed that the *Aero and Hydro* Great Lakes Reliability Cruise would stimulate the growth of aviation and, more important, his own business. He made a special trip by train to Chicago to ensure that the Benoist fliers were the first to be registered for the race. A member of the Aero Club of America stated: "This is undoubtedly the most important contest for the good of aviation in America ever organized and it deserves the loyal moral support of every enthusiast."[23]

Many aviation events held in the United States had been dominated by foreign fliers and foreign-manufactured equipment. Whether by design or coincidence, the first article of the general rules stated that this event was open only to manufacturers building aeroplanes or aerohydroplanes in the United States.[24] In early June, the list of entrants had grown to twelve. The most notable addition to the list was the Californian Glenn L. Martin. Only a year earlier, Jannus and Martin had fiercely competed at the Second International Air Meet in Chicago. With the addition of a flier of Martin's caliber, the race promised to be exciting.

By the second week of June, aircraft and fliers were starting to arrive in Chicago. Qualifying trials were not scheduled to commence until

July 5. The pilots representing the aircraft manufacturers were the best in the business. Few people could claim ignorance of fliers such as Jannus, Glenn Martin, Max Lillie, Beckwith Havens, and Weldon Cooke. Glenn Martin had entered a tractor hydroplane; all the other contestants planned to use flying boats.

A week before the event, Jannus and Smith brought the Benoist flying boat to Chicago. Smith dismantled the Roberts engine and gave it a complete overhaul, after which Jannus put the airplane through several test flights. During one of the flights, Jannus, with Smith as his passenger, flew the airplane over the lake for fifty miles. On another flight, Jannus flew for almost an hour while a photographer from the Pathé Motion Picture Company took moving pictures. Satisfied with the test flights and the recently overhauled engine, Jannus was optimistic about his chances for a victory.

He had been practicing in earnest for this race. Six weeks earlier, while flying in Paducah, Kentucky, he had made a 248-mile trip in one day.[25] On May 23, he left Paducah at 11:00 A.M. After four hours and fifteen minutes of flying time, he was sitting in St. Louis at the foot of Cherokee Street. About three hundred people, many of them women, had been anxiously waiting for Tony's arrival on the levee at the foot of Market Street. Fear could be discerned in their voices as they anxiously wondered aloud what had become of Jannus. Finally, a messenger rushed up and alerted Benoist that Tony had arrived at 4:56 P.M. and had landed at Cherokee Street. Running out of gasoline, the hydroplane had been forced to land short of the final destination.[26]

Now the day of the Great Lakes race arrived and everything was looking good, that is, everything except the weather. At 11:00 A.M., pilots and crews had assembled at Grant Park. By noon, the machines had been started and were ready for the starter's signal. In order of their entrant numbers, the fliers were to start every five minutes, until all were under way for Michigan City. Harold F. McCormick, chairman of the giant International Harvester Corporation and owner of a Curtiss flying boat, was serving as the starter. Exactly at 12:30 P.M., he waved his flag and the race began. Jannus was first off the line. Beckwith Havens followed.

The race that started from Chicago's Grant Park on July 8 was to conclude in Detroit on July 17. Between Chicago and Detroit were eighteen intermediate stops or control points. The first stop in the race was Michigan City, fifty miles from Chicago. Only twenty-five miles into the race, Jannus had problems. Near Gary, Indiana, his propeller was damaged in flight, but he managed to land. While Jannus's flying boat floated in the water, Beckwith Havens flew overhead in his Curtiss F-boat and seemed to assess the situation. If fliers were down in the water with their engines dead but requiring no assistance, they were supposed to fly a square white flag. If in need of assistance, they were to fly a white flag with red stripes. Perhaps Jannus was flying no flag or the wrong flag when Havens flew over, or perhaps Havens wanted to win the race at any cost and simply ignored Jannus's plight and flew off. Trying to reach the shore by rowing, Jannus was making little progress. The flying boat was in danger of sinking because a storm was building over the lake.

Jannus began waving a red flag of distress at a passing boat, which pulled alongside the disabled aircraft. Jannus tied a rope from the engine to the motorboat, and off they went. Because of the storm and the surging waves, the connecting rope came untied when they were still about a mile offshore. The flying boat sank.

Beckwith Havens made Michigan City the first day of the race. His aircraft had a broken rudder and was disabled for a time. Jannus and Havens were not the only aviators to have problems. Glenn Martin had smashed his airplane in Chicago only three days before the race so he was out. Weldon Cooke met a fate similar to Martin's when he broke his engine four days before the race. Walter Johnson's aircraft was smashed in the storm during the first day of the race. Jack Vilas became ill and couldn't compete. If things had worked out differently, Jack Vilas might have been entered in the race with a Benoist flying boat, but the unreliability of the Roberts engine had precluded that possibility. Years later, Vilas recalled, "I almost bought a Benoist flying boat from him in the early spring of 1913. The biggest drawback to the old Benoist machine was the two cycle Roberts motor that Tom used. These motors were very undependable."[27]

A FALL FROM GRACE

The winner of the Great Lakes Reliability Cruise was Beckwith Havens, the Curtiss pilot. He was also the only pilot to finish the race, taking ten days to make it to Detroit. Havens's total flying time was less than fifteen hours.[28] That Beckwith Havens was the winner of the race cannot be disputed, nor should it be. The conditions under which the race was flown were difficult. But it was not publicized at the time that Havens was a ringer thrown into the race by Glenn Curtiss. The flying boat Havens piloted was the only privately owned aircraft in the race; all the others were owned by manufacturers. Its owner, J. B. R. Verplanck of New York, was not a licensed pilot, although Aero Club rules required competitors in sanctioned events to have licenses. Havens was provided by Curtiss as pilot, while Verplanck flew as passenger.[29]

Benoist had expected Jannus to win. When Jannus not only failed to win but even to finish, Benoist was upset and disappointed. He questioned Jannus's decision to start the race in bad weather when several other competitors decided to wait. As pilot in command, it was up to Jannus to make the "go" or "no-go" decision. But it had been a broken wing strut that damaged Jannus's propeller and forced him to the water, not pilot error.[30]

After the race, J. D. Smith stated, "We are out a $5,000 machine, but that's all in the game and we're used to it."[31] Smith the "mechanician" may have been used to it, but Tom Benoist, the man who had to replace the lost airplane, was not. Two years later, in a letter to Smith, Benoist harshly criticized Jannus for his part in destroying the airplane at Gary. He wrote, "It was the same old story like the Great Lakes Cruise boat . . . Tony laid it on somebody else. It is a peculiar thing that Tony could go through a whole season with an old Benoist Boat when it belonged to him, but he is so careless when the outfit belongs to somebody else that he can lose six or seven thousand dollars worth of machines in one season."[32] *Aero and Hydro* reported, "The fact that the trip was finished only one day late, in spite of two occupants being obliged to stay on shore for four days through weather, speaks well for the Curtiss airboat."[33] Benoist had three airplanes entered in the contest; only one actually participated in the race, and it never finished. Glenn Curtiss, his competitor, was complimented on the reliability of his aircraft. Losing efforts did not do much to help the sale of airplanes. Benoist's team may have lost the race, but that did not stop him from writing a congratulatory letter to Verplanck. He still hoped to sell Verplanck a Benoist flying boat.[34]

More misfortune befell Benoist's fliers on August 13, 1913. With Edward Korn as pilot and his brother Milton flying as a passenger, their biplane went into a nose dive. Edward Korn tried but was unable to pull entirely out of the dive before striking the ground. Milton was killed; Edward was badly injured, requiring several years of rehabilitation before making a complete recovery. His flying career was effectively finished, however.[35]

The marriage between Robinson and the Benoist Aircraft Company had also proved short-lived. After disagreements about design changes which Benoist felt were needed, Robinson left the company. His crash in the Benoist flying boat at Duluth may have played a part in the decision. Robinson was married, in his thirties, and the father of several children, and perhaps he and his wife realized that it was time to end active flying. He had probably flown more than six hundred exhibition flights. Money should not have been his motivation; he was financially well-off, having earned nearly a quarter of a million dollars by flying. The rift was a bitter one. Robinson had considered Benoist a true friend; Benoist had thought of Robinson as his first pupil. In later years, Robinson would barely admit that he even knew Tom Benoist, let alone acknowledge that he had ever been a part of the Benoist Aircraft Company.

Less than six months after the "great rivers" flight, Jannus and Benoist were making plans to fly across the Atlantic Ocean. John Henning recalled sitting on a Mississippi River levee at St. Louis while en route to New Orleans when Jannus laughed his usual short chuckle and said, "Ha, Jack, some day somebody is going to fly across the ocean."[1] Jannus wanted to be the first. It would be a perfect fit for a pilot of his skills because his experience in over-water flying was unparalleled.

Early Sunday morning, May 5, 1913, the *St. Louis Globe-Democrat* heralded, "St. Louis Man Will Try to Cross the Atlantic in an Aeroplane."[2] That year, Alfred, Lord Northcliffe, an early protagonist of the usefulness of aviation, had offered a $50,000 prize to whoever made the first transatlantic flight.[3] Jannus and Benoist wanted that prize, but in 1913, there was no airplane capable of crossing the Atlantic. Northcliffe hoped that the $50,000 would provide an incentive to aircraft manufacturers and aviators—the flying skill existed, the scientific knowledge and suitable equipment did not.

A flying boat capable of crossing the Atlantic would have to be larger and stronger than any currently in existence. Both airframe and engine would have to be greatly improved. A seventy-five-horsepower engine was capable of powering a machine with a gross weight of fifteen hundred pounds, but it would be inadequate for an ocean crossing.

Jannus estimated that a nonstop flight from Newfoundland to Ireland would take forty hours.[4] The fuel requirement would be five hundred gallons. Weight of the fuel alone would be nearly thirty-four hun-

Benoist flying boat with *Jannus* painted on the underside of the upper wing, 1913. Courtesy of the Florida Aviation Historical Society.

dred pounds, twice the weight of Jannus's fully loaded Benoist Cross Country Model XII hydroplane.

Their greatest hindrance was a lack of money.[5] Frank Orndorff, a Mattoon, Illinois, representative of Benoist's, petitioned Roberts for a one-hundred-horsepower engine free of charge for the flight. If the flight was a success, it would, Orndorff wrote, be worth "many thousand dollars to you in after sale of motors, as they would have fame."[6] Jannus and Benoist began plans for a transatlantic flight in July 1913.

Roberts took more than a month to respond to Orndorff and then agreed to sell Benoist an engine at the regular price of a thousand dollars. If the flight was successful, the complete cost of the engine would be refunded. Roberts's reason for refusing Benoist an engine was that "at least ten aviators have asked for a loan of a motor for this flight. The Roberts Motor Company could not undertake to furnish such a number of motors free of charge."[7] It is more probable that the Roberts company knew its engines were incapable of such a flight. If a

Benoist aircraft powered by a Roberts engine were lost at sea, the negative worldwide publicity would damage the company's reputation.

According to Orndorff, Benoist would "establish a hangar at Newfoundland near St. Johns. Wait until the weather gets just right at the same time a steamer crossing by the Northern Route which takes them near Newfoundland. Then fly to the steamer and keep alongside or ahead until at least 100 miles off the coast of Ireland, then fly ahead to the coast."[8]

Jannus and Benoist were overly optimistic about their ability to build an aircraft of adequate size and weight-bearing capacity, especially in such a short time. It would have been a quantum leap. The Benoist Model XII that Jannus used in 1912 was state-of-the-art from Benoist's factory. It had a range of only 120 miles and weighed 925 pounds. Less than one year after the Model XII was built, they were talking about building an airplane with a range capacity nearly seventeen times greater. Their experience and design work were not adequate for accomplishing such an undertaking. Airplanes, at least Benoist's, were still designed by eyeball. There was no wind tunnel, no static testing—the experimental laboratory was the airfield. The airplane either flew or it didn't.

Many aviators besides Jannus and Benoist were planning for the conquest of the Atlantic Ocean, with an eye on Lord Northcliffe's $50,000 prize. The Americans Joseph Pulitzer, James Gordon Bennett, and Rodman Wanamaker were more than willing to give their money to further the advancement of early aviation. The wealthy Wanamaker had aligned himself with Glenn Curtiss. Tony Jannus may have been more involved with Curtiss and Wanamaker than anyone knew. Theodore Roscoe claimed, "Tony Janus, one of the ace civilian pilots of the period, announced that a day would soon arrive when a plane would fly across the Atlantic. Rodman Wanamaker embraced the idea; he thought a trans-Atlantic flight might promote science and world peace. In company with Commander John Cyril Porte, a retired British naval officer, Wanamaker had approached Curtiss in 1912 on the matter of building a flying boat for the ocean attempt which Janus had charted from New Foundland to Ireland."[9]

At the time, Curtiss was working on his own flying boat, complete with dual two-hundred-horsepower engines designed solely for this purpose. Roland Garros, Mark Pourpe, and Brindejonc des Moulinais of France had declared their intent to cross the Atlantic from east to west. Garros never crossed the Atlantic; instead, he died a hero in the war in Europe.[10] Wanamaker had deep pockets and was able to bear the entire financial burden himself. Benoist could not hope to cross the Atlantic without additional sponsorship, and that was not forthcoming.

In May 1913, Jannus had told the editor of *Aero and Hydro*, "All things considered I think a trans-Atlantic flight is the next natural step in the development of the flying machine. . . . I don't consider an ocean flight a dream or a fancy, but simply a scientific problem of building a flying boat that will be big and strong enough to make the distance, and I hope to be the first man to pilot that boat across the waters."[11] Orville Wright in 1913 said categorically that a flight across the Atlantic Ocean was not possible and "would be the height of folly."[12]

The *Aero and Hydro* Great Lakes Reliability Cruise had been intended as the means for Jannus to gain additional over-water experience. Benoist and Jannus hoped to test the pilot and gain a further understanding of the rigors to be faced in crossing the Atlantic.

Supposedly, as early as the fall of 1913, Benoist had designed and built a twin-engined flying boat that boasted a seventy-foot wingspan. Benoist and Jannus planned to use this flying boat, constructed in the shops of the St. Louis Car Company, to cross the Atlantic Ocean. Unknown to Benoist, one of his mechanics took the flying boat out for a test flight and the behemoth aircraft crashed and was destroyed beyond repair.[13] This story is doubtful and without any supporting evidence. Benoist probably did not construct a two-engined flying boat until 1915 at the earliest.

Nearly a year later, Benoist and Jannus would still be making plans to navigate the Atlantic. On March 4, 1914, Benoist announced in the *St. Petersburg Daily Times* that Jannus was making plans to fly from St. Petersburg, Florida, to New York City. The proposed flight was to be a practice run for a later transatlantic flight. A new flying boat under construction at Benoist's St. Louis facility was said to be nearing completion and was expected to be shipped to St. Petersburg sometime during the middle of March. Benoist was expecting the *New York Times* to provide not only extensive coverage of the flight but also funding.

The flight along the Missouri and Mississippi Rivers, though a great accomplishment, would pale by comparison to a flight across the Atlantic Ocean. The earlier trip had taken forty days, and actual flying time had been only thirty-one hours and forty-three minutes.[14] The trip to New York was expected to take no more than forty-eight hours of nearly continuous flying.[15] But the Florida to New York excursion never occurred because of a lack of money. The *New York Times* refused to sponsor the trip.

A flight across the Atlantic Ocean was not doomed by the equipment, underpowered engines, weather, or lack of suitable navigational aids. What postponed such a flight was far more complex than a compass, understanding a weather system, or ginning up a pair of engines to deliver a hundred horsepower. It was war.

Fresh from the disappointing Great Lakes Cruise, the Benoist team set out to redeem themselves. Their next challenge was New York City, where the *New York Times* American Aerial Derby was to be held in commemoration of Orville Wright's historic first flight less than ten years earlier.

The sky was heavily overcast from a mid-October cold front. The wind blew from the northwest at forty-three miles per hour. The sixty-mile course for the race was designed to be primarily over water. From their start at Oakwood Heights, the fliers would take off at two-minute intervals and head in a straight line to Governor's Island. The course was plotted to follow the East River to the point where it intersected the Harlem River. From this observation point, the aviators would fly in a northwesterly direction to the junction of the Harlem and Hudson Rivers. Where the two rivers merged, the contestants would turn their aircraft in a southerly direction and follow the Hudson River back to Oakwood Heights.

The aerial race began with the drop of a flag on October 14, 1913. Only five aviators took off from the Staten Island field. The fliers were Tony Jannus, William S. Luckey, Frank Niles, C. Murvin Wood, and

J. Guy Gilpatrick, the local hopeful. Of the original thirteen entrants, eight did not start the race.[16] Flying a one-hundred-horsepower Curtiss biplane, William Luckey was the winner of the *Times* Aerial Derby. The fifty-year-old Luckey was nicknamed "Old Bill." He crossed the finish line with a time of fifty-two minutes and fifty-four seconds. Frank "Do-Anything" Niles, piloting a Curtiss one-hundred-horsepower biplane, crossed the finish line in fifty-four minutes and fifty-five seconds. Third prize went to C. Murvin Wood. Fourth was J. Guy Gilpatrick in an eighty-horsepower Sloane-Deperdussin monoplane. Jannus and his seventy-horsepower Benoist tractor biplane were outmatched. He finished a distant fifth, with an elapsed time of one hour, fourteen minutes, and seven seconds.

Collier's Weekly described the *New York Times* American Aerial Derby as "The Aeroplane's Birthday Party—A Derby Above the Skyscrapers." City officials estimated that the crowds in New York City and eastern New Jersey numbered in the millions for this event.[17] At Washington Bridge, there were so many observers that streetcars and automobiles were prevented from crossing. Though Jannus was the last to finish the race, nearly twenty minutes after first-place finisher Luckey, he was greeted by a boisterous and enthusiastic crowd at the end.

Jannus believed that the race had been one of his most difficult flights and a terrific test of endurance. He said, "Though the element of danger was always present there was never, I believe, any time when my personal safety or the safety of the aeroplane was at stake. . . . I am very thankful that my motor did not stop or other trouble develop, for it would have been a hard task to land. Just imagine a leaf tossed in an Autumn gale and you will have some idea of my experience."[18]

It was not uncommon for the pilots to be cruising at sixty miles per hour in level flight and suddenly find their aircraft rising uncontrollably thirty or forty feet. Just as suddenly, they would be thrown fifty feet toward the ground. The wind made it a race of extremes. While flying north up the East River, the pilots ran into howling head winds. They were reduced to speeds of no more than fifteen miles per hour, close to a stall. It took all of the pilots' skill to avoid being forced to the ground. As they headed south along the Hudson River, the tail winds propelled the rickety machines to speeds of 110 miles per hour. Jannus described his experience in the race as "akin to riding a bucking horse."[19]

Albert J. Jewell had disappeared while flying his Moisant monoplane from the Hempstead Plains aviation field on Long Island to the Oakland Heights field on Staten Island. Several aviators decided to undertake their own search for him the next day. Early on the morning of October 15, Jannus and J. Robinson Hall, the race's promoter, went out to the field on Staten Island. Heavy winds continued from the previous day, forcing Jannus to postpone the flight. They intended to fly over Jamaica Bay and Far Rockaway, where Jewell had last been seen. Optimistically, they carried ropes and tackle for rescue or salvage work.[20]

At 2 P.M., Jannus decided that although the wind continued strong, it had abated enough to undertake the flight. Hall sat in the front seat, directly behind the engine. Jannus sat at the wheel behind Hall. J. D. Smith cranked the engine of the Benoist biplane; Jannus gave the word to let go. As they sped across the field for a hundred or so yards, everything was fine. Having built an adequate speed to allow takeoff, Jannus nosed the biplane off the ground.[21] At an altitude of five feet above the field, they were hit by a wind gust that sent the plane's wheels crashing to the ground.

Automatically, Jannus pulled back on the controls. The heavy weight of the machine did not allow sufficient lift, slowing its response. The biplane skimmed and hopped across the field, finally running into a marsh. High grass in the running gear retarded the aircraft's speed. Not ready to give up, Jannus managed to lift the plane several feet off the ground, only to be hit by another blast of wind. Down they went again.

Looming directly in front of them was a shallow ditch. When Jannus saw it, he tried to get enough lift to leapfrog across the ditch. The wheels struck the far side, forcing the plane to go nose down and throwing the tail into the air in a somersault.

The long wings and broad wing surface provided drag, slowing their forward momentum. The airplane slowly fell over. When the propeller, still spinning at over a thousand revolutions per minute, hit the ground, it broke into pieces. Jagged shards flew hundreds of feet through the air. Flames from the engine exhaust set fire to fuel pouring from a broken gasoline line, igniting the cloth-covered machine. Jannus was able to free himself. He attempted to cover the flaming fuel line with his gloved hands to stop the fire. His actions were too late, but he was slightly injured in the attempt.

Hall was unable to escape from the plane as Jannus had. He became an unwilling captive and was thrown over with the plane. Landing on his arm, with his left knee jammed against the inside of the front of the airplane, he struggled to free himself. Hall was burned on his right forearm when he was thrown against the hot engine. Shortly after, he too was successful in escaping from the plane and was quickly dragged to safety by Jannus. By the time help from the hangar reached the burning aircraft, both men were safe. An ambulance from the S. R. Smith Infirmary took Hall to the facility ten miles away. After being treated for his minor burns and bruises, Hall retired to the Hotel McAlpin for a much needed rest.

Benoist was very disappointed in Jannus.[22] He was angry that Jannus had been flying in poor weather and had lost another of his aircraft. Benoist could hardly afford to lose one more airplane. Reginald Woodcock claimed the accident was caused by carelessness.[23]

At the time of the accident, there was more than a little confusion about what had really happened. The *St. Louis Star* reported, "Jannus badly hurt when plane burns." An unidentified source claimed that the accident had taken place in the water. An October 15, 1913, entry from J. D. Smith's diary set to rest any confusion. Smith wrote, "Tony hitting a high ditch which turned the machine upside down and it caught fire. The whole machine was about ruined."[24]

The intensive search for Jewell continued without Jannus. The builders of Jewell's Moisant airplane hired six motorboats which conducted an exhaustive water search, zigzagging across Jamaica Bay. Lifesaving stations along the New Jersey coast and the south shore of Long Island were all on alert. A reward of $250 was offered for the recovery of Jewell's body and plane. Nearly two weeks later, on October 25, Jewell's badly bloated and disfigured body washed ashore on Long Island's Fire Island.[25]

Jannus snaps his own photograph as he flies over St. Louis, November 1913.
Courtesy of the Florida Aviation Historical Society.

The trip to New York was a total disaster for Tom Benoist and his
team. They not only lost the race but were out the cost of transportation of their aircraft and themselves by railroad, as well as the entry
fee for the race. One airplane was destroyed, and Benoist failed to sell
any others.

Back home again, Jannus, as chief pilot, continued to do most of the
test flights on the flying boat, as well as design work on new aircraft.
In October 1913, Jannus flew a new aircraft, the Benoist Model XIV
tractor biplane, in Detroit, Michigan. With the exception of an increase in wingspan from thirty-six to thirty-seven feet, the new model
was largely unchanged.[26]

One of the most significant events of 1913 for Tom Benoist had been
a letter that he received from Percival Fansler, the sales representative
in Jacksonville, Florida, for Kahlenberg Brothers, a manufacturer of
marine diesel engines. Like many other Americans, Fansler had read
of Tony Jannus's 1,973-mile flight with great interest. Fansler had traveled extensively throughout the states of Florida and Georgia. While
selling road-building equipment, he frequently visited the cities of Tam-

pa and St. Petersburg. No one was more aware of the need for a convenient means of transportation in the area than the farsighted Fansler. A trip of less than twenty miles between Tampa and St. Petersburg by water could take hours by steamship; the overland train trip required several hours. Impressed by Jannus's feat as well as Benoist's meticulous recording of flight costs for the trip, Fansler wrote to Benoist. Benoist responded enthusiastically. As Fansler recalled in a 1929 interview, "After receiving two or three letters that dealt with the details and capabilities of the boat, the idea popped into my head that instead of monkeying with the thing to give 'jazz' trips, I would start a real commercial line running from somewhere to somewhere else."[27]

Now Benoist and Jannus were getting ready to head south with their flying boat.

11   A New Enterprise

ON DECEMBER 4, 1913, Percival Elliott Fansler arrived in St. Petersburg with the idea of operating a scheduled passenger airboat operation between St. Petersburg and Tampa. His original plan had been to operate a flying service in Jacksonville, but the idea received a less than enthusiastic reception from city leaders.

Rebuffed but still determined, Fansler headed south by railroad to Tampa. In early December 1913, Fansler made a spirited presentation to Tampa officials, who were no more interested in Fansler's proposal than those in Jacksonville had been. When the idea of the airboat line was mentioned, nine out of ten people regarded the project as a fake. Tampa officials' belief that airboats could not fly was probably one factor in their negative decision, but if that was the reason they gave to Fansler, their rationale lacked credibility. Lincoln Beachey, "the man without nerves," had flown in Tampa nearly two and a half years earlier.[1] One of Tampa's most influential and highly respected citizens, Morton F. Plant, had been an original stockholder when the Wright brothers incorporated and capitalized their company for $1 million in 1909. In reality, Tampa officials did not care whether travelers could get to St. Petersburg quickly and easily. Rivalry, jealousy, and animosity between the cities was rife. Tampa did not want to lose visitors or potential business opportunities to the city across Tampa Bay.

After his meeting with Tampa officials, Fansler took the train to St. Petersburg. The trip covered sixty-four miles and could take anywhere from three to twelve hours. St. Petersburg in 1913 was a backwater southern town of less than ten thousand people. The city consisted

Jannus at the controls of a Benoist flying boat. J. D. Smith, his trusted mechanic, is the passenger. Courtesy of the Florida Aviation Historical Society.

mainly of scattered frame buildings; many of the streets were unpaved. But Fansler thought the city held promise. Built on the lower tip of a peninsula, St. Petersburg was held captive by the railroad and steamship lines. Travelers bound for St. Petersburg took the train to Tampa and then traveled to St. Petersburg via steamship. The Sarasota Line Steamers and Favorite Line Steamers both operated scheduled service between Tampa and St. Petersburg.

Fansler had a ready-made introduction to one of St. Petersburg's most influential citizens, Major Lew Brown. As owner and publisher of the *St. Petersburg Evening Independent*, Brown could open many doors. Fansler's trump card was his wife, Mary. She and Brown had attended college together and, though not close friends, were acquainted.

After arriving in St. Petersburg, Fansler called on Brown and announced the purpose of his visit: a proposal to start air service between St. Petersburg and Tampa. A born salesman, Fansler flashed a smile as he pulled photographs, as well as newspaper and magazine clippings, from his briefcase. Fansler handed Brown the copy of *Aero*

A NEW ENTERPRISE

and Hydro that publicized Tony Jannus's 1,973-mile trip down the Missouri and Mississippi Rivers. His arguments impressed Brown, who suggested that Fansler meet with L. A. Whitney, the secretary-manager of St. Petersburg's Board of Trade. Whitney supported the idea almost immediately. His only concern was that the airboat operation and the airboats must be safe. Fansler impressed Whitney with his photos and positive clippings, one of which may have been from *Collier's Weekly* of November 9, 1912, entitled "Growing Wings, Aviation Rises Though Aviators Fall, and Aeroplanes Steadily Become Safer." The author, Henry Woodhouse, made the point that "an industry is here."[2] It would not be surprising that a man of vision such as Whitney was impressed with such arguments.

Whitney was a keen businessman and had succinct dollars-and-cents questions for Fansler. Of primary concern was the cost of the proposed fare from St. Petersburg to Tampa. If priced too high, no one could afford to use the service and it would become nothing more than a novelty. Fansler was proposing a one-way fare of five dollars, which would barely cover the direct operating costs of the airplane. He explained that Benoist was willing to sacrifice profits to get an airline up and running. Obviously, the per-mile cost of operating the railroad or steamship service was a great deal less because they dealt with a large volume of passengers, as well as carrying freight. Five dollars a trip would be a premium fare when compared with the railroad or steamship fare, but the airboat line would offer speed. Fansler and Benoist hoped to cover their additional operating costs by flying exhibitions and charters and teaching students to fly. Benoist, when asked how he could cover his costs and make a profit, replied logically, "There are at present about 30,000 tourists in the area and I believe a great many of them will patronize the airboat line to save time. Besides, I am anxious to demonstrate the capability and practicability of aerial transportation at a price anyone can afford even if such a low rate means a revenue loss to me, for today's loss could very well be tomorrow's profit."[3]

Whitney personally pledged $1,200 as a subsidy to guarantee the expenses of the airboat company in the event of inadequate revenue. He had only one proviso beyond that of safety—Fansler would have to persuade other St. Petersburg businessmen to match his pledge.

Fansler's next step was to meet with Noel E. Mitchell, one of the town's more fervent boosters. Mitchell was no newcomer to aviation; nearly two years earlier he had promoted aerial exhibitions over the west coast of Florida. He had financed and promoted an exhibition by Leonard W. Bonney in February 1912.[4] Mitchell had recently returned from a trip to New York City, where he had witnessed the *New York Times* American Aerial Derby in Manhattan on October 14, 1913, with Jannus piloting the Benoist biplane.[5]

Nicknamed the "Sandman," Mitchell was a well-known real estate salesman with a knack for promotion. He pledged $1,000 to underwrite the project. Successful or not, the airboat line would generate publicity for St. Petersburg, as well as his own real estate business. Whether Mitchell was motivated by civic altruism or personal gain is irrelevant. What is important is that he wanted to be involved with Fansler and his airboat operation. Because of this interest, he was responsible for the goodwill and financial backing provided by St. Petersburg's businessmen.

Mitchell and Fansler agreed in principle on the airboat operation. Fansler already had a contract drawn up, but Mitchell wanted some changes. He drew up a contract of his own.[6] Mitchell, Fansler, C. D. Hammond, and two others signed the contract written on the back of a piece of Mitchell's office stationery.

Elated, Fansler wrote to his wife in Jacksonville, "It's in the bag, Mary! Seventeen-hundred dollars pledged. I'm writing Tom that I've found the place to start operations."[7] Mitchell lined up several prominent St. Petersburg businessmen willing to contribute financially to the project. The other backers were Charles A. Hall, O. T. Railsback, C. D. Hammond, Arthur Johnson, C. M. Roser, Lew B. Brown, George Gandy, Perry Snell, G. B. Haines, Soren Lund, and G. T. Bailey. With the support of the city and private financial backing firmly behind him, Fansler wired the good news to Benoist. That same day, Friday, December 5, 1913, the *St. Petersburg Daily Times* headline read, "Regular Air Trip Here to Tampa May Be Run—A Line of Flying Boats Across Tampa Bay May Be Established Here in 30 days—Will Be Novel and Safe Trip." The paper reported, "With a fleet of hydro-aeroplanes running on regular schedule between St. Petersburg and Tampa, making the trip in 18 minutes, and carrying passengers, a new 'boat' line which is likely to be established in the city will in all probability instantly become popular."

Jannus was first mentioned in the *St. Petersburg Daily Times* on December 7, 1913. It reported: "Mr. Benoist will probably send his right hand man, Tony Jannus, who is noted as one of the most careful aviators in the world. His flying has been devoid of such spectacular features as have made the names of other aviators famous, but he set a long distance record two years ago that has not been equalled and that is remarkable, as progress in this line is so rapid that many records hardly stand the test of a day. Jannus has carried hundreds of passengers and has not had one single accident to date—he believes, with his chief, that more harm will be done the aircraft industry through one accident due to carelessness or foolhardiness than could be remedied in years; and following this feeling has kept his record clear."[8] By the time Jannus arrived in St. Petersburg, he had already been involved in several major accidents so this statement was patently false.

The boosters of St. Petersburg may have embraced the project because they believed an airboat line would be good for the people of southwest Florida. Perhaps it was just a publicity stunt by excellent promoters and publicists, concerned only with their own fortunes. Whatever the reason, they were backing the airboat company.

Aerial accidents were commonplace in 1913; newspaper headlines that screamed of men falling from airplanes were not unusual. Aerial death and burning airplanes would not have made positive press for St. Petersburg. The safety of the airboat itself was repeatedly stressed. The *St. Petersburg Daily Times* reported, "The Benoist Airboat has several important features not shared by other machines. The most important, perhaps is that the engine is placed down in the hull of the boat, behind and below the operator. This lowers the center of gravity and, in case of a tumble, is much less dangerous. . . . The hull of the Benoist airboat is built of three thicknesses of spruce with special fabric between. It must be tight, strong and stiff, as the machine is really a boat with wings and not a set of aeroplane wings with pontoons to support it on the water. There are six water tight compartments, making it practically unsinkable."[9]

On December 7, 1913, the local newspaper headlines read, "Local Boosters Back Airboat Line" and "Subscriptions Already Begin and Line Looks Like Sure Thing." Only three days had passed since the signing of the contract. Rapid progress was being made. Nearly half the financing had been committed; the rest would soon be forthcoming. The progress of the airboat line received almost daily publicity in the *St. Petersburg Daily Times*. It was estimated that the airboat line would bring $50,000 worth of publicity to the city.[10]

The reason why a St. Louis manufacturer of airplanes wanted to establish an airboat line in St. Petersburg was obvious—money. Benoist hoped to promote and sell his aircraft. While he may have wanted to provide a scheduled air service to the community, St. Petersburg was also another exhibition venue. St. Louis had begun to charge Benoist $15 each time he took a plane off the ground and required him to have a city as well as a state license. Benoist had reported that St. Louis wanted $5 for a license to fly an airboat and the state added another $10. Whether this was $15 per day, flight, or year is unclear.[11] Benoist wanted a more friendly environment in which to conduct business and sell airplanes. The successful establishment of an airline operation in St. Petersburg would lead to operations in other cities. Demand for air service would create a need for additional aircraft. In a discussion with the press about the airboat line, Fansler said, "If it is successful the Benoist company stands ready to extend their airlines all over Florida. . . . It is contemplated to extend these lines during the coming summer further along the New Jersey, Connecticut, and New York shores—as well as in other sections suited to this method of transportation."[12] Fansler was proposing a hub-and-spoke system years before the idea occurred to anyone else.

Exactly when the first meeting between Fansler and Tom Benoist took place is uncertain. They may have met as early as 1904 during the Louisiana Purchase Exposition in St. Louis when Fansler was working there as an assistant electrical engineer. Benoist and John Berry, the balloonist, had a booth on the eleven-acre aeronautics field, which was the gathering area for balloons, gliders, and airplanes. A purely coincidental meeting is doubtful, however. The fairgrounds "were large, very large," according to an official publicity brochure.[13] The more likely explanation is that the two men first crossed paths following Jannus's record-breaking flight from Omaha to New Orleans in 1912. Fansler read of Jannus's accomplishments, was impressed, and wrote to Benoist asking if Benoist's airplanes were sufficiently advanced to start an airline.

According to Fansler, "I wrote to Tom about the scheme and he immediately became enthusiastic. He agreed to build and furnish two boats if I would work out the operating details, select a route and handle the business end. By August 1913 my experience in Florida had led me to conclude that a line could be operated between St. Petersburg and Tampa. The distance was about 23 miles; some fifteen of which was along the shore of Tampa Bay and the remainder over open water." Benoist responded: "My safety-first airboats are sufficiently advanced . . . besides an airboat when it crashes simply gives the pilot a good bath."[14]

While Fansler negotiated, Jannus and J. D. Smith were flying passengers at Cairo, Illinois, and making plans. In addition to the airboat line, they intended to open a flying school in St. Petersburg.[15]

On December 17, 1913, the final contract making the St. Petersburg–Tampa Airboat Line a reality was signed by Benoist, Fansler, and St. Petersburg officials. The date of the signing was ten years, to the day, after the Wrights' first flight. The contract establishing the St. Petersburg–Tampa Airboat Line read as follows:

> We, the undersigned businessmen of St. Petersburg, do this day promise to pay to the officials of the St. Petersburg–Tampa Airboat Line, fifty dollars a day through January and twenty-five dollars a day, through February and March, for every day, Monday to Saturday of each week over a period of three months, on which regularly scheduled flights from St. Petersburg to Tampa are made, regardless of passenger or cargo, and on scheduled time.
>
> It is understood that if the public takes to the air in sufficient numbers to pay costs of the Airboat Line, such payments will be forfeit.

The Benoist Aircraft Company, through its president, Thomas W. Benoist, does hereby promise and agree to furnish airboats, pilots and crew and maintain service on schedule two round trips daily for three months.

Furthermore, the city of St. Petersburg agrees to build a hangar on the seawall of the North Mole to house the airboats when not in operation, and agrees to keep the Central Yacht Basin and Bay in front of the Basin, free from boat traffic during the hours of scheduled flights. Given under our hands and seal Seventeenth day of December, 1913, at St. Petersburg, Fla."[16]

On December 20, Benoist left St. Petersburg by train, headed for Paducah to assist Jannus and Smith with the crating of Benoist Airboat Number 43. Tuesday, December 23, the aircraft left on a railroad freight car expected to arrive in St. Petersburg no later than Christmas Day. Benoist returned to St. Louis. Percival Fansler was back in Jacksonville, preparing to move his pregnant wife to St. Petersburg.

As Tony, Roger Jannus, and J. D. Smith prepared to catch the 2:30 P.M. train, Tony announced, "I'll be back in Paducah not later than April."[17] He went on to predict that when he returned, he would be making daily round-trip flights between Paducah and Cairo.

The hangar promised to the promoters of the St. Petersburg–Tampa Airboat Line was a long time coming. City commissioners had quickly approved use of the north breakwater of the city's yacht basin for the Benoist School of Aviation. The piece of land measured four hundred feet long by three hundred feet wide. On this site, two hangars, each forty feet by fifty feet and twelve feet high, were to be erected.[18] Only one was for the Benoist operation. The other was built to accommodate Raymond Morris's Curtiss Model M flying boat. The location selected was perfect. The yacht basin, encircled by the breakwater, was long enough to allow a sheltered and calm takeoff, regardless of conditions in the bay. C. D. Hammond, the commissioner of public works, had awarded the contract to a builder who intended to employ outside labor even though many of St. Petersburg's local contractors were out of work. A compromise settling the resultant dispute was hammered out, but the completion of the hangar was delayed for several weeks.[19]

The flying boat, which had been expected days earlier, was lost in transit somewhere between Paducah and St. Petersburg.[20] Local railroad authorities claimed that the matter was out of their control. Jannus and Fansler attempted to put their missing aircraft out of their thoughts and concentrated instead on details still to be finished. Traveling by steamship to Tampa, they met with city authorities to arrange a landing place. Returning to St. Petersburg, they went directly to the site of the proposed hangar. Little progress was evident, and the site was littered with construction lumber.

City officials were becoming skeptical that an airplane really existed. Fansler later recalled the pressure they felt, wondering if the missing aircraft would ever be found, let alone arrive in time for New Year's Day. He stated, "We deluged the freight officials with telegrams." Railroad officials thought that the flying boat had been sidetracked somewhere between St. Petersburg and Jacksonville. Fansler continued, "As the days went by and the car failed to materialize, even the backers of the enterprise began to josh us about the phantom boat. The 28th became the 29th, and the 30th passed into the 31st, and—our frantic joy can be imagined when the local freight agent announced that the car had arrived and would be switched down to the dock within the hour. It was about 4:47 A.M. when the first news was received. Later, aboard freight car No. 65032 of the Missouri Pacific, the airboat was shunted to a spur running down the railroad dock in St. Petersburg. Half a dozen of us clustered around and struggled with our composure while the freight agent fussed over the necessary papers. Literally, that car was a great cocoon, enshrouding a giant moth that was to write a new page in the history of transportation."[21]

Fansler's reference to the passing days as "the 28th became the 29th, and the 30th passed into the 31st" made it appear as if the lost aircraft did not arrive in St. Petersburg until the waning hours of the last day of 1913.[22] Actually, that was not so. In his excitement, Fansler had confused both the freight car number and the date of arrival. The airboat was received at the St. Petersburg freight yard at 4:47 P.M. on December 30. On December 31, the local newspaper reported, "L. S. and M. S. freight car No. 45033 arrived in St. Petersburg yesterday afternoon at 4:47, bearing the Benoist Airboat which is the idol of Tony Jannus' heart."[23] As soon as the morning's passenger train pulled away from the depot, the flatcar carrying the aircraft was pushed to the Atlantic Coast Line track, which ended in a spur just below First Street. The men walked alongside the railroad car as it was hustled from the freight yard to the waterfront. After days of worry, they were not about to let the freight car containing the flying boat out of their sight.

Fansler remembered the frenzied activity that followed. He recalled, "The seal was broken. Jay Dee Smith and Tom Benoist crawled into the car and hastily inspected the contents to see that no damage had been done in shipment." Once uncrated, the flying boat was reassembled. Fansler continued, "Then skids were fastened into place, and slowly and tenderly we lowered the hull to a strip of sand beside the track. Then the wing sections came out. Whitney, a man of great personal charm and one who had not lost faith, took off his coat and helped."[24] The flying boat received at St. Petersburg had undergone several changes since its original manufacture. Its hull was still painted green, but it had been signed by nearly fifty thousand people who had witnessed its flights since June. This was almost certainly the only Benoist equipment of any kind to be painted green. Reinhardt Ausmus, a onetime employee of Benoist's, wrote, "This was the only plane that he painted green and it was rather dark green. I think the hull may have been from another flying boat and painted dark green to cover any wear that may have been shown. As to the color of his planes where painted were nearly all grey."[25] Its yellow wings had been expanded by ten feet and still bore traces of the painted-over legend *Lark of Duluth* on the underside of the upper port-side wing.

The airline crew had plenty of help in assembling the flying boat from young boys drawn to the waterfront activity. Sixteen-year-old Luke Atkins was swimming with a friend near the site. Atkins later recalled, "We hung around every day until he asked what we were doing and we told him we were looking for a job. He handed us a can of axle grease and told us to grease the ramps that they used to push it into the water. We were supposed to get a ride on the airboat, but never got it."[26] Obviously, Jannus had more important things on his mind and forgot that he had promised a ride to the young helpers. Many years later, J. Leland "Jack" Seale recalled, "It was my job to sleep beneath the wings to protect it from the public. I told Tony Jannus there was no need for this because the people of St. Petersburg would not harm the plane, but he had some bad luck up north with souvenir hunters so I kept my job. I guess I was the world's first line boy."[27]

12 ✈ An Airline Is Born

THE OFFICIAL WEATHER REPORT for the first day of 1914 was favorable. Cloudy skies on Wednesday night would lead to light variable winds on Thursday, New Year's Day. "Tony Jannus Will Make First Flight Thursday," read the headline of the *St. Petersburg Daily Times* on December 30, 1913. The *St. Petersburg Evening Independent* informed its readers, "Jannus to Set up Airboat Tomorrow."[1] The *Tampa Morning Tribune* devoted no front space to either Jannus or the St. Petersburg–Tampa Airboat Line on January 1, 1914. That day, Tampa residents were more interested in events in Mexico.[2]

Three thousand people crowded St. Petersburg's waterfront in anticipation of the big event. At 9:15 A.M., R. C. Bannister, the auctioneer, held up his left hand to begin the auction. Bidding for a seat on the first commercial flight of the St. Petersburg–Tampa Airboat Line was spirited. Thornton Parker began with a bid of $100. The opening bid was matched, then raised to $150 by Abe Pheil. Parker countered with another raise. Noel Mitchell threw in his offer of $275. On and on, it went.

Finally Abe Pheil's bid of $400 won the coveted seat for the flight across the bay. In 1935, Noel Mitchell recalled, "I was determined to see it sold for one thousand dollars and was running the price up in the bidding, when someone came to me and suggested that we should allow our ex-mayor, A. C. Pheil to be the first to take the trip. His next bid was four hundred dollars and we all stopped bidding and Mr. Pheil was the first passenger."[3]

To L. A. Whitney, secretary of St. Petersburg's Board of Trade, went the honor of saying a few words before introducing Percival Fansler. The flying boat was pointed toward the water, almost ready to go. Three men continued tinkering with it, ridding themselves of last-minute jitters. Fansler stood behind the trailing edge of the wings. A Benoist pennant hanging from a wing strut barely moved in the breeze. Fansler surveyed the expectant crowd before speaking. Suddenly his words flowed: "The Airboat Line to Tampa will be only a forerunner of great activity along these lines in the near future . . . what was impossible yesterday is an accomplishment of today—while tomorrow heralds the unbelievable."[4] With the conclusion of these words spoken by Fansler on January 1, 1914, the "world's first airline," the St. Petersburg–Tampa Airboat Line, was officially inaugurated. That the St. Petersburg–Tampa Airboat Line was the world's first scheduled, passenger, heavier-than-air airline is indisputable, but technically it was not the first airline. That honor rightfully belongs to Deutsche Luft-schiffarts AG (DELAG), which was founded on November 16, 1909. DELAG carried thousands of passengers in a lighter-than-air Zeppelin airship.[5]

When the applause for Fansler ended, he introduced Tony Jannus, who had quickly become the best known and most popular of all the Benoist group. Jannus appeared ready for a night on the town, not a twenty-one-mile flight in an open cockpit. He was dressed in white duck pants, a dark jacket, and his usual bow tie. Black leather gloves nearly to the elbow and a visored cap completed his outfit.

When he stood to speak, he was met with a tumultuous greeting. His broad smile was nearly outmatched by the emotion visible in his eyes. He was ready to go. In his brief remarks, he told the crowd that he "would do his utmost to make this line what people expected of it." In closing, he promised to "always keep the maxim 'safety first' foremost in my mind."[6]

If Jannus was nervous, it was not evident in the many photographs recording the day's events. Other than the historical significance attached to the first flight, there was nothing to differentiate it from any other. Jannus had flown almost daily since his first flight in the Rex Smith biplane in November 1910. Before the airline's birth, Jannus claimed that he had made more than nine thousand separate flights in Benoist flying boat Number 43 and had carried more than three thousand passengers.[7] Although Jannus was a highly competent and very experienced aviator, there is no way that he could have logged nine thousand flights in flying boat Number 43. That machine had not come out of the Benoist factory until June 1913. It was then taken to Duluth, Minnesota, where it was flown by William Jones. Jannus could take credit, however, for having flown more than nine thousand flights since 1910. On many days, it was common for him to fly twenty to thirty short flights.

Jannus, as well as everyone involved with the airline, did everything possible to make people comfortable with the idea of flying. Only a few days earlier, Jannus had stated, "I never attempt those spectacular flights you read about every day in the newspapers the kind that break aviator's necks, and I likely never will, certainly not while the life of a passenger is entrusted to my care. . . . Afraid? Bah. Why should anyone be afraid?"[8]

Jannus climbed into the flying boat and began checking the control surfaces. He primed the engine, retarded the spark, and switched the lever on the coil into the "start" position. Fansler and Benoist helped Abe Pheil into the passenger seat. Jannus donned a long slicker as protection from the cool morning air and the spray generated by the airboat sliding through the water. He stood up and cranked the engine with the starting bar. The Roberts engine coughed to life. When it was cranked over and running, Jannus switched the coil lever to "run." He was almost ready to go. Standing three feet from the airboat, Percival Fansler raised his right hand as if starting his three-two-one countdown.

"What time is it?" Jannus asked Fansler. "One minute before ten," was the answer. At exactly 10 A.M., Jannus gave it the throttle. The flying boat slid down the boarded runway into the calm waters of the yacht basin. Jannus circled the enclosed harbor before taxiing out between the breakwaters and heading for the open waters of the bay. Two American flags tied to the wing struts waved in the wind. A Benoist pennant flying on the starboard side was countered by one on the port side emblazoned "St. Petersburg." Opening the throttle and increas-

Jannus in a formal pose. The photograph was probably taken in January 1914, while Jannus was in St. Petersburg, Florida. Courtesy of the Florida Aviation Historical Society.

Jannus, Percival E. Fansler, and financial supporters of the St. Petersburg–Tampa Airboat Line, the world's first scheduled passenger airline service, January 1, 1914. Courtesy of the Florida Aviation Historical Society.

Just before the first flight of the St. Petersburg–Tampa Airboat Line, January 1, 1914. *Left to right:* Percival Elliott Fansler, Abram C. Pheil, Tony Jannus. Courtesy of the Florida Aviation Historical Society.

ing speed caused water to stream over the bow and into the pilot's face until the flying boat slid onto its step. Two hundred feet later, the aircraft took to the air at about thirty miles an hour. Fifteen feet above the water, Jannus headed east across Tampa Bay.

At about the halfway point, he crossed over a small spit of land named Gadsden Point. From there, he flew over Hillsborough Bay and then up the Hillsborough River. As soon as Jannus and Pheil faded from sight, the crowd rushed to the telegraph office to await news of their arrival in Tampa. Years later, Fansler recalled the moment: "Rapidly old 43 dwindled in size, winging her way towards Tampa. The crowd settled down to wait. I heard many interesting comments during the next few minutes. Some said she'd fall into the water before she got half-way across, and I doubt if many actually believed the trip would be carried out on schedule. At 10:26 a.m. the telephone rang and my elation could not be concealed as I heard the attendant at the Tampa terminal say, 'Tony's coming up the river, and there's a big crowd yelling their heads off.'"[9]

Flags flutter as Jannus taxies out of the yacht basin, January 1, 1914. Courtesy of the Florida Aviation Historical Society.

Twenty-three minutes after his departure, Jannus landed his aircraft and brought it to rest near the Tampa Electric Company. The crowd waiting for Jannus's arrival had been estimated to be almost as large as that at St. Petersburg. Jannus and Pheil were treated to a series of cheers as the aircraft taxied to a stop. The handshakes and congratulations were unending. Mayor Donald B. McKay of Tampa belatedly turned out to offer his congratulations to the pair. The city of Tampa had missed a golden opportunity, and McKay had missed his chance to be the first person to welcome Jannus officially to his city.

On January 2, 1914, the *Tampa Tribune* reported, "First Commercial Air Ship Line in World Inaugurated." Finally, Tampa was giving credit to the airboat line. The front-page story reported, "When the airboat arrived yesterday morning a crowd of two thousand was waiting near the temporary landing, another 1,000 saw what they could from the Lafayette Street Bridge, and 500 more were across the river. When the dock was reached an enthusiastic cheer went up, and there was a clapping and the waving of hats and handkerchiefs. A moment later there was a rush down the three narrow planks connecting the

JANNUS, AN AMERICAN FLIER

platform with the shore, men, women, and children fighting to get down to the boat and its two occupants. The police were called to hold back the crowd so that W. C. Burgert could take motion pictures during which Messrs. Jannus and Pheil bowed and smiled."

At precisely eleven o'clock, Jannus began his westbound trip to St. Petersburg. With the wind at his back, the return flight took only twenty minutes. Word spread like wildfire that Jannus had been sighted on his approach to St. Petersburg. Hundreds of people scurried for positions along the waterfront. Climbing from the airboat, Jannus dropped his flight goggles, breaking the glass. Ten-year-old Judy Bryan ducked under the rope that had been hastily erected to hold back the crowd. Running up to Jannus, she asked him if she could have the broken goggles. Without hesitation, he gave them to her. Then he removed one of the brightly lettered Benoist pennants from the wing strut and handed it to her with a smile. Posing for photographs, Fansler, happy and triumphant, uttered only, "So I was crazy!" Tony Jannus, quiet and confident but understated as ever, remarked that it was "just a routine flight."

As tired as Jannus may have been from the first flight, the excitement of the morning, and the anxiety about the arrival of his aircraft, it did not slow him down. No sooner had he arrived back in St. Petersburg, than he was off again. Jannus took Johnny J. Jones, the owner of the carnival show, for a short flight around the harbor. Jones's show featured a flea circus and the Regnalls, who dived ninety-two feet into a miniature lake of fire. No stranger to excitement, Jones must have believed the flight with Jannus would be as exciting as his own carnival show because he paid $15 for his short flight around the harbor.

Later that afternoon, the auctioneer Bannister was back at work. Noel E. Mitchell made a high bid of $175 for the second flight to Tampa. Several other short flights were also made that afternoon. At the end of its first day of operation, the airline had racked up an impressive array of statistics. The company had made nine flights, including the two scheduled round-trips between St. Petersburg and Tampa. Nine passengers had been carried; 134 miles and 138 minutes of flying time had been entered into the log book. Financially, the first day of the operation had been a tremendous success; the company had earned

$615. The money was donated to the city of St. Petersburg to purchase a pair of harbor channel lights.

For years, other fliers had transported people from one place to another, but it was always on an informal basis, never defined by a schedule. The St. Petersburg–Tampa Airboat Line was the first airline in the world to operate a scheduled passenger service.

On the first day of the airline's operation, Jannus defined the joys of flying. He stated, "To me flying is not the successful defying of death—but the indulgence in the poetry of mechanical motion—a dustless, bumpless, fascinating speed; an abstraction from things material into infinite space; an abandon that is yet more exciting but less irritating than any other form of mechanical propulsion."[10]

Fansler, Benoist, and Jannus were not small-minded men mired in provincial thinking. Even before they received a definite go-ahead for the St. Petersburg–Tampa Air Boat Line, they envisioned expansion. St. Petersburg would serve as their hub, with ever-increasing spokes to surrounding towns such as Bradenton, Safety Harbor, Tarpon Springs, and Pass-a-Grille. Once the Florida expansion was successfully accomplished, they would push north like the American frontiersmen who had opened the West. They hoped by summer to connect several coastal cities in New Jersey, Connecticut, and New York.

The one-way fare to Tampa was $5. A round-trip earned no discount and cost $10. For the regularly scheduled flights, the airline earned nearly twenty-five cents per passenger mile. The company was not profitable, at least not if expenses such as fuel, capital costs, personnel expenses, and salaries were considered. If a financial profit-and-loss statement had been prepared, the St. Petersburg–Tampa Airboat Line would probably not have broken even. To think that Fansler and Benoist entered into this agreement to operate the airline for money alone, however, would be missing the point. To be sure, both men were capitalists and hoped to make money eventually. Initially they wished to persuade the public that a scheduled airline could be viable and to prove that their idea was practical in any weather. In that, they were successful.

An advertising flyer for the St. Petersburg–Tampa Airboat Line was distributed the day after the inaugural flight. The company promised "fast passenger and express service." Initially, the flight schedule called for two trips daily, except Sunday. The advertisement stated that special flight trips "can be arranged through any of our agents or by communicating directly with the St. Petersburg Hangar. Trips covering any distance over all-water routes and from the waters' surface to several thousand feet high AT PASSENGERS' REQUEST." All of this could be had for only $15. For the one-way fare of $5, "Passengers are allowed a weight of 200 pounds Gross including hand baggage, excess is charged at $5.00 per 100 pounds, minimum charge 25 cents." The company offered "EXPRESS RATES, for packages, suit cases, mail matter, etc., $5.00 per hundred pounds, minimum charge 25 cents." Tickets for the daily trips could be purchased at either of the hangars or at the City News Stand on Central Avenue in downtown St. Petersburg.

Eager to garner publicity, the owner of the *St. Petersburg Daily Times* contracted with the airline to carry its newspapers to Tampa. The front-page headline boasted, "The *Times* Will Deliver Papers in Tampa by Speedy Benoist Airboat." The story informed readers that the *St. Petersburg Daily Times* would be the first newspaper in the world to use flying machines for delivery purposes. Each morning on the ten o'clock flight, a bundle of newspapers would be flown to Tampa, where they would be distributed to the newsstands. Unfortunately, the first shipment did not go well. While attempting a takeoff in rough seas, the aircraft took on water and had to return to the hangar to be pumped out and have its cargo offloaded.

Although the Benoist company carried newspapers to Tampa, it did not have the distinction of making the first aerial newspaper delivery. As early as July 1912, nineteen-year-old Art Smith of Michigan delivered newspapers by airplane. Acting as a flying newsboy, Smith dropped neatly bound packages of the *Hillsday Daily* at the Michigan towns of Osseo, Pittsford, Hudson, and Adrain.[11] But the *St. Petersburg Daily Times* would have the honor of being the first newspaper company to make deliveries by a regularly scheduled airline.

Several milestones were recorded for the airline on its second day of operation. In addition to the handbill advertising the airline's schedule and the carriage of a cargo of newspapers, the airline's first woman passenger was carried.

St. Petersburg-Tampa
AIRBOAT LINE
Fast Passenger and Express Service
JANUARY 1, 1914
SCHEDULE:
Lv. St. Petersburg 10:00 A.M.
Arrive Tampa 10:30 A.M.
Leave Tampa 11:00 A.M.
Ar. St. Petersburg 11:30 A.M.
Lv. St. Petersburg 2:00 P.M.
Arrive Tampa 2:30 P.M.
Leave Tampa 3:00 P.M.
Ar. St. Petersburg 3:30 P.M.
Special Flight Trips
Can be arranged through any of our agents or by communicating directly with the St. Petersburg Hangar. Trips covering any distance over all-water routes and from the waters' surface to several thousand feet high AT PASSENGERS'REQUEST.
A minimum charge of $15 per Special Flight.
Rates: $5.00 Per Trip.
Round Trip $10.
Booking for Passage in Advance.
NOTE--Passengers are allowed a weight of 200 pounds GROSS including hand baggage, excess charged at $5.00 per 100 pounds, minimum charge 25 cents. EXPRESS RATES, for packages, suit cases, mail matter, etc., $5.00 per hundred pounds, minimum charge 25 cents. Express carried from hangar to hangar only, delivery and receipt by shipper.
Tickets on Sale at Hangars or
CITY NEWS STAND
F. C. WEST, Prop.
271 CENTRAL AVENUE
ST. PETERSBURG, FLORIDA

The St. Petersburg–Tampa Airboat Line's advertisement, January 1914. Author's collection.

Early that morning, the weather was threatening and the winds were heavier than usual. Mae Peabody of Dubuque, Iowa, had arranged for a special flight before the regularly scheduled morning trip to Tampa. When the young woman showed up, Jannus did his best to dissuade her from flying. She informed him that she was unafraid; all he had to do was to fly into the gale. Peabody was not disappointed. Jannus took off and ascended to an altitude of two hundred feet above Tampa Bay. For her perseverance, Peabody earned the distinction of being the first woman to fly in St. Petersburg, as well as the first female passenger on the world's first scheduled airline, although hers was not one of the daily scheduled flights.[12]

Jannus, with a Benoist student, Harry Railsback, made the first scheduled flight to Tampa that day. The morning flight was uneventful. Glenn Smith, another Benoist student, was the passenger for the afternoon's round-trip. With a slight wind at their back, Jannus and Smith made the flight to Tampa in only nineteen minutes. Their return flight from Tampa would take longer and would probably be rougher because they would have to fly directly into a westerly wind.

Flying at sixty miles per hour into the wind, Jannus suddenly felt his power drop. They had just left Hillsborough Bay and were at only the halfway point on their trip home. Gadsden Point was on their right as they headed into the open waters of Tampa Bay. Because of his experience with the Roberts engine, Jannus knew that he still had sufficient power to complete their flight to St. Petersburg safely. He decided to land because of the head wind and decreased power. Gradually he spi-

Mae Peabody, the airline's first woman passenger, booked a charter flight with Jannus on January 2, 1914. Courtesy of the Florida Aviation Historical Society.

AN AIRLINE IS BORN

raled down. Jannus had long been a proponent of the flying boat because it offered, as he had stated only days earlier, "the advantage of miles and miles of unobstructed aviation field."[13] Splashing into the windswept waters of Tampa Bay, the flying boat quickly came to a stop. Bobbing helplessly up and down as the waves carried the lightweight aircraft, Jannus and Glenn Smith drifted aimlessly.

Only a minor repair was necessary. The gasoline feed pipe that ran to the forward three cylinders had become clogged, reducing engine power. People on shore in St. Petersburg had seen Jannus land in the bay; a motorboat was immediately dispatched to provide assistance. When the boat arrived, Jannus advised the would-be rescuers that everything was all right and that he would fly his aircraft to shore under its own power. Glenn Smith, an employee at the post office in St. Petersburg, was concerned that he might be late for his afternoon shift. Believing that a ride back to St. Petersburg in the motorboat was more certain than a promised flight back with Jannus, Smith dived out of the disabled flying boat and swam to the motorboat. Once Smith was safely on board, the launch headed to shore. Shortly afterward, Jannus had the clogged fuel line cleaned out and was ready to go.

As it headed into the wind for takeoff, the flying boat was hit by a huge wave crashing over the right wing. The force of the wave caused the airboat to slide sideways across the water with the wing tip partially submerged. The combined force of the wave that had crashed over the wing and the subsequent underwater drag resulted in several broken wing ribs.

Undaunted by what he considered to be minor damage, Jannus continued with his takeoff and was soon airborne and headed for port. On the last leg of the trip to St. Petersburg, he passed above the motor launch carrying Glenn Smith. Jannus arrived at the hangar fifteen minutes ahead of the boat.

Two things were clearly proven on the airline's second day of operation. As Jannus had claimed, flying in an airboat was safe. The damaged wing was quickly repaired and only one flight had to be canceled.[14] The company needed an additional airplane, not so much for a spare as to meet passenger demand.

Less than one week after the airline was launched, the *St. Petersburg Daily Times* issued a report about its performance. The article noted that the airline was an overwhelming success, and "St. Petersburg is now coming to be known in a way she was never before heard of by people who otherwise would likely never hear of the city."[15]

Jannus and Fansler kept pushing Benoist for additional aircraft. On January 7, Benoist announced that he planned to ship three additional airplanes to St. Petersburg.[16] No one recognized the need for additional aircraft more than Benoist. He hoped that the increased publicity generated by the airline would help him sell airplanes and was anxious to get more aircraft south.

Benoist Number 43, the flying boat that was being used to meet the airline's schedule, had supposedly been constructed in only three days, then taken to Duluth, where it was flown for several months. Tom Benoist stated, "The airboat which is being used here has received a great deal of comment on its unfinished appearance and this is accountable by the fact that it was built in three days."[17] To construct a Benoist flying boat in only three days would have been impossible unless it had been assembled from an existing hull, wings, and tail assembly, as indeed it had been. Because of its hasty construction and its heavy use, the aircraft looked old and unfinished. Several people had commented on its rough-looking appearance. Christy Magrath, a St. Louis writer, claimed that he was told by an associate of Benoist's that "he absolutely could build one plane in 10 days in 1914."[18]

Benoist planned to ship three additional aircraft to St. Petersburg within three to four days. He explained that the construction was taking longer than usual because extra effort was being taken with the machines' fabrication and appearance.

As Benoist hastened construction and worried about the transportation of additional equipment, Jannus and Fansler were about to become involved with problems of their own.

13 🛩 Bureaucrats and Hams

JANNUS'S FIRST FLIGHT on January 6 was little different from any
other scheduled flight during the week. Glenn Smith was flying with
him. After reaching Tampa, Jannus taxied up the Hillsborough River
to his mooring. As he climbed from the flying boat and headed toward
a small crowd, Jannus heard a voice calling him. Expecting a friendly
conversation, he was instead greeted by a barrage of questions from
the Tampa port inspector H. L. Whitney, who wanted to know if Jannus
had life preservers, foghorn, charts, pilot rules, and running lights on
board. Jannus informed Whitney that his flying boat did not come
under the government's small craft ruling.[1]

Was Whitney's action politically motivated by someone in Tampa
to ease the sting of being upstaged by St. Petersburg? Probably not. A
month later, W. Stevenson MacGordon, owner of his own flying boat,
was preparing for a takeoff. John Havens, collector of the port at Palm
Beach, demanded to see MacGordon's motorboat license before allowing him to proceed. The port collector threatened arrest if Mac-
Gordon attempted to depart without the equipment required under
the law governing motorboats. Not willing to be held up any longer
than necessary, MacGordon hastily purchased two life vests, a foghorn,
a pilot's book of rules, charts, fire extinguisher, and lights.[2]

If the airboat line was unable to produce a license issued by the United
States Department of Commerce's Steamboat Inspection Service, it
would not be allowed to carry passengers. Under an act of Congress
approved June 9, 1910, a license was required "to operate or navigate
vessels not more than sixty-five feet in length propelled by machinery,

Above: On the morning of January 1, 1914, an anxious crowd lined St. Petersburg's waterfront waiting for Jannus's return from Tampa. Courtesy of the Florida Aviation Historical Society.

Left: Jannus in January 1914. Courtesy of the Florida Aviation Historical Society.

The city of St. Petersburg built a hangar for the St. Petersburg–Tampa Airboat Line at a cost of approximately $400. It was not completed until February 1914 because of a labor dispute with workers. Courtesy of the Florida Aviation Historical Society.

and carrying passengers for hire." In theory, the flying boat met the criteria for licensing. There was one minor catch. Benoist's equipment was not a steamship or technically even a boat. It was a flying boat.

Without a license, the airline could be forced to cease operation. Fansler immediately contacted Benoist in St. Louis. Instead of being opposed to the licensing of the airline, Benoist was pleased with the news. He responded, "Federal jurisdiction over planes and pilots would be invaluable. I'm being forced out-of-business in Missouri by state and city taxes on aviation which cost me $15 to take a plane off the ground. Encourage Federal intervention; apply for licenses and comply with all regulations."[3]

Inspector Whitney had not been acting on his own; his meeting with Jannus and his subsequent inspection of the flying boat had not been by chance. Whitney had been directed by James D. Calhoun, the deputy collector in charge of the Treasury Department's Customs Service, to seek out Jannus and inspect his equipment. On January 2, Whitney informed Calhoun, "In compliance with your instructions to me to

JANNUS, AN AMERICAN FLIER

inspect the Hydroplane, or flying boat plying between this port and St. Petersburg, Fla. under a regular schedule carrying passengers for hire, I beg to say that I have today made such inspection and find as follows. . . . Mr. Jannus carries no license as provided for under the Act of June 9th 1910. The boat carried neither life preservers, whistle, fire extinguisher or Pilot Rules."[4]

Was the Benoist flying boat to be classified as a motorboat or an airplane? On January 2, Calhoun had sent a letter to the collector of customs in Jacksonville asking for "specific instructions as to what course I shall pursue in connection with Mr. Anthony Jannus and his boat named 'BENOIST.'"[5] The Jacksonville collector of customs sent a letter of his own to the secretary of commerce in Washington, D.C. Short on information as well as imagination, his thoughts were little more than a rehash of the Whitney and Calhoun letters. He wanted to know "whether or not the Hydroaeroplane in question is deemed to be a vessel within the meaning of the Act of June 9th 1910, and is required to carry the equipment specified therein for a vessel of class one."[6]

Acting on Benoist's belief that licensing would be good for the business of aviation, Jannus wrote his own letter to the Department of Commerce. He promised to comply with the rules governing a class one vessel, equip the flying boat as directed, and apply for licenses for its pilots. In his letter of January 21, he wrote, "The writer has had a large and varied experience in designing, building, and operating aircraft, having covered over 80,000 miles including one continuous trip of 1,900 miles from Omaha to New Orleans. This experience might be of value to your Department when the time comes to formulate rules and regulations governing the equipping and operation of airboats, and I am at your service at any time if I can be of any help to you."[7]

On January 10, E. F. Sweet, assistant secretary of commerce, ruled that "the Department has held that hydro-aeroplanes while navigating the water are to be considered as motor boats and must be equipped accordingly, they also must obey the rules of the road."[8] On January 28, Sweet wrote to Jannus, acknowledging receipt of his correspondence.

The second flying boat in the fleet, February 1914. The Benoist Number 45 was capable of carrying the pilot and two passengers. *Left to right:* Tom Benoist, Roger Jannus, Tony Jannus, Heinrich Evers, and J. D. Smith. Courtesy of the Florida Aviation Historical Society.

The issue should have been closed, but it was not. On February 7, the supervising inspector general of the Department of Commerce sent a letter to the secretary of commerce. He explained that on February 3, the local port inspectors at Apalachicola, Florida, had written to the Board of Supervising Inspectors questioning whether the Benoist flying boat was to be "considered as a motor boat with the contemplation of the law while engaged in water traffic and carrying passengers for hire."[9] The inspector general stated, "It is a most peculiar situation and it is requested that we may have an opinion in order that the matter may be determined as to whether or not it is necessary for this craft to be in charge of a licensed operator while navigating in the water and carrying passengers for hire."[10] The request was referred to Albert Lee Thurman, solicitor of the United States. Finally, on February 17, 1914, Thurman issued an opinion resolving the matter.

It took six pages for Thurman to decide that "in my opinion, the hydroaeroplane at present plying between St. Petersburg and Tampa is a 'motor boat' within the letter as well as within the spirit of the Motor Boat Act, and is subject to the provision thereof."[11] The St. Petersburg–Tampa Airboat Line and its pilots complied fully with the Thurman opinion and never again had a run-in with either Whitney or Calhoun.

While this controversy was raging, Mrs. L. A. Whitney, wife of the secretary of St. Petersburg's Board of Trade, became the first woman to fly on one of the airline's scheduled flights. Her trip across the bay took place on January 8 and earned a spot on the front page of the newspaper. Mrs. Whitney must have enjoyed her flight. She described it "as enjoyable as being rocked to sleep in your mother's arms and yet every muscle and fibre of your body tingles and the blood courses through your veins, seemingly with new life! It would be hard to describe the exact sensation and I can find no words that are suitable to express it."[12]

On January 12, a unique advertising opportunity had fallen into the laps of the managers of the airline. In 1914, the Hefner grocery store was a popular vendor of Swift meats in St. Petersburg. When a long-time customer wanting his favorite brand of ham for dinner had to be told that the store was temporarily out of Swift products, L. C. Hefner got an idea. The nearest place to get a new supply was from the Tampa distributor; that would take at least a day, probably longer. He placed a telephone call to Fansler and inquired if it would be possible to carry a shipment of hams and bacon on the flight from Tampa that morning. The answer was a resounding yes. At 8:52 A.M., Hefner cabled to Swift & Company, "Ship via first Benoist airboat express one case each Premium hams and bacon, five cases hams to follow on evening boat." That morning, a mule dray drove up Pratt Street in Tampa, headed toward the airline's riverside ramp. Twenty-two pounds of ham and eighteen pounds of bacon were loaded onto the flying boat. Once the shipment was safely on board the scheduled eleven o'clock flight, Swift cabled, "Your wire for case each Premium hams, bacon, airship delivery, rec'd 9 A.M. Shipment left via Benoist airboat eleven-four and will reach you in twenty minutes. Answer when shipment rec'd and when this telegram rec'd." By 11:25 A.M. the shipment of hams Hefner had ordered was in St. Petersburg. The cargo received major news coverage in magazines such as *Collier's Weekly*. Hefner's newly coined slogan claimed, "Although they came high, the price is low."[13]

The same Tampa officials who had been unwilling to sponsor the airboat line were also reluctant to give credit where credit was due once it was up and running. Not only had they refused to participate in Percival Fansler's project, they seemed to go out of their way to throw roadblocks into the path of the fledgling airline. Tampa and St. Petersburg had long been rival communities in Hillsborough County. In May 1911, a bill creating an independent Pinellas County had become law, further dividing the two cities. When Fansler had requested a landing and mooring spot at the Tampa Bay Hotel, where many passengers would be available, his request was refused. Fansler was advised that the airline would have to use the riverbank where the steamers docked.

After the first flights proved the merit of Fansler's airline, Tampa officials tried to benefit from the free publicity. Tampa newspapers went so far as to take credit for the idea. Published stories also claimed that the flights originated in Tampa, not St. Petersburg.

The first volley in the war of words between St. Petersburg and Tampa newspapers had appeared in the *St. Petersburg Daily Times* on January 3. An editorial boasted with tongue-in-cheek:

> Tampa is a great city—of its kind—and we are all proud of her—in a way. And she is something more than a city too, and something different—she is an institution. . . .
>
> And so, friends across the bay—instead of trying to appropriate for the benefit and glory of yourselves all or any of the great things being done by St. Petersburg it will pay you best to begin preparing for yourselves a frame of mind that will permit you to accept and absorb and thrive upon, the reflected, brilliant glories that soon will reach from St. Petersburg entirely over South Florida.

Before city officials from Tampa had a chance to respond, the *St. Petersburg Daily Times* loaded another shell into its public relations cannon and aimed for a direct hit. According to the *Daily Times:*

Tampa is at her old tricks trying to steal the honor from her little sister across the bay. . . . The latest thing to come to light is a page one dispatch in the *New York Times* from Tampa under the dateline of December 31, 1913.

This just shows how the land lies and to what lengths Hillsboro people will go. The dispatch follows: "Airboat to be run from Tampa, Florida on 23 Mile Run, Tampa, Fla., December 31.—Aero Boat transportation is to be begun on a commercial scale between Tampa and St. Petersburg on January 1, 1914."[14]

The *St. Petersburg Daily Times* went on to charge, "The *Tampa Tribune* of yesterday morning carried a page one story under a four-column headline using a connecting cut under the caption of 'Tampa–St. Petersburg Airboat'—just as it made the landing at the foot of Hill Street yesterday morning with Aviator Jannus at the wheel.' There is not a penny of Tampa capital in the enterprise. Tampa does not figure in the line save as a terminal point—Pass-a-Grille, Gulfport, or Ruskin would have done as well but Tampa isn't satisfied with getting all this for nothing she goes ahead and tries to swipe everything."[15]

Back and forth the charges flew between the rival newspapers. On January 9, the *St. Petersburg Daily Times* shot itself in the foot with its own headline, which promised, "More Boats for Tampa–St. Petersburg Line." The next day, an editorial in the *St. Petersburg Times* apologized for the erroneous juxtaposition of the names of the cities.

As the editorial ripostes between the newspapers of St. Petersburg and Tampa abated, a third source of antagonism entered the fray. Like a jilted suitor, the *Jacksonville News* exhibited its jealousy, when on January 21 the paper charged, "St. Petersburg papers might secure an obituary sketch of aeroplane passengers at the same time they take the passenger manifests." St. Petersburg's supporters retorted, "But ours is not an aeroplane. It is an airboat—that is, when in the air it flies, and when it isn't in the air it is on the water; and when it is on water it floats; and as long as it floats there's no-biy-o-airy about it!"[16] Throughout the controversy, the people responsible for operating the St. Petersburg–Tampa Airboat Line remained unaffected and continued to do what they were being paid to do; they carried passengers. Through the first ten days of operation, the airline logged twenty-six flights, 682 miles, and carried fifty-two passengers.[17]

In response to high demand, Benoist shipped an additional flying boat to St. Petersburg during the waning days of January. Benoist flying boat Number 45, capable of carrying two passengers, was nothing more than a larger version of the flying boat that had been in service since the airline's beginning. A small aircraft was also used for training. Named the *Kitten*, it was wrecked beyond repair by Heinrich Evers, the German flying student.[18]

On February 7, the St. Petersburg–Tampa Airboat Line was confronted with competition, not for the carriage of passengers but for attention.[19] Raymond V. Morris, a Curtiss pilot, arrived in St. Petersburg and was awaiting the arrival of his own flying boat. Only a week earlier, construction on a hangar to house Morris's monoplane had begun adjacent to the Benoist hangar. Morris's Curtiss M boat, characterized as one of the most attractive flying boats ever built by Curtiss, had been designed and constructed specifically for Morris.[20] He intended to train for several international flying races in Europe during the coming summer. Curtiss engines were well-known for their reliability and durability, but Morris's engine had problems. Fansler recalled an episode in which the famed Curtiss OX engine proved embarrassing to Morris. Fansler related:

> The Navy had wanted some data on flying boats and detailed two officers to come to St. Petersburg and report on the Curtiss boat.
>
> One morning these two officers appeared in a hangar that had been built next to ours for Morris's boat. Down they sat, in comfortable chairs, tilted back against the wall, only five feet from our wall. Ray and his mechanic were tinkering over the motor. It wouldn't turn over. From time to time Ray would come over and explain that the trouble would be rectified in half an hour. The afternoon was a repetition of the forenoon. The next day passed as had the former. That night, acting on orders, the Navy men departed. Ray had not been able to get his boat into the air.[21]

Subsequently, Morris was able to prove his mettle by beating Jannus in an aerial race, but the real victory went to Glenn Curtiss. In spite of the engine trouble experienced by Morris's Curtiss M flying boat, the United States government had ignored Benoist's more dependable equipment.[22] During World War I, the government bought thousands of airplanes from Curtiss.

The Curtiss and Benoist flying contingents in St. Petersburg enjoyed a spirit of camaraderie. The fliers attempted not only to make money but to become part of the community. The Jannus brothers had an opportunity to put their musical talents to good use. Chauncey Brown recalled, "Ray Morris was in the cast of 'A Miss Amiss,' a musical we gave at the Plaza theatre in which both my wife and I took part. Morris did an English music hall type stunt from one of the balconies of the theatre. Both Tony Jannus and his brother, Roger, were in the orchestra of that amateur production."[23]

Tony became an especially well-known celebrity in the small southern city of St. Petersburg. He was only twenty-five years old and a bachelor in demand. Though not wealthy, he was well-off financially. He was handsome; with his dark, brooding good looks and twinkling eyes, he was certainly more than capable of turning feminine heads. The whole crew of the St. Petersburg–Tampa Airboat Line, particularly Tony Jannus, was famous and royally treated.

One of the people who spoke most glowingly of Jannus was Eleanor C. Reed, the proprietor of the Wigwam Hotel. The hotel had been Jannus's home in St. Petersburg. According to Reed, "Tony Jannus was as handsome as a picture and so refined. He was so thoughtful of others, and had such a winning personality, that he was constantly being sought after by the girls. He did not know some times which way to turn."[24]

By mid-February, the Benoist flying school was up and running. Heinrich Evers, Lloyd South, J. D. Smith, Harry Railsback, and Glenn Smith had already enrolled in the school. Glenn Smith and Railsback were from St. Petersburg; South was from Indianapolis. Heinrich "Heinie" Evers had been sent to St. Louis by the German government to attend Benoist's flying school, and he went along when the operation moved to St. Petersburg. At the outbreak of World War I, Evers was recalled

Jannus was seldom seen without an attractive woman in his company. Courtesy of the Florida Aviation Historical Society.

to Germany, where he eventually became a prisoner of war,[25] incarcerated in Brest until he managed to escape three years later.[26]

The flying school was, at least financially, the most successful aspect of the entire operation. Twelve student pilots went through the school. Julia Wilson of St. Louis was the only woman to sign up for Benoist's St. Petersburg–based flying school. Jannus and Benoist were strongly opposed to admitting her. She was accepted at Noel Mitchell's insistence, but she never took a flying lesson.[27] Roger Jannus and J. D. Smith were also receiving training in flying boats. The other students included Jack Williams, Byrd Latham, Harry Weddington, Chauncey Elliott, Dan and Ira South, and F. H. Mattocks. Pulling in $250 per student, the flying school made a major financial contribution to the operation. More important, it was hoped that every student would end up buying a flying boat from Tom Benoist. Unfortunately, L. E. McLain was the only citizen of St. Petersburg to buy an aircraft from Benoist, and it was secondhand.

With the airline and flying school running smoothly, Jannus was preparing his brother Roger and Weldon B. Cooke to take over the daily operation of the airline. Tony was planning to use the larger three-passenger flying boat for the company's exhibition and charter work. Several months later, Cooke died in an airplane crash in Pueblo, Colorado. He apparently had not followed the Benoist and Jannus credo of "Safety First." According to *Aeronautics*, Cooke died in a home-built aircraft that had been constructed with cheap parts from a Woolworth store.[28]

Supposedly, Cooke had once proposed that he and Percival Fansler travel to San Francisco, where they would establish an airline similar to the one in Florida and operate it during California's Panama-Pacific Exposition in 1915. It is possible that the prospect of an airline in California was discussed, but with Weldon Cooke, it could not have been much more than talk. His lack of concern for safety was notorious. Mrs. Fansler recalled forty years later, "Mr. Cooke was a good aviator but very careless in the upkeep of his planes. He was killed on a barnstorming flight, tho he had been warned that some of his wires needed replacing. I vaguely remember some talk of the San Francisco Exposition but do not remember Mr. Fansler's giving it any serious consideration."[29]

On February 17, W. J. Bennett, the local forecaster for the U.S. Department of Agriculture's Weather Bureau, visited St. Petersburg to locate a site for an anemometer in connection with the airline.[30] Fansler had broached the idea a month earlier.[31] Following his visit with Fansler and Jannus and his firsthand observation of the airline's operation, Bennett recommended that "an anemometer, set of cups, and 100 ft of 2 conductor cable be sent direct to St. Petersburg–Tampa Airboat Line."[32] Bennett's supervisor rejected the suggestion because the operation was not permanent.[33] Bennett felt strongly about it, persevered, and finally received authorization to furnish Jannus with rudimentary weather forecasting equipment. The equipment was not installed until near the end of March, only weeks before the airline's contract was due to expire.

Over the years, many conflicting accounts have arisen in regard to the St. Petersburg–Tampa Airboat Line. Many claims to the honor of being the first scheduled passenger airline in the world have been made. In 1938, Alan F. Bonnalie claimed, "About 1913 Silas Christofferson operated a flying boat across San Francisco to Oakland in the world's first regularly scheduled airline passenger service. Lack of customers soon ended its existence, but it is very probable that the first paying passenger to ride a scheduled airline patronized this early effort."[34] H. P. Christofferson, the brother of Silas, however, wrote, "My brother Silas flew this flying boat himself. He took Mayor James Rolph on one trip. But it was not run on schedule, or did we carry mail or express."[35] Will D. Parker, a past president of the Early Birds organization, stated, "I have been in touch with Allen [Alan] Bonnalie and he still was under the impression that Christofferson might have run a scheduled airline. I assured him that Harry Christofferson told me they did not run a scheduled service, and I think Al is satisfied now."[36]

On January 1, 1939, the U.S. Department of the Interior made a nationwide radio broadcast, "Early Wings for Commerce," in which it stated, "The carrying of passengers by heavier-than-air craft scheduled over an established route was first achieved in America. This was the St. Petersburg–Tampa Airboat Line, organized by L. A. Whitney and P. E. Fansler of those Florida cities, using flying boats produced by Tom Benoist at St. Louis. . . . The Florida airline was inaugurated January 1, 1914."[37]

Many individuals involved with the airline, even though only on a peripheral basis, attempted to claim credit for themselves. F. R. Bannister, son of the auctioneer of the airline's first seats, claimed, "My father was the organizer of this commercial airline."[38] In fact, Bannister's presence at the inauguration of the airline added fun and drama to the event, but he was definitely not one of its organizers.

In 1954, forty years after the St. Petersburg–Tampa Airboat Line ceased operation, J. M. Lassiter claimed, "I was one of others who helped to make the Jannus flights a success."[39] In 1914 Lassiter was manager of the Hibbs Dredging Company, which dredged the channel from the yacht basin to the seawall and to the end of the hangar's ramp. That service was no greater a contribution than that performed by the men who built the hangar or those who sold rides.

James M. Eaton, a resident of Tampa at the time, stated, "I unofficially assisted Tony Jannus, who had arrived in Tampa with his Benoist Flying Boat, in establishing a scheduled operation between Tampa and St. Petersburg. I offered Jannus the use of machine shop facilities at the Tampa Electric Company."[40] Eaton's use of the word "assisted" was correct; that was the only contribution that Eaton, Lassiter, Bannister, and others made to the success of the airline. The credit belongs exclusively to Jannus, Fansler, Benoist, and several members of St. Petersburg's Board of Trade.

Ownership of the airline and the flying boats used by the St. Petersburg–Tampa Airboat Line has also been disputed. Letters from Frank Merrill Bell to his wife and daughter reportedly stated that "he had not been too keen about using his flying boats for a 12 week contract to fly passengers on a regular schedule, twice a day round trip. But his partners were confident and enthusiastic and they had won him over . . . with certain conditions to be met . . . no risk-taking, no bad-weather flying, just low daylight flights, etc."[41]

That Bell owned and flew a Benoist airplane is not in dispute. In fact, Frank Bell died while flying a Benoist airplane in February 1914 in Meridian, Mississippi. Bell had earned a doctorate in electrical engineering and was the holder of at least one patent.[42] There is, however, no proof that even if Frank Bell was in St. Petersburg for the first flight of the airline, he was anything more than an interested observer. The flying boat, Benoist Number 43, was owned by Julius H. Barnes of Duluth, Minnesota.

In 1943, Barnes wrote, "With the adventurous disposition of a mere child of 40, I bought a flying boat. . . . Because of my status as the largest wheat exporter in the world, the local bank advised me in no uncertain terms, that I was not to fly. Instead my friend, W. D. 'Bill' Jones, took lessons in the plane from Tony Jannus. As fall approached that year, the Jannus brothers came to me with a proposition. They would like to take the 'Lark' down to Florida and set up a flying service."[43]

Some have claimed that there is photographic evidence that Glenn H. Curtiss was present at the inauguration of the airline.[44] Had someone of Curtiss's reputation visited St. Petersburg, surely the press would have covered the event. The man in the photograph was Heinrich Evers, the German flying student, not Glenn Curtiss.

Nearly half a century later, Elliott Fansler, son of Percival Fansler, stated, "This was not Tom Benoist's airline by any stretch of the imagination and the statement 'he was the first aviation manufacturer to envision scheduled airlines' was incorrect, if he were he would have started one on the Mississippi in his own backyard—it was my father's idea." In reality, it was a collaborative effort. Unarguably it was Fansler's idea to situate the airline in Florida, and he was the man who went out and sold the idea. The statement that seemed to incense Elliott Fansler was probably true. There is little doubt that Benoist "was the first aviation manufacturer to envision scheduled airlines." Clearly and indisputably, Benoist was a manufacturer and Fansler was not. Elliott Fansler went on to say, "My father was at that time a resident of Jacksonville, and was never at any time an employee of Tom Benoist. If anything, they were associates."[45] Elliott Fansler's assessment was correct; the two men were equals in every way.

As successful as the St. Petersburg–Tampa Airboat Line was from an operational standpoint, financially it was not profitable. Percival Fansler's wife recalled that the company was probably self-sustaining only during February and March.[46] In a roundabout way, Fansler, while complimenting Jannus on his aerodynamic skills and questioning mind, brought to light the financial difficulties the group faced. Fansler wrote, "Tony had some advanced ideas regarding construction and details, and we all were constantly itching to try these and others of our own brewing . . . experiments cost money, and there was just about enough of that to keep the gang from being hungry. The operation of the airline at five dollars for a one way trip simply was not making enough money to support several people and the upkeep of aircraft."[47]

In accordance with the contract, Fansler submitted his request for reimbursement in the amount of $540 on February 9.[48] Under the agreement that promised "fifty dollars a day through January and twenty-five dollars a day, through February and March," $540 was all that Fansler and Benoist ever requested.[49] In January the company had eighteen flying days and was able to earn $360. The difference between the airline's earnings and the promised $50-per-day January subsidy was $540. The airline claimed no subsidy for the months of February and March. Fansler wrote, "In view of the fact that the guarantee for the months of February and March was only $25.00 per day, we have waived any assessment for these two months so that this $36.00 assessment is all that stands against your subscription to date."[50]

On March 28, the contract with St. Petersburg ended. The accomplishments logged by the airline in three months were impressive. The total miles flown with only two aircraft exceeded eleven thousand. The airboat line had carried more than one thousand passengers.[51] National Airlines, another home-grown St. Petersburg airline, fell far short of this mark during its first year of operation in 1934, when it carried only four hundred passengers.[52] Benoist summed up the operation of the world's first scheduled airline when he said, "Many of the formulae, methods and details that have been worked out were and are still being worked on, will become a part of the classics of the science of aeronautics, but the most encouraging thing about this experiment was the discovery of how easy the whole thing was."[53]

On March 31, the St. Petersburg–Tampa Airboat Line made its last flight. Benoist left the city almost immediately and headed back to St. Louis.[54] When Benoist left St. Petersburg by train, he was quoted as complaining that "his greatest misfortune is that he was unable to devote more time to getting acquainted with the people of this town as he would like to have met more of them than the comparatively few with whom he came in contact during the slight cessation between his busy hours."[55] These do not sound like words Tom Benoist would have uttered. He was not a warm, people-oriented man concerned with making friends. Brusque and taciturn, he was portrayed in photographs as a man who was highly uncomfortable in social situations and mixed company. Benoist was probably happy to be leaving Florida. Fansler had been ill, forcing Benoist to assume control of day-to-day operations of the airline when he should have been in St. Louis. Benoist made no money from the airline and, while in St. Petersburg, sold only one aircraft—the used Benoist Number 45 flying boat which L. E. McLain bought.

Although Benoist had departed, the others seemed reluctant to follow suit. Tony announced that he would continue to provide scheduled service between St. Petersburg and Tampa three times a week, as well as charters and exhibition flying. Several of his flying students were not yet licensed; Glenn Smith, Byrd Latham, Roger Jannus, and Heinrich Evers had not finished their training. Latham became the only flight student to qualify for his Aero Club of America license while in St. Petersburg.[56]

Fansler did everything possible to keep the airline in operation. On April 7, he went before the Board of Trade and made a pitch for a permanent locally owned airline to replace the expired contract.[57] He was advised to prepare a written proposal which the Board of Governors would consider. The Board of Trade was doing little more than offering Fansler lip service. Its interest in an airline as a practical means of daily transportation had faded. St. Petersburg now sought to acquire the Tampa and Gulf Railroad.

Throughout the month of April, stories persisted that a local group of businessmen were making a last-ditch effort to keep the moribund airline alive.[58] Fansler, in concert with Charles A. Hall, was trying to form a company with a proposed capitalization of $50,000. Fansler also invited several city officials to enjoy a complimentary flight, but the hospitality was wasted. Neither the private company nor city support ever materialized.[59]

On April 27, Roger and Tony flew their last flight before leaving Florida. The brothers put on an air race over Tampa Bay. Roger piloted the newer, larger, seventy-five-horsepower Number 45, while Tony was behind the controls of the smaller and older airboat. The course was four miles out and four miles back. Roger won the first leg in three minutes and twenty seconds; Tony trailed by nearly a quarter of a mile. Fighting a head wind on the return, Tony was the winner of the second leg, but it took him more than six minutes.[60] They then crated Benoist flying boat Number 43 and headed to Paducah, Kentucky, by train.

Fansler had had big ideas for the airline. The development of these plans was frequently limited by the narrow vision of others. Fansler claimed in *Aero Digest* in December 1929, "I also attempted to interest Post Office officials in the transportation of mail by air between the two cities, but aside from the postmaster in St. Petersburg, (Roy Hanna) there was no one who could picture the U.S. Mails attaining such speed."[61] He should have realized that any project requiring Tampa's cooperation would be difficult to accomplish.[62] Tampa was unwilling to support anything that would benefit St. Petersburg.

Fansler also claimed that he had attempted to interest the Seaboard Airline Railroad in a joint promotion and interline scheme. Under the suggested program, passengers would arrive in Tampa by train and connect with the airline to be flown to their final destination. The railroad expressed no interest.[63]

L. E. McLain of St. Petersburg bought flying boat Number 45 shortly before the operation was dismantled.[64] On May 20, McLain reported to the *St. Petersburg Daily Times*, "I want it understood that Byrd Latham and I are not quitting St. Petersburg. We will be taking No. 43 to Conneaut Lake, Pa. for the summer and will be back in September to reopen the Airboat Line. We are prepared to buy additional airplanes and make the airboat line the biggest thing of its kind in this country."[65] Three days later, Byrd Latham, accompanied by Heinrich Evers, who was to serve as his mechanic, set out for Conneaut Lake with McLain's flying boat. McLain and Latham may have believed that they owned Benoist flying boat Number 43, but actually McLain had purchased Benoist Number 45; Number 43 was purchased by Roger Jannus in August 1914. *Aero and Hydro* reported, "Roger W. Jannus, the pilot, has just obtained ownership of the Lark from W. D. Jones."[66]

ON MAY 6, 1914, J. D. Smith left St. Petersburg. Roger and Tony Jannus departed three days later. The original plan called for the three men to travel together, but Tony had delayed his plans.[1] Tony anticipated being called into active duty with the United States Volunteer Aviation Corps to serve in Vera Cruz, Mexico, but was never called.[2]

With the St. Petersburg–Tampa Airboat Line behind them and odds of resurrecting the company improbable, Tony and Roger severed their relationship with Tom Benoist. Understandably, Benoist must have felt deserted and deeply betrayed by people with whom he had been involved, personally and professionally, for the past several years. He had given almost all of his energies and resources to the airboat line, had not made any money from it, and had neglected his business in St. Louis. With his business in a near shambles, he now found himself virtually alone and without his most famous flier.

There were several reasons why Jannus left Benoist. The Jannus brothers and J. D. Smith wanted to start their own flying company. During the past few years, they had flown thousands of miles in equipment belonging to other people; the brothers had been in more midwestern and southern cities than a traveling medicine show. Tony was tired of flying from city to city to make a daily wage as a hired hand. Typically, the owners of the aircraft would receive upward of several hundred dollars a day for an exhibition and pay the pilot only a small percentage. More important, he wanted to escape the mantle of being known only as a flier. He wanted to move into the design and production side, as had Glenn Curtiss, Glenn Martin, and the Wrights. Tony

Jannus was one of the most famous aviators in the United States during the years before the outbreak of the war. Based on his experience and reputation, he expected the Jannus brothers' flying boat to be a big seller to the warring European nations. In 1914, the Jannus name eclipsed that of Benoist, the aircraft manufacturer. Tony may not have been as well known as Louis Blériot, Farman, Curtiss, and the Wrights, but he was not far behind. The founding of his own aviation company was a logical progression.

Undoubtedly, Tony Jannus was also greatly concerned about Benoist's ever-worsening financial situation. Uncharacteristically, Benoist's integrity may have come into question. In late August 1914, in a letter to Henry Woodhouse, editor of *Flying*, Jannus wrote, "I am surprised at any act of Mr. Tom Benoist that could be construed as a reflection upon his character. However, the affairs of the Benoist Company have been in pretty bad shape for about a year and being hard pressed often demands subterfuge that additional hardship makes impossible to cover."[3]

Paducah, Kentucky, was their first stop. Benoist Airboat Number 43 arrived by rail on May 18. At the time, the flying boat was still owned by Julius Barnes of Duluth.[4] When Jannus stepped off the N. C. and St. Louis train, he cracked a big smile and said, "It's good to be back in old Paduke again."[5] Later he told the townsfolk, "I have just closed one of the most successful seasons of my life, and I'm feeling like a fighting cock, but somehow, I feel better in Paducah—seems like home to me."[6] Tony Jannus hoped to establish an airline operation similar to that which he had left behind in St. Petersburg, but the idea proved unfeasible. The three young men flew for ten days in Paducah, then packed up their airplane and headed for the beach.

In Peoria, Illinois, on July 4, 1914, Jannus's flying boat, the *Flying Fish*, was inspected and charged with several violations. Lieutenant James Pine, collector of customs, cited Jannus for "Carrying passengers for hire without license, Navigating without pilot rules," and "Carrying passengers for hire without life preservers of kind approved by Supervising Inspectors of Steam Vessels."[7]

The secretary of commerce was drawn into the fray when Jannus wrote to him on August 8 requesting relief from the payment of a $400 penalty. Accompanying his letter was a two-and-one-half-page deposition in which he cogently argued his case. A. L. Thurman ruled, "As Mr. Jannus has in the past endeavored to comply with all of the requirements of the Department, the penalties for violation of the above-cited Acts are hereby remitted."[8]

The summer of 1914 saw Tony and Roger Jannus and J. D. Smith flying in Cedar Point, Ohio. The trio brought Benoist Airboat Number 43 there to provide rides for guests at the Breakers Hotel, a popular summer resort on Lake Erie. Until Roger and Smith arrived with Number 43, Tony worked and flew on his own. After departing St. Petersburg, he had purchased another Benoist flying boat which he kept moored at a boardwalk directly in front of the hotel.

While at Cedar Point, Tony met a young Cleveland woman by the name of Edna Dagmar Hansen. She later reflected on her initial meeting with Jannus: "On Friday, June 26, I had that famous air-plane ride with Tony Jannus. From then on until July 20 I had 21 dates with Mr. Jannus." Commenting on their joint interest in music, Hansen wrote, "Tony played the flute and liked music—so we spent many hours together."[9]

Jannus was in great demand at Cedar Point. He carried more than thirty passengers in his first five days there. Edna Hansen's recollections shed light on how much money Jannus was making. She wrote, "He took patrons up for a ride over the Bay—& out over Lake Erie— for about a ten minute ride for $25." Hansen also wrote, "Mr. G. A. Boeckling—who managed Cedar-Point, brought Tony there, and he took passengers out for about ten minutes or so—for $25 a trip."[10] An advertisement offered an aerial ferry service to and from Sandusky for $15 round-trip or $10 one way. Scenic trips were offered at the rate of a dollar per mile.[11] About her own flight with Jannus, Hansen recalled, "We had the Cleveland Newspapers take pictures of me—standing by his air-plane—and they said I was learning to be a pilot, etc.— Of course—this was all for publicity—to help people overcome their fear."[12] According to Hansen, "He was the big attraction that summer."[13]

Reinhardt Ausmus related, "Tony was very popular, had a great personality, and took to everyone. He carried on a very successful passen-

Left to right: Roger Jannus, Julius Barnes, and Tony Jannus in front of the Benoist Number 43, the *Lark of Duluth*. This flying boat was originally owned by Barnes and was sold to Roger in August 1914. Courtesy of the Florida Aviation Historical Society.

ger carrying service there. He would bet someone he could beat them in a footrace—or give them a free trip in the plane. He would let them win, take em for a ride, they would tell others and Tony was busy all day as a result of this popular stunt."[14] A Roberts Motor advertising circular claimed Jannus made 376 passenger-carrying flights while at Cedar Point.

Many of Tony Jannus's passengers at Cedar Point were well-known to the readers of American newspapers. They included Eugene V. Debs, the five-time Socialist candidate for the presidency of the United States, and Hugh Chalmers, owner of the Chalmers Motor Car Company.[15] Chalmers encouraged forty-two of his employees to fly with Jannus.[16]

On one of his trips to Cleveland, Jannus carried the well-known English aviatrix Lily Irvine in a heavy rainstorm. Many years later, James Martin would claim that Irvine had been the first woman to fly over water from Sandusky to Euclid Beach in Cleveland. There, Martin claimed, Jannus and Irvine were met not only by the mayor of Cleveland but by a crowd of fifty thousand people.[17]

While Tony was in Cedar Point, Roger Jannus was in Duluth, Minnesota, where his flying was proving to be just as popular as Tony's. Roger was flying the Benoist Number 43 airboat. During the first week of August 1914, while flying at an altitude of a hundred feet, Roger nearly lost his engine when one of the pistons seized and knocked off the cylinder. Before Roger could shut off the engine, the adjoining cylinder jacket was badly damaged. Because of the engine trouble as well as a rainy Minnesota summer, Julius Barnes decided that he was not getting his money's worth from his investment. When Barnes expressed his dissatisfaction, Roger offered to buy the flying boat. Barnes accepted the proposal.[18]

Once ownership of *The Lark of Duluth*, Benoist Number 43, was transferred, Roger and Friothiof Gusaf "Fritz" Ericson, his flying student, made plans to take the airboat to Cedar Point, Ohio. Roger's arrival at Cedar Point was most opportune. Tony claimed, "Ever since my machine wore out on me at Cedar Point, I have kept my brother busy with bookings, and our first week here, although we had expected to do practically nothing, netted $745.00 in passengers alone."[19]

In the fall of 1914, the Jannus brothers did almost as much exhibition flying as they had in all of 1912 and 1913. While in Sandusky, Ohio, in the summer of 1914, Tony Jannus claimed "280 engagements, 280 successful contracts filled and 3745 passengers carried during four successful years."[20] In early August, Roger Jannus was in Duluth flying three or four times a day. In mid-August, Tony and J. D. Smith headed to Grand Rapids, Michigan, where they had been hired by the Grand Rapids Railway Company as entertainment for a company picnic. Smith wrote, "The Grand Rapids Railway Company gave a picnic to their employees which cost thousands of dollars, besides lasting two days." Smith analyzed the treatment of American workers when he added, "Now, I think if some of the other companies would see this they would feel ashamed of themselves because as a rule the majority of them work their men 365 days each year and never as much as give them a pleasant look. Speaking from experience, I know."[21] Tony and Smith then took the flying boat to Put-in-Bay, Ohio, to take part in the centennial celebration commemorating Commodore Oliver Hazard Perry's victory over the British during the War of 1812. From August 19 through 22, Tony Jannus controlled the sky over Lake Erie.

Heading to Iowa in September to take advantage of the heavy county fair business, Roger took his flying boat to Muscatne. On September 2, Roger was in Oquawka, Illinois, then was booked for several flights on the waterfront at Burlington, Iowa, on September 15. Next, Roger was hired to appear at Fort Madison, Iowa, only seven days after Tony had performed there as the main attraction at the Pioneers and Old Settlers Reunion.

By mid-October, Tony and Roger had settled in Baltimore. Fritz Ericson and Knox Martin had traveled with the Jannus brothers from Toledo. J. D. Smith joined them by the end of October. Shortly after their arrival, they rented space in an old warehouse used by Spencer Heath's American Propeller Company. Almost immediately, the group began working on their own design—the Jannus flying boat, a large biplaned aircraft capable of carrying several passengers. *Aeronautics* magazine reported that Tony had designed and was building his first monoplane.[22]

The Jannus brothers' first attempt at flight in Baltimore was not an immediate success. They announced their intention to fly out of Yockel's Park in the Brooklyn section of the city. The Jannus team arrived an hour early for their 3 P.M. flight. The wings, tail, and hull of the well-worn Benoist Number 43 flying boat were still packed in crates. As Roger, Tony, and several assistants carefully fit the aircraft parts together under the watchful gaze of hundreds of would-be helpers, three o'clock came and went. Little had been done except for unpacking the numerous wooden crates. By four o'clock, the men were still running control wires to the rudder and elevator. Eventually the biplane's wings were lifted up and attached to the body of the flying boat.

Finally, at five o'clock, Tony and Roger Jannus were satisfied that everything was ready. They settled into their seats, the engine was cranked to life, and the machine slowly eased its way down the wooden incline into the Patapsco River.

As the aircraft floated through the water, Roger prepared to take off. A wire on one of the control surfaces snapped, and the aircraft swerved, snakelike, through the water. As Roger shut off the engine, both brothers grabbed paddles and steered the aircraft toward the shore. Once they were headed in the right direction, the engine was restarted and maneuvered back to the starting point.

Several minutes later, the broken wire had been replaced, and the flying boat was headed back into the currents of the river. After skimming along for two hundred yards, the nearly one-ton airboat leaped several feet out of the water. Flying almost level with the river for another hundred yards, it slowly gained altitude, settling at about two hundred feet.[23]

Headed northward, the aircraft soared over Fort McHenry. Up and down the river they flew until they reached an altitude of one thousand feet. After making several lazy circles around Baltimore, the aviators turned back toward the river and Yockel's Park. Thousands of people were on hand to greet their return.

On November 5, Roger Jannus showed the citizens of Baltimore how dangerous an instrument of war the airplane could be. Roger was at the controls while his passenger, Lloyd D. Norris, a photographer for the *Baltimore Sun*, served as bombardier. From an altitude of two thousand feet, Norris dropped make-believe bombs. The *Baltimore Sun*, sponsor of the bombing, reported, "The bombs hit surprisingly close to their marks. Had the bombs been of greater weight, had a man like Antony Jannus, who has had considerable practice at bomb dropping, been the marksman, had there been less wind, and had the bombs been filled with high explosive instead of good reading matter, there would have been a vastly different tale to be told of yesterday's flight over Baltimore." An eyewitness to the flight said, "Roofs of all the office buildings in the downtown section were alive with men and women, while the streets were also thronged with many who were unable to obtain such advantageous places from which to view the flight."[24] In less than two years, Roger and Tony would be involved in the war in Europe, no longer engaged in make-believe.

The licensing brouhaha followed Tony Jannus to Baltimore. The *Baltimore Sun* reported on November 6, 1914, "To see that he had complied with the law the local board of U.S. Steamboat inspectors, Wright and White, and Chief Marine Clerk Thalheimer made an investigation yesterday. They found the Jannus brothers fortified with all the credentials prescribed by the navigation laws to fly or swim."

As Christmas approached, Roger Jannus, dressed as Santa Claus, flew over the city of Baltimore. Landing at the Light Street Wharf, he was met by a large, enthusiastic crowd. To the accompaniment of the band from St. Mary's Industrial School, Roger was paraded through the streets of Baltimore. This was perhaps the first time that Santa Claus rode in an airplane.[25] At the time, the Jannus brothers were at work on the design and construction of the Jannus flying boat. Bills to be paid necessitated taking any flying jobs they could get. These same expenses necessitated the sale of Benoist Number 43 to Knox Martin.[26]

In mid-December, Roger Jannus and J. D. Smith headed to San Diego, California, shipping Benoist Number 43 by railroad. There they opened a flying school and offered passenger rides, hooking up with Knox Martin and O. S. T. Meyerhoffer. Meyerhoffer became manager of the operation, while the others concentrated on flying. Tony and Fritz Ericson remained in Baltimore, operating a flying operation and working on the Jannus flying boat. Tony had intended to go but decided to stay behind, probably at the last minute. J. D. Smith wrote, "We have been flying every day here in Baltimore carrying passengers and teaching pupils. Next month we go to California with two machines. We probably will not get back to the east for a year or more."[27] There were two reasons why Tony did not go to California. Smith stated that they planned to ship two machines to California. They sent only the aircraft owned by Knox Martin because that was the only one they had available. The brothers had expected to have their own flying boat completed by then, but it was not. With only one aircraft, there was no need for four fliers. Tony had to stay in Baltimore to finish his flying boat.

The California contingent had no trouble convincing people to fly. After only a couple of months in San Diego, they had carried over seven hundred passengers.[28] While flying out of San Diego, Roger Jannus endeared himself to the United States Navy, or at least to two of its men. After a heavy night of drinking and carousing while on a

The Jannus Brothers' west coast operation at San Diego, California, January 1915. J. D. Smith and Roger Jannus (first and second on the right) pose in front of the rebuilt Benoist Number 43 originally used in St. Petersburg. Two of the three unidentified men are probably Knox Martin and O. S. T. Meyerhoffer. Courtesy of the Florida Aviation Historical Society.

twenty-four-hour pass, the two sailors fell asleep, missing the liberty boat that would have returned them to their ship. The next ship would not sail for another twenty-four hours; by then, the sailors would have been considered absent without leave. At the foot of Market Street, they ran into Roger and talked him into flying them to their ship. J. D. Smith wrote, "First time anyone delivered on board a battleship from a flying boat in San Diego harbor . . . officer G. M. Kriebie and sailor J. M. Brandon both of the U.S.S. Glacier."[29]

In February, while flying near the Santa Fe Wharf in San Diego Harbor, Smith attempted to bank too close to the water. One wing hit the water and the airboat crashed into the bay.[30] Smith and his passenger were pulled under water after the impact but managed to surface and climb onto the aircraft's buoyant wings, where they waited to be rescued by a navy torpedo boat. Smith suffered a lacerated nose and lost seven teeth. Still enamored of flying, Smith said, "Flying is a great life—while it lasts."[31]

While Roger and Smith were in California, Tony had been occupied with his own business ventures. In late November, Tony had sent letters to several people in St. Petersburg telling them he would soon be returning.[32] On January 12, 1915, the front page of the *St. Petersburg Daily Times* declared, "'Tony' Coming Back to Fly Over Route He Made Famous.'" Jannus would be flying Benoist flying boat Number 45, owned by L. E. McLain.

Arriving by train on January 20, accompanied by his mechanic Harry Rau of Baltimore, Jannus said, "I feel that this is my winter home and am more than glad to be back."[33] As the conquering hero, Jannus spent the next day on St. Petersburg's Central Avenue, greeting friends and shaking hands. The plan was for Jannus to fly exhibitions and non-scheduled services to Tampa, Sarasota, Bradenton, and Pass-a-Grille in the old Benoist Number 45 airboat, rechristened the *Florida*. Jannus and McLain intended to charge a rate of one dollar per mile.

After Jannus had settled in, he and Rau went to work on the flying boat to ensure its airworthiness. The previous summer at Conneaut Lake, Byrd Latham had crashed the aircraft, necessitating a complete restoration. The hull was entirely new and heavier than the original. All that remained of the original aircraft were the engine and the wings.

TAKE CORONADO BEACH CARS NO. 9 OR NO. 10 TO
H STREET, OPP. OLD BARRACKS

JANNUS BROTHERS
FLYING BOATS

AVIATORS: TONY JANNUS, ROGER JANNUS, KNOX
MARTIN AND JAY D. SMITH

MANAGER: O. S. T. MEYERHOFFER

Round Trip Prices For One Passenger:
San Diego Sight-Seeing Flight $5.00

CIRCUIT AROUND CORONADO BEACH............$10.00
CIRCUIT AROUND NORTH ISLAND................$15.00
FORT ROSCRANS $15.00
NATIONAL CITY $15.00
OCEAN BEACH $25.00

OTHER POINTS BOOKED ON APPLICATION

We strictly adhere to your wishes regarding altitude and
general character of flight. We will keep within five feet of
the water if you desire, or ascend to 1000 feet.

The machines are equipped with 75-horsepower motors
They have a wing spread of 45 ft. Weight, empty, 1300 lbs;
fully loaded, 2000 lbs. Maximum speed, 60 miles per hour;
minimum, 30 miles per hour.

3100 PASSENGERS CARRIED DURING 1914, AND
EVERY ONE DELIGHTED.

 39

Handbill advertising the California operation of Jannus Brothers, January 1915.
Author's collection.

The pair spent nearly a week working on the *Florida*. The projected start-up date of January 29 came and went without a flight.[34] Jannus and Rau still had the machine apart. With their first flight now re-scheduled for Sunday, January 31, Jannus and Rau got little sleep. They worked through Saturday night and by Sunday morning still were not finished. The wings were in the hangar but had not been attached to the flying boat. Working all day, they finally had the aircraft assembled and were ready to fly by three o'clock that afternoon. The newspaper claimed that ten thousand people turned out on the waterfront to watch Tony's first local flight since May.[35] Soloing, Jannus took the rebuilt aircraft up to an altitude of six hundred feet. When he was satisfied with the feel of the aircraft and the sound of the engine, he took Rau for a short flight over St. Petersburg's harbor.

It did not take long for Jannus to make news. On February 25, 1915, he crashed the *Florida*.[36] Jannus had taken Ruth Crawford of Balti-more for a short flight around Tampa Bay. Piloting the airboat through the channel, he circled around the bay and nosed the Benoist back toward the yacht basin. As the wind increased in strength, Jannus pulled back on the controls. When he attempted his ascent, a wing broke. The flying boat, now off balance and with no lift, crashed into Tampa Bay. As the aircraft slapped into the water, Jannus and Ruth Crawford were pitched from the hull.

Crawford sank under the water but was rescued by Jannus, who pulled her back to the buoyant overturned hull. Jannus helped her onto the floating carcass of the airboat, then climbed up beside her. Floating in Tampa Bay on the partially submerged flying boat, the pair awaited rescue. The *Evening Independent* reported, "The sight of the breaking boat caused one great shiver to run through the crowd, but with the sight of the intrepid little pilot and his pretty passenger scrambling through the planes to safety changed the fear to admiration for their exceptional nerves and presence of mind."[37]

Captain H. H. Kramin of Atlantic City, New Jersey, was standing at the Home Line Dock, having just come in from a cruise around the yacht basin with Percival Fansler, when the accident occurred. He jumped into his boat, the sixteen-foot *Flying Eagle*, and within two minutes reached the floating airboat. Ruth Crawford must not have been too frightened. She and Jannus sat atop the overturned airboat, casually waving at the spectators who were now crowded on the pier. Concerned about the safety of his passenger, Jannus told Kramin, "Get the lady out of the wreck, never mind me."[38] Captain Kramin had the soaked duo back on shore only seven minutes after the crash. Jannus was unhurt; Ruth Crawford sustained a minor injury to her right knee.

After the accident, Jannus was at a loss to explain how the misfortune had occurred. He was certain that the aircraft had been in fine flying condition; the machine had been overhauled only a few days earlier. Less than two weeks later, Benoist claimed that the accident had been the fault of poor workmanship on the part of Tony Jannus.[39] According to the *St. Petersburg Daily Times*, "Mr. Jannus stated that his only fear was for the safety of Miss Crawford who he was afraid would go down with the aircraft."[40]

Kyle Smith and Harry Rau went out to the *Florida* in a powerboat, hooked a line to it, and towed the craft back to shore. The *St. Petersburg Daily Times* reported that the airboat required $200 worth of repairs.[41] McLain estimated a prohibitive repair cost of $1,200.[42] On February 28, Tony took the steamer to Tampa. He expected to bring the Jannus flying boat to St. Petersburg and needed to communicate with Fritz Ericson in Baltimore. He wanted the airboat in Florida within ten days; Ericson advised him that there was no way the untested flying boat could be sent in less than three weeks. Although barely one month had passed since Tony's return to St. Petersburg, without an airplane to fly he had no reason to remain in Florida. On March 21 he took the train from St. Petersburg back to Baltimore.

Shortly after Jannus's departure from St. Petersburg, McLain decided that the *Florida* was salvageable for only $500. The engine was largely undamaged and only the wings and hull needed a major overhaul. McLain cabled J. D. Smith in San Diego and offered the flying job to him. When Smith agreed to come, McLain set about rebuilding the *Florida*.[43] It needed new cable as well as complete replacement of both the left and right wings. Jannus's crash into Tampa Bay had not been as severe as the wreckage of the *Florida* seemed to indicate; the salvage effort by Rau and Kyle Smith had caused the bulk of the heavy damage.

Benoist flying boat Number 45, the *Florida*. This flying boat was crashed by Tony Jannus in February 1915 and later rebuilt. Courtesy of the Florida Aviation Historical Society.

Traveling by train across the United States, J. D. Smith arrived in St. Petersburg during the first week of April. First he completely overhauled the engine. Smith may have become a flier, but he still thought like a mechanic. After making only eight flights for McLain, Smith left St. Petersburg.[44]

Back in Baltimore, Tony Jannus took his untested flying boat out for its trial run in April 1915. On April 28, an aviation magazine reported that the first Jannus flying boat was completed and that another was in the works, scheduled for completion in five weeks. Christened the *Lark*, the Jannus flying boat was the brainchild of Tony, but the actual construction was largely the work of Fritz Ericson. Highly competent and skilled with engines, he was the inventor of the Ericson four-cycle, gasoline, reversible marine engine.

When designing their airboat, the builders had decided that several objectives had to be met. These included air and seaworthiness, speed, quick and easy assembly, comfortable and clean accommodations, and general all-around efficiency. To achieve these goals, they incorporated old and new designs into the construction.[45]

Tony Jannus behind the controls of the Jannus flying boat, the *Lark*, in Baltimore, March 1915. Courtesy of the Florida Aviation Historical Society.

The aircraft was designed with a low center of gravity. When the flying boat was first built, a Roberts engine was used. Later, a 125-horsepower Maximotor engine was installed. The Maximotor engine placed in the hull was tremendously powerful compared to the Roberts with which Jannus was most familiar.[46] The aircraft was capable of a maximum speed of sixty-five miles per hour.

The Jannus flying boat could be disassembled in three stages. The tail was easily disconnected behind the forward compartment holding the engine. The wing assembly was of one piece and could also be easily removed.

The aircraft had the capacity to carry three passengers and the pilot. The engine was placed behind the passenger compartment and was isolated from the rest of the aircraft to facilitate cleanliness. The Jannus flying boat was designed to carry a useful load of nine hundred pounds, and it had a range of 240 miles.

The first test of the flying boat went well. Jannus flew at thirty to fifty-five miles per hour with only sixty-indicated horsepower. To test the stability, he taxied in the lee of large boats to record the effects of

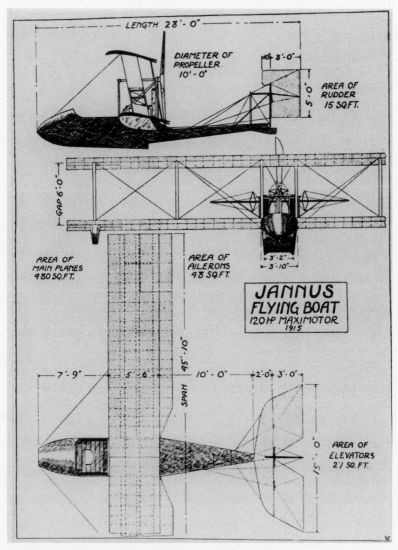

Drawing of the Jannus flying boat, 1915. Author's collection.

wake turbulence. To test the struts and staggered wing design, the aircraft was flown in dangerously heavy winds.

According to Spencer Heath of the American Propeller Company, Roger and Tony built two, possibly three, flying boats while they were in Baltimore. Jannus's *Lark* was eventually sold to W. E. Davidson of Detroit, Michigan.[47] If more Jannus flying boats were built, their history is unknown.

How did the Jannus brothers capitalize their fledgling operation in Baltimore? They taught a few students and sold Benoist Number 43 to Knox Martin. Potential sources of funds included Weightman family money. Between January and April 1915, Tony Jannus visited the Weightmans in Philadelphia on several occasions. While in Philadelphia in April, Jannus gave a lecture at the Academy of Sciences on the subject of flying and airplanes. Of this lecture, Nell Coursen recalled, "I do remember him saying that he had made up to then 10,000 flights and had never had an accident." Mrs. Coursen went out to the Patapsco River one Sunday afternoon at Tony's invitation to fly in the *Lark*, but Tony was unhappy with the engine's sound and would not allow her to fly. Coursen was not disappointed at the cancellation of her flight, remembering that "he flew around the water and when I saw the construction of the boat was kind of glad I was on dry land."[48]

On April 30, Tony wrote Edna Hansen that he had recently "finished a new machine that is sold in Detroit and will arrive there Monday. I should arrive about next Saturday. I would stop on my way out but business demands that I route via the Canada route and stop off at London, Ontario."[49] Jannus's short stint as entrepreneur and flying boat manufacturer was about to come to a close. The side trip to Canada would hold great importance for Tony; he was about to meet with John A. D. McCurdy, general manager of the Curtiss operation in Canada.

A Russian Test Pilot

THINGS WERE NOT going well for the Jannus brothers. Tony had smashed the *Florida* flying boat in St. Petersburg. J. D. Smith had met the same fate in San Diego. Their aircraft company, with only limited production, had not been particularly successful. Tony knew only one trade, and that was flying. Forced to evaluate his options, he considered running an engine production factory for the Roberts Motor Company in Toledo, Ohio.[1] Instead, he decided to go to Canada.

The Curtiss Aeroplane Company had designed the original Curtiss H–1 flying boat in 1914 for a proposed transatlantic flight. The British Royal Naval Air Service was impressed and asked Curtiss to construct a version capable of taking off from land. Because the Curtiss operation in America was already heavily involved in fulfilling war orders, Curtiss decided to create a Canadian subsidiary, Curtiss Aeroplanes and Motors, Ltd., to meet the increased demand. The new aircraft was to be based on the design of the H–1 *America*, and would use the same tail surfaces and wings. A new fuselage and undercarriage were to be developed in Toronto.[2]

Antony Jannus and Fritz Ericson were both hired by Curtiss in the spring of 1915, Jannus as test pilot and Ericson as chief engineer. The two men arrived in Toronto in early June. Under a veil of secrecy because of concerns about espionage, workers were busy assembling flying machines for various governments, including Russia and the United States. In July 1915, *Aeronautics* alluded to Curtiss's construction of "the big machine for Russia with two 160 H.P. motors."[3]

The Curtiss facility in Toronto was the largest flight training school on the North American continent. Trainees in early June included thirty-eight students of British or Canadian nationality, and total enrollment numbered nearly eighty flight students.[4] Before being accepted for training, each student had been approved by either the British Admiralty or the British Army, under the auspices of a British Army representative in Ottawa. The Curtiss instructors pushed aviators through their courses as quickly as possible. In June there were six to seven hundred anxious students waiting for the few precious training spots in the Curtiss school. *Aeronautics* reported that Tony Jannus "was now associated with the Curtiss Aeroplanes & Motors, Ltd., in the construction of various machines which they are building for various governments."[5]

J. A. D. McCurdy was the managing director of the Curtiss plant. He must have had great respect for young Jannus's skills and experience as a test pilot to allow him the *Canada* project; Jannus had been with the company for less than two months. If anyone at the facility was in a position to judge Jannus's flying skills, it would have been McCurdy. John Alexander Douglas McCurdy held the distinction of having made the first flight of a heavier-than-air machine in Canada when he flew the *Silver Dart* in 1909.[6] McCurdy's awareness of Jannus's skills went back to 1911, when both flew together in Washington, D.C.

Curtiss's redesigned bomber was named the *Canada* to complement the name of the H–1 *America*. Unattractive and aerodynamically cluttered in appearance, the aircraft's long fuselage resembled a cigar. The body was supported by a set of four-wheeled tandem landing gear. It carried a crew of three with the pilot in the rear and two passengers side by side in the front cockpit. Construction was completed surprisingly quickly.

The *Canada* was designed to be fitted with a pair of Curtiss VX 160-horsepower engines. When they were not ready, Curtiss OX–2 engines were installed instead. Although Jannus initially flew the *Canada* on September 3, 1915, the news was first published in the *New York Times* on September 6. It reported, "Tony Jannus was the pilot and went up for a short flight and then came down and the machine was thoroughly gone over, while the motors were left running. Then on

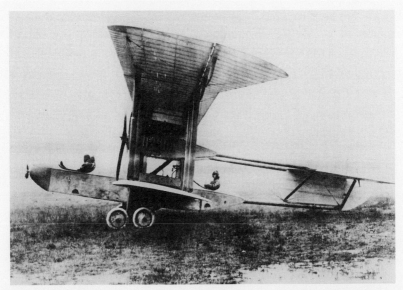

Curtiss *Canada* aircraft manufactured by Curtiss Aeroplanes and Motors, Ltd., in Toronto. Tony Jannus test-flew the *Canada* in 1915. Courtesy of the Glenn H. Curtiss Museum, Hammondsport, New York.

the second flight, he took up a passenger and they made a more extended trip. Everything worked beautifully."[7] On September 7, the aircraft was again flown by Jannus in a demonstration flight for British Squadron Commander John C. Porte. An aviator who witnessed the flying test told of the day's events in a letter to the *New York Times* mailed across the border to avoid Canadian censorship. The *Times* reported, "Antony Jannus flew the *Canada*, both with and without load, and a number of the military men went up. Carrying a load of 2,000 pounds, it rose from the ground with ease and great speed, and when in full flight attained a speed of ninety-five miles an hour."[8]

On at least two occasions, Jannus broke the oath of secrecy. During the summer, he had written a letter to Edna Hansen, his girlfriend from Cedar Point. He wrote that he was "engineering and testing the greatest air dreadnaught the world has ever known."[9] Jannus was not the only one talking about a dreadnaught. An *Aeronautics* article was titled "Curtiss Making Air Dreadnaught."[10] On another occasion, he sent pictures of the *Canada* to his friend Nell Coursen. After Tony's death, Coursen recalled, "I also have pictures of the *Canada*, the one the boys said they had helped design. Those pictures were given me and told not to show a soul as they were the first of their kind."[11]

It is doubtful that Jannus did much designing on this aircraft because it was already in production when he arrived in Toronto. Nevertheless, his test flying of the *Canada* would have led to engineering and design modifications. Jannus's statements about engineering may have been a young man's attempt to enhance his image with a member of the opposite sex. John P. Tarbox, a former patent attorney with the Curtiss company, added credence to the idea that Jannus was test pilot on the *Canada*. Tarbox wrote, "The so called dreadnaught designed by Curtiss and his engineers and produced mainly in the Toronto, Canada, plant was a twin engined plane. It's quite possible that Jannus piloted it on its test flights."[12] Jannus's inability to keep quiet also may have led to his eventual exile to Russia. Imperial Russian Navy Lieutenant Victor Utgoff wrote, "Mr. Jannus was sent to Russia after he had participated in the first twin-engined Curtiss landplane, model C-1 *Canada*, trials. This was a sort of exile that occurred because of Tony Jannus' talkativeness."[13]

Jannus had a reputation as a gifted talker. Following the bitter break between Jannus and Tom Benoist, Benoist had accused him of being a better talker than a flier. He had written that Jannus's "conversational ability is the only thing that has kept him going so far."[14] Tom Benoist had earlier blamed the crash of the *Florida* in St. Petersburg on poor workmanship on the part of Jannus. Comments such as these reflected the animosity he felt toward his former flier.

In 1915, the Curtiss company built the JN–2, powered by an eight-cylinder, V, 110-horsepower Curtiss Model OXX engine.[15] Used primarily as a scout or observation airplane with Brigadier General John J. Pershing's forces in Mexico, the JN–2 was the result of the marriage between the Curtiss Model J and Model N.[16] The combination of the Curtiss designators of J and N led to the joint designator of JN, which resulted in the widely used nickname "Jenny." A merger does not always produce the desired results, however, and such was the case with the Curtiss JN–2. The Model J's performance in the field was lacking, especially in its rate of climb. The JN–2 inherited this same weakness.

The first of the Canadian-built JN–3s was tested satisfactorily on July 14, 1915, by Jannus. Shortly after, the JN–3s were shipped to England. It is believed that all eleven JN–3s were completed in time to be tested by Jannus before he left for Russia. According to authors K. M. Molson and H. A. Taylor, not only did Jannus fly the JN–3, but he was the first to do so.[17] The wingspan of the JN–2 had been thirty-six feet, with both wings of equal length. The JN–3 featured an upper wing of forty-three feet, nine inches, while the lower wing had a span of nearly thirty-four feet. The JN–3's fuselage had grown by almost a foot to slightly over twenty-seven feet, two inches. The ninety-horse-power Curtiss OX engine allowed a rate of climb of nearly 325 feet per minute. The improvements to the JN–3 proved to be of little value; the aircraft was still underpowered, and the rate of climb continued to be unsatisfactory.[18]

Claims have been made that Jannus was involved with the design and engineering of the Curtiss JN–4 *Canuck*. This belief probably originated with Gay Blair White. In 1952, she wrote to several former Curtiss employees, "We have it on hearsay that he [Jannus] engineered the Curtiss 'Jenny' or JN–4D models used so extensively in World War I."[19]

J. D. Smith was also responsible for the belief that Jannus's involvement with the Curtiss Jenny was greater than it really had been. Many years after the deaths of both Jannus brothers, Benoist, and Fansler, Smith was asked to write a brief history of the St. Petersburg–Tampa Airboat Line. In this account, he wrote, "Jannus was taken on as engineer for the Curtiss plane company, where he helped engineer the Curtiss Jenny models."

The similar appearance of one of Tom Benoist's airplanes may also have led to the confusion surrounding the Curtiss Jenny. In 1917, the Benoist Aircraft Company designed and constructed its Model H–17 cross-country airplane. An all-metal design except for the wings, the two-passenger biplane looked much like the Curtiss aircraft.

The issue was resolved by a former Curtiss official. John P. Tarbox stated that Jannus "positively did not engineer either the Curtiss 'Jenny,' or the JN–4D. They were both engineered wholly by Glenn Curtiss and Henry Kleckler, with the aid of their young technical assistants and Dr. Albert Zahm."[20] Modifications by Ericson to the earlier models of the Jenny led to the development of the Curtiss JN–4D, or *Canuck*, in 1917. After the war ended, Ericson formed Ericson Aircraft Ltd. of Toronto, buying surplus aircraft, primarily the Curtiss JNs or Jennies of the Canadian Royal Air Force. Once refurbished, the aircraft were sold throughout Canada and the United States.

In 1914, the Curtiss company began building the standardized Model F flying boat.[21] The F boat, single-engined and the smallest of the Curtiss flying boats, proved to be one of the most popular and widely used of all equipment produced by Curtiss. Originally marketed to sportsmen, it eventually went on to gain wide acceptance by the military of the United States and Europe.

When it came time to build a larger flying boat with greater range, albeit no greater speed, the most expeditious way was to copy an existing model. The Curtiss Model K flying boat was cloned from the highly successful Model F. Production figures for the number of K boats vary from fifty-four to fifty-six.[22] Attorneys for the Curtiss-Wright Corporation wrote to J. D. Smith seeking information on the Curtiss K flying boats used by the Imperial Russian Navy. Attorney Thomas L. Howe claimed, "48 flying boats of type K were sold to the Imperial Russian Navy."[23] The Romanov government in Russia was desperately in need of the Curtiss flying boats. At the outbreak of war with Germany, the woefully weak Russian naval fleet consisted of only 195 ships, mostly small destroyers. Although the czar had a massive army, the navy numbered only fifty thousand men.

Tony Jannus may have test flown the Model K in the later stages of its design and production in Toronto. Walter E. Johnson had tested at least one Curtiss K boat in Hammondsport on November 14, 1914, several months before Jannus began working for Curtiss. Following that, Theodore C. McCaulay was responsible for most of the test flying of the K boat in Toronto. Since Jannus eventually went to Russia as a Curtiss representative to test the K boats on site, it is almost impossible to imagine him taking such an assignment without many hours of flying the aircraft in friendly waters.

In 1915, the $1 million Russian order was big business. In addition to the fifty-four K flying boats, the Russian purchase included twelve

Curtiss Model K flying boat, 1916. Tony Jannus went to Russia to assist with the delivery of approximately fifty Model K flying boats to the Russian Imperial Navy. Courtesy of the Glenn H. Curtiss Museum, Hammondsport, New York.

OX 90, 100-horsepower engines and nineteen V model 160-horsepower engines worth $125,000.

Less than fifteen months after the outbreak of the Great War in Europe, Tony Jannus made his long-awaited transatlantic crossing, though not by air. On October 1, 1915, Jannus sailed from New York City to Archangel, Russia. German submarines were a constant threat; the ocean liner had to take the longer, less direct northern route, instead of through the Mediterranean Sea and the Suez Canal.[24] From Archangel, Jannus traveled to Sevastopol, where he met Charles C. Witmer, Curtiss's representative, and Walter E. Johnson, the test pilot and instructor whom Jannus was replacing.[25]

Tony met with immediate frustration. At the time of his arrival in Sevastopol, approximately twenty-five Curtiss Model K flying boats had already been delivered. Some were in various stages of assembly, and many were still in crates.[26] Progress had been slow; only a few of the K boats had been accepted by the Russians. Another half dozen had been partially completed; hulls and wings were assembled, awaiting engine installation.

The relationship between Curtiss and the Russians was plagued with difficulty almost from the very beginning. On August 31, 1914, the

Russian Imperial Navy had placed an order for two Curtiss Model H–4 flying boats. When Curtiss refused to commit to Russian specifications on the rate of climb and payload capability, the order had been canceled. Early in 1915, the Russians again ordered two Model H–4 flying boats. Orders were eventually placed for Curtiss H–7 flying boats, but the H–7 was destined for nothing but problems.

Russian aviators were immediately impressed with Tony's skills as a flier. Senior Lieutenant Ivan Ivanovich Stakhovsky, commander of the Black Sea Fleet, wrote, "Jannus is flying daily. First time—carefully and little. Now—much more boldly and often. Yesterday, there was a gusty wind accompanied by a rain—nobody flew here and at the Kacha. Jannus still took off with me and a mechanic. We flew about an hour, then making a landing in the sea and taking off from heavy waves. Neither coastline nor ships at the harbour were visible because of the rain. After this flight our pilots have confidence in the apparatuses and ask to fly as passengers."[27]

After only four months in Russia, Jannus returned home. Senior Lieutenant A. A. Tuchkov, commander of the Aeronautical Department of the Russian Navy General Staff, advised, "Pilot Jannus has his work ended and leaves for America because he considers the slow acceptance trials of the K boats unfavorable to him."[28] By the time Jannus left for the United States, only ten Model K boats had been successfully demonstrated and accepted by the Russian government.[29] On February 12, 1916, Jannus departed Sevastopol on the American ocean liner *St. Paul*, headed for New York City.[30]

Upon his return to the United States, he praised the Russian fliers. It was Jannus's opinion that the Russian air fleet was "the finest and most efficient of all the belligerent countries." He also related a story of flying with the Russians as they attacked and destroyed a Turkish seaport. He claimed that "all the Turkish ports on the Black Sea were dominated by Russian hydro-aeroplanes." Of his involvement, Jannus wrote, "I did witness an attack by four torpedo boats on what probably was a submarine." He also recalled, "I saw a bombardment of the town of Sangoeack by a portion of the Russian fleet from the air. A heavy cloud bank hung over the town. Each airship emerged from the mist long enough to drop a bomb and then drove back into the clouds."[31]

The aggressive attack in which Jannus participated was a combined effort by the airplanes and ships of the Black Sea fleet squadron against the Turkish port of Zunguldak. The Turks were attacked by a Russian armada composed of the battleship *Imperatritsa Mariya*, the cruiser *Almaz*, two aircraft carriers, and two torpedo boats.[32] The port of Zunguldak was attacked from the sea; the coup de grace was an aerial attack that bombed the Turkish ships moored in the harbor. Ten flying boats dropped thirty-eight bombs, sinking the Turkish steamer *Irmingard*.

In 1915, the approximately four hundred Russian fliers had little military experience.[33] The Russian war effort was hampered by a shortage of useful aircraft. In Canada, Glenn Curtiss's company was turning out aircraft for Russia as fast as humanly possible. On the Russian front, Curtiss aviators were training pilots as quickly as they could.

Jannus longed to do more than simply test fly and teach the Russians how to fly the Curtiss H and K flying boats. He applied for combat service with the Russian air fleet. Lieutenant G. V. Piotrovsky cabled, "Anton Franklendovich Jannus, an American subject and Curtiss Company pilot, offers his service to fly the flying boats, Model K, during Fleet's operations expecting to have the anti-submarine patrol as a main combat mission. I think the proposal of Mr. Jannus gives a possibility to test the K boat in combat."[34] The commander of the Black Sea Fleet issued an order prohibiting Jannus's involvement as a combatant because he was a citizen of a neutral country. The decision did not reflect the reality of the situation; Jannus was frequently more than an observer. On several occasions, he ended up in the thick of battle. While on a Russian warship, he observed the surfacing of a Turkish submarine. Once above water, the submarine launched a torpedo at one of the Curtiss flying boats floating unprotected on the water. The torpedo grazed it without causing any damage. The Russian flying boat took to the air, jettisoned its load of bombs on the submarine, and destroyed the fleeing Turkish submarine.[35]

Philosophizing on the use of aerial tactics in war, Jannus reflected,

"It is the first time in history that physical control of a large body of water has been maintained by the air. Practically every Turkish ship that attempts to move in the sea in good weather is observed by an aeroplane. If the ship is not destroyed or driven back to its harbor by bombs, the aeroplane within a short time has several Russian warships in pursuit of it."[36]

Jannus had been in Washington, D.C., only ten days before plans changed, necessitating a hurried return to Russia.[37] His scheduled replacement, Theodore C. McCaulay, had suffered an accident while flying a Curtiss H–7 flying boat near Mt. Vernon, Virginia.[38] When McCaulay's injuries prevented him from traveling to Russia, Jannus was recalled.

On April 1, 1916, Jannus boarded a ship for his second eastbound ocean crossing. What was so important that Jannus had to return to Russia after only ten days at home? Jannus and Emily Prettyman of Chicago were rumored to have become engaged and were to be married on Christmas Day 1916.[39] If this was true, why would he leave his fiancée?

On his return to Russia Jannus was charged with two primary responsibilities.[40] McCaulay's crash was an important factor in his return, but there were larger issues at hand. Curtiss's million-dollar aircraft deal with Russia was in jeopardy. Jannus's immediate duty was to ensure the smooth delivery and testing of two H–7 flying boats that had recently been shipped from the Curtiss factory to Sevastopol. The delivery test flight for the first of the two Curtiss H–7's had proven unsuccessful. The ability to reach a prescribed altitude of 750 meters within a certain time frame was a requirement for the H–7.[41] During the first test of the H–7, Jannus reached the specified altitude in only thirteen minutes, making that part of the test a success.[42] Unfortunately, the aircraft sustained considerable damage on landing. Jannus then decided to test fly the second Curtiss H–7 flying boat.

Assembly and testing of the Curtiss K boats had not gone well in Tony's absence. The Russians were not pleased with the results and were seriously contemplating voiding the purchase agreement. The Russian Naval General Staff had gone on record as saying, "In view of the fact that up to the present time the K flying boats have not been brought into condition that the Government might accept them, the Aviation Department of the Naval General Staff requests us to take steps for clearing the premises of the staff which is occupied by the above stated K boats."[43] Jannus was desperately needed in Sevastopol.

Immediately after Tony's return to Russia, his brother Roger arrived. Roger's primary duty was to handle the hundreds of details associated with the shipment of the Curtiss Model H and K flying boats. Tony's only mention of Roger was in a cablegram sent to Curtiss Aeroplane in Buffalo, New York. Tony wired, "Have consulted Russian Worthington pump company regarding commercial combination new aeroplane and motor business their London or New York offices advised to consult you stop they are strongly recommended by Army Staff as advisable ally here full advices arriving by Roger about August twentieth."[44] The information to which Tony referred was personally delivered by Roger when he left Russia in August after only four months.

Tony Jannus's flying skills were as well regarded by the Russians as by his American contemporaries. On December 12, 1915, Lieutenant Piotrovsky wrote to Senior Lieutenant I. I. Stakhovsky, the commander of the Black Sea fleet, "Flying boats of the K type have some peculiarities which are characteristic for all flying machines of heavy weight and high inertia . . . that is why they demand a pilot to a particular ability and skill. . . . This is why it is necessary to have a special school for piloting of high inertia apparatuses to train pilots not only for K-boats but for flying boats of the Transatlantic type too. . . . At first, it would be possible to draw Mr. Jannus for this purpose, until Mr. Utgoff returns."[45]

The financial and communication difficulties Jannus faced were made clear in two cables that he sent from Petrograd on June 23, 1916. The initial cable stated, "All desperately need money rush five thousand dollars why no answer telegrams. Jannus."[46] The second communication was a letter to Lieutenant Commander A. A. Tuchkov in which Jannus wrote of design problems, the seriousness of a lack of communications from America, and a shortage of funds.[47]

16 🛩 A Mysterious Ending

"JANNUS DIES IN RUSSIA" read the bold black letters of Tony's belated obituary in the *Baltimore News* on November 2, 1916. The telegram Spencer Heath of the American Propeller and Manufacturing Company received on the morning of November 2 was terse. Fritz Ericson had been given the miserable task of informing Jannus's relatives in Washington. Few details about his death were offered by anyone in the Curtiss organization, perhaps for several reasons. The Curtiss company in Canada remained subject to the wartime secrecy that had existed since 1915. The fate of a lone American airman doing support work in Russia was not enough reason to risk the loss of business. Lack of information was probably also tied to Curtiss's fears of a lawsuit by the Romanov government in Moscow.

Roderick Wright, a 1911 Wright brothers' flying school graduate, added more mystery to an already cloudy story. Wright claimed to have been with the Curtiss sales group at the time Tony Jannus took the Curtiss K flying boats to Russia in 1916. He said, "No one will ever know what happened to Tony. One report is that he crashed and burned at sea." Wright claimed that in 1950 "two Russian Officers called on him. They learned he had something to do with the sale of two planes to the czar's government in 1916. Also they just learned that these machines failed because of defective motors never replaced by Curtiss and wanted the U.S. government to pay for them in 1950! The whole thing was hush hushed by the F.B.I., and the story closed for reasons best known to our G boys."[1]

In 1949, the FBI conducted an investigation of the Curtiss Aeroplane Company and its sale of flying boats to Russia. On December 1, Lester S. Jayson, special attorney, wrote to the special agent in charge of the investigation, "These K-boats were powered by a Curtiss Model V engine which was an earlier motor than the Model VX. It was also rated 160 h.p. but was different in physical shape and, we are informed, was much cruder and had many and various defects."[2]

Part of the problem with the single-engined K boats headed for the Black Sea lay in the long transpacific shipping time. The large flying boats were shipped from Vancouver to Vladivostok by boat, then loaded aboard the Trans-Siberian Railroad for overland shipment to Sevastopol. From departure to destination, the trip took three months. The lengthy journey frequently resulted in warped propellers, rusted parts, and weakness to structural surfaces.

Jannus's predecessor, Walter E. Johnson, had complained of logistical problems, lack of support by Curtiss, and Russian intimidation. Johnson had once been forced by the Russians to remain in Sevastopol against his will. Earlier, Pluym Ochs, the Curtiss representative, had been arrested and jailed as a spy.[3]

Chauncey Brown of the *St. Petersburg Evening Independent* wrote to Raymond V. Morris, a Curtiss agent, to ask what had happened to Jannus. Morris replied, "The company was merely advised that Jannus was killed—no further information was obtained, though every effort was made to get the details."[4]

In 1994, several official communiques between various Russian agencies following Tony Jannus's crash into the Black Sea became available. One communication between A. V. Kolchak, commander of the Black Sea Fleet, and the naval minister advised, "Today, during a delivery flight of an American apparatus of the Atlantic type, the machine has fallen into the water from the altitude of 700 metres; American pilot Jannus and two (our) men have been killed, Podporuchik Kasatkin has been badly injured, the apparatus has sunk quickly."[5] Kruglaya Bukhta, one of several small bays at Sevastopol and the site of Tony's crash, had been used as a training and experimental base for Black Sea Fleet Aviation since May 1915. Jannus had used Kruglaya

Bukhta for most of his training and test flights and was intimately familiar with the area. What the cable failed to say was that Jannus had been flying a Curtiss K boat for several days until bad weather stopped the flights. When the Russians demanded that Jannus fly the Model H–7 to demonstrate the aircraft's performance in bad weather, Jannus went up under protest. The Curtiss company's anxiety over the Russian acceptance of the H and K boats and intimidation by the Russians had been persuading factors.

The Curtiss company was notified of Jannus's death sometime between October 12, the date of the accident, and October 22. On October 22, the Russian naval attaché in Washington sent the following wire to the Russian Naval General Staff headquartered in Petrograd: "Curtiss has asked Lieutenant Utgoff to organize a transportation of the body of Jannus to New York, at Curtiss' expense. If any money are necessary immediately, they can be granted by the office of Ochs. I ask to cable the name of that steamer which will be used for the transportation of the body."[6] On October 27, I. I. Stakhovsky, commander of the Black Sea Fleet Aviation, transmitted a seven-word communique to the Naval General Staff in Petrograd: "The body of Jannus is not discovered."[7]

Although the Black Sea covers an area of approximately 169,000 square miles and in places is more than a mile deep, it is not easy to understand why Jannus's body was not recovered. Pieces of the wreckage were found, as were the bodies of two Russian airmen. Podporuchik Kasatkin, although badly injured, was rescued.[8] Perhaps Jannus's body was discovered and given a burial at sea or brought to shore and quickly buried in an unmarked grave. The truth will probably never be known. One theory was that Jannus did not die in a Curtiss H flying boat but instead was kept in Russia to strengthen the inferior Russian aerial forces. Another story was that instead of dying in a streetcar accident, Tom Benoist was kidnapped by a forerunner of the Russian KGB and spirited off to Russia. There, the former partners supposedly joined in designing and building airplanes for the czar. Though these are romantic and interesting ideas, they are not true.

The whereabouts of Jannus's body may remain a mystery, but the cause of the accident on October 12, 1916, was determined. The Russian Aviation Committee concluded, "When wreckage of the plane had been examined, the Committee came to decision that the machine fell from the altitude of 450 metres because of an inadequate low speed which took place during a turn. Apparently, the speed was lost because of too intensive climb which was carried out by Jannus who tried to lift to the contract altitude (750 metres) as soon as possible. Apparently, after the speed had been lost, Antony Jannus was unable to fly the plane level because of shortcomings of the aircraft design."[9] On impact with the water after an uncontrolled dive of nearly half a mile, the hull of the Curtiss H flying boat splintered into thousands of pieces. Built of spruce and covered with canvas painted in battleship gray, the flying boat could never have withstood such a crash.

Almost certainly, Jannus's accident was caused by mechanical failure rather than pilot error. The Curtiss H–7 in which Jannus was killed was powered by two Curtiss V 160-horsepower engines. According to Andrei Alexandrov, an expert on the Imperial Russian Navy and the relationship between the Russians and the Curtiss company, "The engines of this type were relatively powerful but unreliable powerplants and, I believe, this is quite possibly the motors were a reason of the fatal accident."[10]

At least one lawsuit had been brought against the Curtiss Aeroplane Company alleging various mechanical shortcomings in the Curtiss flying boats. The first legal challenge arose in 1915. Shortly after Tony's arrival in America from Russia, he had been required to provide a deposition regarding the K boats. Jannus testified under oath on March 21, 1916, about the shortcomings of the Curtiss equipment.[11] His unexpected return to Russia after only ten days in the United States may have been an attempt to prevent further damaging testimony.

In 1949, the United States government brought a second suit against Curtiss in the Southern District Court of New York. Lester S. Jayson, attorney for the government, stated that on many occasions Jannus had complained by either cable or letter to Curtiss about engine problems, shortages of tools, faulty crankshafts, extreme engine vibrations, faulty magnetos, and propeller problems.[12]

During March 1949, James L. Ferris, a onetime employee of the Curtiss company, was questioned about the soundness of the Curtiss flying boats, as well as Jannus's competency as a pilot. Ferris, an airplane and engine mechanic, had been in Russia in 1915 and 1916. When questioned about problems the Russians may have had with the Curtiss aircraft, Ferris generally claimed any problems were the fault of Russian incompetence or inexperience. When interrogated about carburetor problems, Ferris replied, "The only trouble they [the Russians] had with the carburetor was their own fault, they didn't keep them properly. The air and water—the Black Sea is very salty, and you had to do the same as we do, protect the aluminum alloy parts from salt corrosion, and if you don't you fall into trouble, and they didn't do it."[13]

Ferris was twice asked specifically about Tony's skills. "According to your observation was Janus a competent pilot?" asked the government's lawyer. "Janus was a very competent pilot," responded Ferris without hesitation. The questioning continued:

> QUESTION: "Would he check his plane before he took flights?"
> FERRIS: "Yes, Tony was pretty fussy."
> QUESTION: "He also checked his motors?"
> FERRIS: "He definitely did."[14]
> QUESTION: "I think you said you regarded Janus as a fairly competent fellow in his field?"
> FERRIS: "Janus was, to my mind, a very competent pilot."
> QUESTION: "He was also quite zealous in connection with Curtiss interests in Russia, was he not?"
> FERRIS: "I never knew anything to the contrary."
> QUESTION: "It was his job to get the K boats built?"
> FERRIS: "Flown and accepted."
> QUESTION: "And as quickly as possible."
> FERRIS: "Yes."[15]

The government attorneys repeatedly grilled Ferris about faulty magnetos, engine vibrations, and defective propellers. The death of the world-renowned Jannus, at the height of his career, may have been caused by something as simple as dirty magneto brushes.

Streetcars and Cigarettes

THE YEARS FOLLOWING the collapse of the St. Petersburg–Tampa Airboat Line were unkind to the company's founders. Tony Jannus was only twenty-seven when he died in 1916. Life for the others was not easy.

In 1915, Tom Benoist tired of the inhospitable attitude displayed by the city of St. Louis toward his company and moved his operation to Chicago. One year later, Benoist relocated to Sandusky, Ohio, where he built airplanes capable of carrying five to seven passengers. While in Sandusky, Benoist designed and constructed his first metal-framed and metal-covered aircraft.

The relationship between Jannus and Benoist at this time was anything but friendly. A letter from Benoist to J. D. Smith in early 1915 provided insight into Benoist's feelings about Jannus. Benoist accused Tony Jannus of being duplicitous, careless as an aviator, a "joke" as a designer of aircraft, and a second-rate flier. He claimed: "Tony is impossible as an Aeroplane designer, and only average as a flyer, and his conversational ability is the only thing that has kept him going so far."[1] Benoist's spite was evident. Jannus's departure had been a major blow, and Benoist was unforgiving.

Benoist and Percy Fansler continued to correspond after their short-lived and financially unsuccessful partnership. Fansler asked Benoist to build a twin-engined, twelve-passenger flying boat.[2] The new airplane seemed to go the way of everything else in Sandusky—very poorly. Flying from Battery Park, Elmer Straub and Otis Klein crashed, destroying the Benoist airboat ordered by Fansler.[3] Lack of financial resources prevented the aircraft from being rebuilt.

Tom Benoist had labored under a black cloud of undercapitalization for most of his adult life, as Percival Fansler pointed out when talking about the first airboat used in the St. Petersburg–Tampa Airboat Line. He recalled, "Tom Benoist had one finished, but not entirely paid for, as he had almost no working capital."[4]

Benoist always lacked the important element of a sponsor in the success of his business. Glenn Curtiss had had several. Early on, Alexander Graham Bell and the collective group of the Aerial Experiment Association were of paramount influence. Later, he had the financial as well as psychological patronage of the very wealthy Rodman Wanamaker. The Wright brothers could claim the support of the United States Army's Signal Corps. Benoist had only the allegiance of Albert Bond Lambert of St. Louis. Confined to St. Louis and not worldwide, the relationship with Lambert was never financial.

In Sandusky, barely able to afford the $6.50 for his weekly room and board, Benoist scrimped everywhere he could, except in the building of his aircraft. Reinhardt Ausmus, a student at the Benoist flying school and a buyer of one of Benoist's aircraft, recalled, "Benoist roomed and slept on the third floor of the attic of the old Longmore place. We had room and board for $6.50 a week, while the boys with money had rooms upstairs for $12.00 a week. Tom would often sew a patch on his pants so that he could buy materials to build planes."[5] At least Tom Benoist never met the fate of fellow airplane designer and manufacturer Armand Deperdussin, who was arrested and jailed by the French police for not paying his bills.[6]

Housed in the Roberts Motor Company facility, Benoist's workshop had become a vestige of his former St. Louis factory; the Spartan surroundings illustrated the dearth of funds. Once capable of producing several aircraft at a time, the workshop was now barely large enough for one. The weakest link in Tom Benoist's operation had been his choice of engines used to power almost all of his aircraft. Unlike Curtiss, Benoist never developed his own highly efficient and lightweight engine. Instead, he became and remained captive to the Roberts, an inefficient, two-cycle engine. Roberts and Benoist were equally dependent upon each other. Because they were symbiotic in nature, once one company ceased to operate, the other was shortly out of business. The Roberts Motor Company closed in 1918. Benoist's production at Sandusky was minimal at best; probably no more than half a dozen aircraft were manufactured.

Tom Benoist's worries about airplanes, production schedules, and payrolls came to an end on June 14, 1917. The official cause of Benoist's death was "a fractured skull, accidentally struck head on pole while leaving out of streetcar, shock and hemorrhage from ears."[7] It is unthinkable that a man of such vision and love of flying would meet his death in anything as mundane as a streetcar accident, but that was exactly what happened.[8] Benoist and Reinhardt Ausmus had boarded the streetcar on the way to the factory when the accident occurred. Ausmus recalled, "Tom Benoist and I went out to the factory on a streetcar. The factory was located on Columbus Ave. At that time, the streetcars had steps all along the side of the car, with a hand railing which was used getting in and out. Tom had the habit of jumping off real quick out at the Roberts Motors, so he could get in the factory quickly. One day, he leaned forward, his head was struck by a telephone pole that leaned toward the streetcar. He hit the pavement with a deadly thud. By the time we got him to the Good Samaritan Hospital he was nearly gone. About three hours after the accident he died and his remains were shipped back to Missouri."[9] Bud Morriss remembered the accident a little differently. According to Morriss, Benoist died on the day that "Admiral Peary was to be at Benoist's plant to place an order for planes for the Navy. Tom heard a plane overhead and leaned out of the trolley to see if it were one of his. He was struck by a telephone pole."[10]

Tom Benoist's contribution to early American aviation can hardly be debated. Not as well-known as either the Wrights or Glenn Curtiss, he nevertheless made his own distinct imprint. P. G. B. Morriss, Benoist's vice president in charge of sales, on two separate occasions claimed that the Benoist company was "making and selling more planes in this country [the United States] than any other company with the exception of Glenn Curtiss." That was probably true. In the first decades of the twentieth century, hundreds of people were manufacturing air-

Tom Benoist, Jannus's onetime mentor, in a formal pose. Courtesy of the Rutherford B. Hayes Presidential Center, Reinhardt Ausmus Collection, Fremont, Ohio.

planes, but only a few companies were producing very many. Benoist built slightly over one hundred airplanes, hydros, and flying boats during his lifetime. When he died, aircraft number 106 was still on the assembly line. Benoist never achieved the reputation of Glenn Curtiss and never became known as much more than a small, midwestern designer and manufacturer of airplanes and flying boats. The St. Petersburg–Tampa Airboat Line, however, was an important milestone in the early history of aviation and transportation.

Following Benoist's death, his company splintered apart. Several people attempted to keep the company operating. Its location was changed several times without success. A lack of information surrounding the events following his death precludes knowledge of what actually happened. On February 18, 1918, an advertisement appeared in *Aerial Age* attempting to sell the remaining property of the Benoist Aircraft Company: "Two 4 passenger flying boats; one passenger (2 place) flying boat; one Baby Tractor in process; one 2 passenger Flying Boat in Process; one Hall Scott motor, one Roberts motor; blueprints, drawings, patterns, all patent rights, and an assortment of aeroplane parts and accessories."

In the spring of 1917, Roger Jannus, accompanied by J. D. Smith, arrived at the Curtiss civilian flying school in Miami, Florida. Roger Jannus was to serve as a civilian flight instructor and Smith as a mechanic. Because flight manuals were nonexistent, Roger completed a long treatise on flying the Curtiss JN–4 titled "Suggestions for Flying Students."[11]

While in Miami, Roger also perfected a lifesaving aerial maneuver. Years later, his onetime commanding officer, Logan McMenemy, recalled, "Rumor had it that a certain civilian Roger Jannus, had learned how to get out of the then deadly tail spin. Due to the nature of our training, it seemed highly desirable that all instructors, as well as students, should gain the experience of how to get out of the tail spin at the earliest date possible. In any event, Jannus was assigned to our command and did prove to be everything and more than we expected. His experience and training must have saved many, many lives. He was a superb graceful flier, and patient with his students, turning out many Birds who later distinguished themselves in combat."[12]

On June 19, 1917, Roger Jannus enlisted in the Aviation Branch of the United States Signal Corps. During the spring of 1918, he was assigned to the Third Aviation Instruction Centre at Issoudun, France. Jannus was assigned to pilot the de Havilland 4, cynically but accu-

From January to May 1917, Roger Jannus served as a civilian flight instructor at the Curtiss flying school in Miami, Florida. Roger Jannus (far left) and four of his colleagues. Courtesy of the Historical Association of Southern Florida, Miami.

STREETCARS AND CIGARETTES

rately nicknamed "the flying coffin." On September 18, 1918, Captain Jannus was killed in the flaming midair explosion of his "flying coffin" over Field Number 7 at Issoudun.

As with his brother's death two years earlier, the events surrounding Roger's death were mysterious. Lieutenant Colonel Hiram Bingham, Air Service Staff commanding officer at Issoudun in 1918, believed that Roger's death was the result of a leaky gasoline tank. Logan McMenemy thought it might have been caused by carelessness. He wrote, "It was nothing unusual for Roger to smoke while he was flying, as he often did when we flew together, and it was not too unusual a matter for other officers to smoke when flying when it was possible to get a light in one of those open drafty cockpits. We all felt that it could have been brought about by lighting a cigarette, but very improbably."[13] Arthur Richmond concurred about Roger's smoking while flying. "Yes, Roger did like to smoke while flying. He used to invariably throttle back our Curtiss Jenneys and give his students the controls while clouds of cigarette smoke would come from the front cockpit as he lit his cigarette."[14] Nell Coursen, who was friendly with both Tony Jannus and Fritz Ericson, gave credence to the idea that Roger's death may have been caused by his own actions. She claimed that Fritz Ericson told her that "Roger was showing some officers with a match that the ship couldn't catch fire in the air, and when he took it up she burnt up in the air."[15]

In the early 1950s, a great deal of time and energy was spent researching the story of the St. Petersburg–Tampa Airboat Line, as well as the lives of Tony Jannus, Tom Benoist, Percival Fansler, and J. D. Smith. Smith, the only member of the airline still alive, seemed to be the logical person to fill in the blanks. He had been with Benoist and Jannus since 1911. Smith seemed reluctant to offer any assistance in bringing the details to light. Gay Blair White, in her attempt to prove that the St. Petersburg–Tampa Airboat Line was the world's first airline, was often stymied in her efforts by Smith. Advanced in age, he refused to cooperate. More often than not, he was petulant and quarrelsome, believing that history had slighted him. Perhaps he had good cause. Settling in St. Petersburg only a few years after the operation of the world's first airline, Smith had become a forgotten man. When

Left: Captain Roger Jannus before shipping out for France in 1918. Author's collection. *Right:* Tony Jannus. The photograph was taken at Cedar Point, Ohio, in August 1914. Courtesy of the Rutherford B. Hayes Presidential Center, Reinhardt Ausmus Collection, Fremont, Ohio.

the airline was spoken of or written about, it was invariably referred to as Jannus's airline, slighting Fansler and Benoist as well as Smith. In July 1952, White summed up the situation with Smith. In a letter to Ross Windom, St. Petersburg's city manager, she stated, "Our position is that though Mr. Smith may be an exceedingly stubborn old man, he has something that the city wants and needs."[16]

The health and well-being of "Smitty the infallible" and his wife ultimately deteriorated to the point that White assumed legal guardianship for them. White continued in this role until September 6, 1952, when she petitioned Judge Richard A. Miller of the County Court to "resign as guardian of the physical case of Mr. and Mrs. Jay Dee Smith."[17]

On March 11, 1963, James D. Smith, the last remaining member of the St. Petersburg–Tampa Airboat Line, died alone in a rest home in

St. Petersburg.[18] His career in aviation may have been short-lived, but it was illustrious. He contributed to the war effort in 1916 and 1917 as a civilian aviation engineer. In 1920, he was with Major R. W. "Shorty" Schroeder when Schroeder made his 33,114-foot stratospheric record.[19]

For Tony Jannus, the most famous of the group and the youngest to die, there was no body to be buried, no grave to be dug, and no funeral to be arranged. Tony Jannus's adoptive family, the Spaldings, had a plain headstone erected in Rock Creek Cemetery in Washington, D.C., as a memorial. The simple inscription carved into the stone read, "Antony Jannus, Died at Sea, 1889–1916." No one happening past the monument would realize the contributions this boy from Washington had made to his chosen field—American aviation.

Notes

CHAPTER I: AN AMERICAN FLIER

1. Gibbs-Smith, *Flight Through the Ages*, 126.
2. R. E. G. Davies to Siobhan M. White, January 21, 1994. In possession of the author.
3. *St. Louis Post-Dispatch*, December 1, 1912.
4. Gibbs-Smith, *Flight Through the Ages*, 134.
5. "Recognition for Gardner," 119.
6. Jannus, "The Aeroplane Engine," 190–92.
7. Jannus and Southard, "Washington Aeroplane Show," 139.
8. "Another Aviator Now Has National License," 122; Department of Commerce and Labor Steamboat Inspection Service license, serial no. 54578, issued to Antony H. Jannus, August 10, 1914.
9. Morehouse, "Flying Pioneers," 276. Morehouse wrote that Waite "holds Department of Commerce License No. 1, and District of Columbia License No. 2."
10. Henry Roy Waite to Gay Blair White, August 29, 1952: "I believe I hold the first license issued by the Dept. of Commerce." All letters to Gay Blair White cited hereafter are from the Gay Blair White Collection, Florida Aviation Historical Society Archives, St. Petersburg. Archives hereafter abbreviated as FAHSA.
11. Woodcock, "Benoist," 1.
12. Birth certificate for Antony Habersack Jannus, 1889; birth certificate for Roger Weightman Jannus, 1886.
13. Johnson and Buel, eds., *Battles and Leaders of the Civil War*, 1:306.
14. Birth certificate for Antony Habersack Jannus, 1889.
15. R. Hanson Weightman to Gay Blair White, September 16, 1952.
16. Ibid.

17. Boise L. Bristor to Gay Blair White, August 18, 1952.
18. Walter E. Lees to Gay Blair White, December 1, 1952.
19. Gay Blair White to James A. Lebenthal, letter published in *Life*, October 4, 1953.
20. "Benoist School Operated on Mississippi," 83.
21. *St. Louis Post-Dispatch*, November 20, 1913.
22. Ibid., May 25, 1913.
23. Ibid., September 7, 1913.
24. Ibid.
25. James D. Smith scrapbook.
26. *Aero and Hydro*, January 4, 1913, 256.
27. Russell Froelich oral history.
28. *Chicago Daily Tribune*, November 2, 1916.
29. *Detroit News*, September 18, 1913.
30. W. H. Burke to J. D. Smith, March 9, 1916.
31. Martha Benoist Davis to Gay Blair White, November 25, 1952.
32. *St. Louis Globe-Democrat*, November 20, 1913.

CHAPTER 2: SKY RIDER

1. Betty Stuart Jannus to Tony Jannus, March 10, 1910, College Park Airport Museum, College Park, Maryland.
2. Jannus, "Flight Progress About the Country," 21.
3. *Aero*, April 1911, 248.
4. *Aero*, January 1911, 22.
5. Jannus, "Flight Progress About the Country," 21, 22.
6. "Latham the Hero at Baltimore Meet," 7.
7. "The Story of Aviation in Baltimore," 12.
8. Gurney, *Chronology of World Aviation*, 14.
9. Mitchell, "News and Gossip of the Nation's Capital," 51.
10. "Dramatic Legislation Proposed," 72.
11. *Washington Post*, March 8, 1911.
12. Ibid., March 26, 1911.

CHAPTER 3: SOCIETY GIRLS AND MUDDY WATER

1. *Washington Post*, March 26, 1911.
2. "Entangled Skirt Kills Two," 226.
3. *Washington Post*, March 26, 1911.
4. Mitchell, "Rex Smith Biplane Highly Favored," 245.
5. *Washington Post*, May 4, 1911.
6. Ibid., May 4, 1911; Boyne, *Smithsonian Book of Flight*, 111.
7. *Washington Post*, May 4, 1911.
8. Casey, *Curtiss*, 5.
9. *Aero*, April 2, 1911, 58.

10. *Washington Post*, April 7, 1911.
11. Ibid., April 10, 1911.
12. James Brough to Thomas Reilly, July 16, 1993. Brough is the author of *Princess Alice: A Biography of Alice Roosevelt Longworth*.
13. Carol Felsenthal to Thomas Reilly, August 18, 1993. Felsenthal is the author of *Alice Roosevelt Longworth*.
14. *Aero*, April 22, 1911, 65.
15. *Washington Post*, April 7, 1911.
16. Ibid.
17. Ibid., April 9, 1911.
18. Brown, *Florida's Aviation History*, 14.
19. Roseberry, *Glenn Curtiss*, 288.
20. *Washington Post*, April 14, 1911.
21. Ibid.
22. Mitchell, "To Standardize Control of Army Planes," 2.
23. Morehouse, "Rexford M. Smith," 2.
24. *Kansas City Star*, June 16, 1913.
25. *Washington Post*, May 19, 1911.
26. *Baltimore Sun*, July 7, 1911.
27. Ibid., November 12, 1954.
28. *Washington Post*, May 23, 1911.
29. Ibid.
30. Ibid., May 24, 1911.
31. Jannus, "Learning How to Fly," 624.
32. Antony Jannus to the Adjustable and Detachable Propeller Company, July 20, 1911. FAHSA.
33. *Aero*, April 6, 1912, 47; "Blanche Stuart Scott," Early Bird Questionnaire, 1952, FAHSA.

CHAPTER 4: NEW FACES, NEW PLACES

1. Woodcock, "Benoist," 1.
2. *United States Patent Gazette* 151 (December 14, 1909): 726.
3. Woodcock, "Benoist," 3.
4. Morriss, "An Early Bird Remembers," *Sportsman Pilot* 6 (May 15, 1935), 26.
5. Woodcock, "Benoist," 5.
6. "Eighty-Two American Pilots Licensed Up to the Close of 1911," *Aero*, January 20, 1912, 12.
7. John C. Henning to St. Petersburg Chamber of Commerce, 1952.
8. Beech, "In the Slip Stream," 345.
9. Orville Wright to Wilbur Wright, July 10, 1908. U.S. National Air and Space Museum, Washington, D.C.
10. "Benoist Undismayed by $20,000 Fire," *Aero*, October 28, 1911, 82.

11. *St. Louis Globe-Democrat*, October 21, 1911.

12. *St. Louis Post-Dispatch*, November 2, 1911.

13. Benoist "Safety First" Airboats and Aeroplanes Catalog, 1916.

14. *Aero*, October 28, 1911, 8.

15. *St. Louis Post-Dispatch*, September 1, 1915.

16. Edward Korn to Gay Blair White, September 8, 1952.

17. *Detroit News*, September 18, 1913.

18. *St. Petersburg Times*, May 31, 1955.

19. "James D. Smith Story," n.d. FAHSA.

20. Edward Korn to Gay Blair White, January 8, 1953.

21. *Aero*, February 3, 1912, 249.

22. Benoist Flying Boats and Hydro-Aeroplanes Catalog, 1912.

23. "Fliers Busy at Kinloch Field," *Aero*, February 3, 1912, 29.

24. Edward Korn to Gay Blair White, January 8, 1953.

25. "Jannus in a Benoist Makes Record," 160.

26. "Jannus Qualifies for His License," *Aero*, December 9, 1911, 202.

27. *St. Louis Post-Dispatch*, December 3, 1911, 2.

28. "Ward Defeats Jannus in Race," *Aero*, April 6, 1912, 25.

CHAPTER 5: LIKE A CRAZY ARROW

1. "1912 Headless Benoist Biplane Described," *Aero*, January 27, 1912, 335.

2. Jannus, "Aeroplaning Unawares," 152.

3. Ibid.

4. "16 Passengers Carried in One Day," *Aero*, January 27, 1912, 342.

5. Lomax, *Women of the Air*, 37.

6. "Tape Recorded Interview with Matilde Moisant," Columbia University Oral History Collection.

7. McIntyre, "Odyssey of the Flyer," 47.

8. J. D. Smith to Gay Blair White, July 18, 1962.

9. The rebuilt and restored Benoist Model XII is at the Smithsonian Institution's National Air and Space Museum, Paul E. Garber Facility.

10. Edward A. Korn to Gay Blair White, January 6, 1953.

11. Gurney, *Chronology of World Aviation*, 15.

12. Jannus, "Dropping a Man and Parachute from an Airplane," 44.

13. *St. Louis Post-Dispatch*, March 2, 1912.

14. Ibid.

15. "Parachute Jump from Aeroplane Is Successful," *Aero*, March 9, 1912, 1.

16. *Aero*, March 9, 1912, 471.

17. *St. Louis Globe-Democrat*, March 2, 1912.

18. Thomas W. Benoist to the Editor of *Aero*, April 27, 1912.

19. *St. Louis Post-Dispatch*, February 13, 1912.

20. "James D. Smith Story," 5.

21. Bell, "Parachute Dropping from Aeroplanes," 208.

22. *St. Louis Post-Dispatch*, February 18, 1912.
23. Russell Froelich Oral History.
24. "Kinloch Sees Tractor's Safety," *Aero*, June 1, 1912, 222.
25. *St. Louis Post-Dispatch*, May 14, 1912.
26. Contract Between Frank M. Bell, John W. Eclaire, and Wood C. Lineback, May 22, 1912.
27. Jannus and Benoist Patent Approval, U.S. Patent Number 1,053,182, February 18, 1913.
28. "Makes Parachute Jump from Plane to Sea," *Aero*, April 27, 1912, 2.
29. *St. Louis Post-Dispatch*, April 29, 1912.
30. Ibid., May 14, 1912.
31. "Inexperience Proves Fatal," *Aero*, May 18, 1912, 174.
32. Edward Korn to Gay Blair White, September 25, 1952.
33. "Kinloch Has Quiet Week," *Aero*, May 25, 1912, 202.
34. *Collier's Weekly*, November 9, 1912.
35. *St. Louis Post-Dispatch*, July 16, 1912.
36. Grahame-White, "The World's Airmen," 7.

CHAPTER 6: HIGH-FLYING SUCCESS

1. Retired Colonel Frank R. Lang to Christopher C. Magrath, November 20, 1953.
2. *St. Louis Post-Dispatch*, June 5, 1912.
3. Beatty, *Cradle of American Aviation*, 27.
4. Gurney, *Chronology of World Aviation*, 12.
5. *St. Louis Post-Dispatch*, July 22, 1912.
6. Ibid., July 15, 1912.
7. Advertising Circular by the Benoist Company, 1912.
8. *Chicago Daily Tribune*, September 12, 1912.
9. Ibid., September 9, 1912.
10. Roseberry, *Glenn Curtiss*, 42.
11. *Chicago Daily Tribune*, September 12, 1912.
12. Ibid., September 13, 1912.
13. "Great Flying Seen at Cicero Meet," *Aero and Hydro*, September 21, 1912, 539.
14. *Chicago Daily Tribune*, September 14, 1912.
15. *New York Times*, September 15, 1912.
16. "Great Flying Seen at Cicero Meet," *Aero and Hydro*, September 21, 1912, 540.
17. *Aero and Hydro*, September 28, 1912, 558.
18. Morehouse, "Flying Pioneers of Aviation," 207.
19. "Great Flying Seen at Cicero Meet," *Aero and Hydro*, September 21, 1912, 538.
20. Friedlander and Gurney, *Higher, Faster, and Farther*, 300.

21. *New York Times*, September 23, 1912.
22. Benoist Advertising Circular, 1912.
23. Glenn L. Martin to Gay Blair White, June 4, 1952.
24. *Chicago Daily Tribune*, September 22, 1912.
25. Ibid., September 20, 1912.
26. Ibid., September 19, 1912.
27. Ibid., September 14, 1912.
28. Ibid., September 21, 1912.
29. *St. Louis Post-Dispatch*, November 17, 1912.
30. Ibid., September 22, 1912.
31. "Hydro Goes Up Mississippi 72 Miles," *Aero and Hydro*, October 12, 1912, 22.
32. *St. Louis Post-Dispatch*, October 13, 1912.
33. *Aero and Hydro*, October 26, 1912, 69.
34. *St. Louis Post-Dispatch*, October 20, 1912.
35. *Aero and Hydro*, November 2, 1912, 82.

CHAPTER 7: THE GREAT RIVERS FLIGHT

1. "Hugh Robinson Joins Benoist Co.," *Aero and Hydro*, November 9, 1912, 108.
2. "Aviator and Builder," *Aero*, November 11, 1911, 112.
3. "Jannus Ready for Long Hydro Trip," *Aero and Hydro*, November 9, 1912, 108.
4. Christy Magrath to Gay Blair White, September 12, 1953.
5. "James D. Smith Story," 10.
6. *Houston Chronicle*, December 17, 1948.
7. John C. Henning Jr. to the St. Petersburg Chamber of Commerce, August 10, 1952.
8. *St. Louis Globe-Democrat*, August 14, 1953.
9. *St. Louis Post-Dispatch*, November 7, 1912.
10. *St. Louis Times*, October 24, 1912.
11. *Omaha Nebraska News*, November 7, 1912.
12. Ibid., November 6, 1912.
13. Jannus, "From Omaha to New Orleans by Hydroaeroplane," 22.
14. Ibid.
15. *Aero and Hydro*, November 16, 1912, 2.
16. James D. Smith diary.
17. Ibid.
18. *St. Louis Post-Dispatch*, November 21, 1912.
19. Ibid.
20. James D. Smith diary.
21. *St. Louis Post-Dispatch*, November 17, 1912.

22. "Jannus Reaches St. Louis on Long Hydro Trip," *Aero and Hydro*, November 23, 1912, 144.

23. "Complete Time Table of the Cruise," *Aero and Hydro*, December 28, 1912, 236.

24. "Jannus Reaches St. Louis on Long Hydro Trip," *Aero and Hydro*, November 23, 1912, 144.

25. Ibid.

26. Instructions for Installing and Operation, Roberts Marine Motors, n.d., 6.

27. *St. Louis Post-Dispatch*, November 21, 1912.

28. "Activity at the Flying Fields and Hydro Havens," *Aero and Hydro*, November 30, 1912, 167.

29. *St. Louis Globe-Democrat*, November 28, 1913.

30. *Fly Magazine*, January 1913, 20.

31. James D. Smith diary.

32. Provenzo, "Thomas W. Benoist," 97.

33. *Memphis Commercial Appeal*, December 3, 1912.

34. James D. Smith scrapbook.

35. James D. Smith diary.

36. Ibid.

37. Ibid.

38. Gurney, *Chronology of World Aviation*, 17.

39. *New Orleans Times Democrat*, December 17, 1912.

40. "Jannus Makes World Record in Benoist Plane," *Aero and Hydro*, December 28, 1912, 235.

41. James D. Smith diary.

42. "Among the Aviators," *Aero and Hydro*, January 4, 1913, 256.

43. James D. Smith diary.

44. "Jannus Arrives at Memphis; Covers 1,159 Miles," *Aero and Hydro*, December 7, 1912, 179.

45. Ibid., 214.

46. "Jannus Arrives at Memphis; Covers 1,159 Miles," *Aero and Hydro*, December 7, 1912, 179; Boyne, *Smithsonian Book of Flight*, 69.

47. Jannus, "Touring with Hydraeroplanes," 23.

48. "Jannus Makes World Record in Benoist Plane," *Aero and Hydro*, December 28, 1912, 235.

49. "Jannus Completes Long Flight in Benoist Hydro," *Fly Magazine*, January 1913, 19.

CHAPTER 8: BARNSTORMING

1. Noel, "Many Opportunities for Good Fliers," 40.

2. Benoist Aeroplane Company to Henry A. Phelps, August 21, 1913.

3. "Demand for Flights Will Be Greater in 1912," *Aero*, October 7, 1911, 6.

4. Noel, "Many Opportunities for Good Fliers," 40.

5. *Aero and Hydro*, July 13, 1912, 342.

6. *St. Louis Post-Dispatch*, June 22, 1912.

7. Ibid., June 23, 1912.

8. *Aero and Hydro*, July 27, 1912, 281.

9. Ibid., August 24, 1912, 464.

10. Poster Advertising Jannus's Flights at St. Cloud, Minnesota, August 7, 1912.

11. Poster Advertising the Memphis Fair, September 1912.

12. *Memphis Reveille*, September 5, 1912.

13. Poster Advertising Union City Fair, Union City, Tennessee, September 1912.

14. Poster Advertising Weakley County Fair, October 1912.

15. Benoist Aircraft Company advertising circular, 1912.

16. Montgomery County Agricultural and Mechanical Society to Thomas W. Benoist, August 1912.

17. *Montgomery Standard*, August 23, 1912.

18. Studer, *Sky Storming Yankee*, 201.

19. Ibid.

20. A. B. Chalk to Gay Blair White, November 24, 1953.

21. "He Has Carried Passengers Without Accident for Twenty-Three Years," *U.S. Air Services*, June 1940, 25.

22. *American Air Mail Catalogue*, 1947.

23. Bilsteen, *Flight in America*, 17.

24. Thomas W. Benoist to James D. Smith, March 9, 1915.

25. *Aero and Hydro*, April 12, 1913, 28.

CHAPTER 9: A FALL FROM GRACE

1. *St. Louis Post-Dispatch*, January 5, 1913.

2. Gurney, *Chronology of World Aviation*, 12.

3. *Aero and Hydro*, December 21, 1912, 214.

4. Knott, *American Flying Boat*, 11.

5. Christy Magrath to Gay Blair White, October 7, 1952; Villard, *Contact!* 167.

6. Russell Froelich Oral History.

7. Casey, *Curtiss*, 111, 102.

8. Mondey, ed., *International Encyclopedia of Aviation*, 302. Henri Fabre's Hydravion is recognized as the first successful float plane; see Crouch, *Dream of Wings*, 131.

9. "The Benoist Flying Boat," *Aeronautics*, January 1913, 16.

10. "Flying Boats Begin to Arrive in Chicago," *Aero and Hydro*, June 14, 1913, 205.

11. Casey, *Curtiss*, 42.

12. "Benoist Boat Flies on Mississippi," *Aero and Hydro*, March 15, 1913, 430.

13. *St. Louis Post-Dispatch*, February 15, 1913.

14. Harris, *First to Fly*, 286.

15. "Benoist Boat Flies on Mississippi," *Aero and Hydro*, March 15, 1913, 430.

16. Woodcock, "Benoist," 8.

17. Morehouse, "Flight from the Water," 176–77.

18. "More Cruise Entries Assured," *Aero and Hydro*, March 22, 1913, 453.

19. "Duluth Sportsman Buys Benoist Boat," *Aero and Hydro*, May 17, 1913, 126.

20. Gertrude B. Fiertig to the City of St. Petersburg, Public Information Office; *Aero and Hydro*, July 25, 1914, 206.

21. Jannus, "Teaching Flying Boat Operation," 348.

22. "Jannus Goes to Duluth with Boat," *Aero and Hydro*, June 28, 1913, 246.

23. *Aero and Hydro*, May 17, 1913, 126.

24. "General Rules Governing the *Aero and Hydro* Great Lakes Reliability Cruise," *Aero and Hydro*, March 29, 1913, 471.

25. "Jannus in Hydro Flies Fast 248 Miles," *Aero and Hydro*, May 31, 1913, 167.

26. *St. Louis Post-Dispatch*, May 25, 1913.

27. L. A. "Jack" Vilas to Gay Blair White, July 26, 1952.

28. Knott, *American Flying Boat*, 15.

29. J. B. R. Verplanck to Gay Blair White, June 27, 1953.

30. Morehouse, "Flight From the Water," 176.

31. "Air Pilots Are in Misfortune," clipping from unidentified newspaper, J. D. Smith scrapbook.

32. Thomas Wesley Benoist to James D. Smith, March 9, 1915.

33. *Aeronautics*, September 1913.

34. Tom W. Benoist to J. B. R. Verplanck, July 22, 1913.

35. Edward Korn to Gay Blair White, 1953.

CHAPTER 10: FLYING BOATS ACROSS THE OCEAN

1. John C. Henning to Christy C. Magrath, August 12, 1952.

2. *St. Louis Globe Democrat*, May 5, 1913.

3. Beaty, *The Water Jump*, 112.

4. "Antony Jannus Will Try Trans-Ocean Flight," *Aero and Hydro*, May 10, 1913, 107.

5. *St. Louis Post-Dispatch*, December 5, 1912.

6. Frank Orndorff to Roberts Motor Company, May 25, 1913.

7. Roberts Motor Company to Frank Orndorff, April 28, 1913.

8. Frank Orndorff to Roberts Motor Company, May 1913.

9. Roscoe, *On the Seas and in the Skies*, 48–49.

10. Villard, *Contact!*, 245.

11. "Antony Jannus Will Try Trans-Ocean Flight" *Aero and Hydro*, May 10, 1913, 107.
12. Delear, *Famous First Flights Across the Atlantic*, 190.
13. Brashear, "Early Birdman."
14. Morehouse, "Flight from the Water," 176.
15. "Jannus to Fly Florida to New York," *Aero and Hydro*, February 28, 1914, 280.
16. *New York Times*, October 13, 1913.
17. *Collier's Weekly*, November 1, 1913, 15.
18. "Fliers Found New York Circuit Severe Test," *Aero and Hydro*, October 25, 1913, 39.
19. *New York Times*, October 14, 1913.
20. Ibid., October 16, 1913.
21. *Aero and Hydro*, October 25, 1913, 248.
22. James D. Smith diary.
23. Woodcock, "Benoist," 12.
24. *St. Louis Star*, October 17, 1913; James D. Smith diary.
25. *St. Louis Post-Dispatch*, October 26, 1913.
26. "New Benoist Tractor Out," *Aero and Hydro*, October 4, 1913, 10.
27. *Aero Digest*, December 1929.

CHAPTER 11: A NEW ENTERPRISE

1. Brown, *Florida's Aviation History*, 14.
2. Woodhouse, "Growing Wings," 14.
3. *Aero and Hydro*, January 10, 1914, 178.
4. *St. Petersburg Daily Times*, February 23, 1912.
5. *New York Times*, October 14, 1913.
6. White, "First Airline," 5.
7. Ibid.
8. *St. Petersburg Daily Times*, December 7, 1913.
9. Ibid.
10. Ibid.
11. *St. Petersburg Independent*, February 16, 1914.
12. *St. Petersburg Daily Times*, December 21, 1913.
13. Allwood, *Great Exhibition*, 110.
14. Fansler, *Aero Digest*, December 1929.
15. *St. Petersburg Daily Times*, December 9, 1913.
16. White, "First Airline," 5.
17. Clipping from an unidentified newspaper, J. D. Smith scrapbook.
18. *St. Petersburg Daily Times*, December 10, 1913.
19. *St. Petersburg Evening Independent*, December 26, 1913.
20. *St. Petersburg Daily Times*, December 30, 1913.
21. Fansler, *Aero Digest*, December 1929.

22. Ibid.

23. *St. Petersburg Daily Times*, December 31, 1913.

24. Fansler, *Aero Digest*, December 1929.

25. Reinhardt N. Ausmus to Paul E. Garber, February 15, 1967.

26. J. D. Smith scrapbook.

27. White, *World's First Airline*, 16.

CHAPTER 12: AN AIRLINE IS BORN

1. *St. Petersburg Evening Independent*, December 30, 1913.

2. *Tampa Morning Tribune*, January 1, 1914.

3. J. D. Smith scrapbook.

4. *St. Petersburg Daily Times*, January 1, 1914.

5. Mondey, ed., *International Encyclopedia of Aviation*, 228; Davies, *Lufthansa*, 2.

6. *St. Petersburg Daily Times*, January 2, 1914.

7. Ibid., December 30, 1913.

8. Ibid.

9. Fansler, *Aero Digest*, December 1929.

10. *St. Petersburg Daily Times*, January 2, 1914.

11. *Aero and Hydro*, July 27, 1912, 381.

12. *St. Petersburg Daily Times*, January 3, 1914.

13. Ibid., January 2, 1914.

14. Jannus, "Benoist Airline Operation at St. Petersburg," 41.

15. *St. Petersburg Daily Times*, January 6, 1914.

16. Ibid., January 7, 1914.

17. Ibid.

18. Christy C. Magrath to Gay Blair White, July 14, 1952.

CHAPTER 13: BUREAUCRATS AND HAMS

1. *St. Petersburg Daily Times*, January 7, 1914.

2. *Aero and Hydro*, March 7, 1914, 111.

3. *St. Petersburg Independent*, February 16, 1914.

4. H. L. Whitney to James D. Calhoun, January 2, 1914.

5. James D. Calhoun, Deputy Collector in Charge, Tampa, to the Collector of Customs, Jacksonville, Florida, January 2, 1914.

6. Collector of Customs, Treasury Department, United States Customs Service, Jacksonville, Florida, to the Secretary of Commerce, Washington, D.C., January 5, 1914.

7. Antony Jannus to Department of Commerce, Washington, D.C., January 21, 1914.

8. E. F. Sweet, Acting Secretary of Commerce, to Antony Jannus, January 28, 1914.

9. Supervising Inspector General, Department of Commerce, Steam Boat Inspection Service, Washington, to the Secretary of Commerce, February 7, 1914.

10. Supervising Inspector General, Department of Commerce, Steamboat Inspection Service, Washington, D.C., to the Secretary of Commerce, February 7, 1914.

11. Office of the Solicitor, Department of Commerce, Washington, D.C., Albert Lee Thurman, Solicitor, February 17, 1914.

12. *St. Petersburg Daily Times*, January 9, 1914.

13. Handbill produced by the Hefner Grocery Co., St. Petersburg Museum of History Archives.

14. *St. Petersburg Daily Times*, January 7, 1914.

15. Ibid.

16. Ibid., January 21, 1914.

17. *Aero and Hydro*, January 24, 1914, 214.

18. Office of the Department of Publicity, City of St. Petersburg to John G. Shea, January 4, 1952; Hagerty, "A Flying School That Made History."

19. *St. Petersburg Daily Times*, January 22, 1914.

20. Casey, *Curtiss*, 166.

21. Fansler, *Aero Digest*, December 1929.

22. Casey, *Curtiss*, 166.

23. L. Chauncey Brown to Gay Blair White, August 28, 1960.

24. *St. Petersburg Evening Independent*, January 18, 1930.

25. *St. Petersburg Daily Times*, October 20, 1914.

26. *Tampa Tribune*, December 31, 1980.

27. *St. Petersburg Daily Times*, January 10, 1914.

28. *Aeronautics*, September 30, 1914, 19.

29. Questionnaire by Mrs. Percival Fansler, May 1952.

30. *St. Petersburg Daily Times*, February 18, 1914.

31. Percival Elliott Fansler to U.S. Weather Bureau, Tampa, Florida, January 21, 1914.

32. W. J. Bennett to Chief, U.S. Weather Bureau, Washington, D.C., February 18, 1914.

33. Chief of Bureau to W. J. Bennett, Local Forecaster, Weather Bureau, Tampa, Florida, January 28, 1914.

34. Alan F. Bonnalie, *Air Transportation*, 2.

35. H. P. Christofferson to G. B. White, July 20, 1952.

36. Will D. Parker to G. B. White, November 6, 1952.

37. U.S. Department of the Interior, Office of Education in Washington, Radio Division, with the Cooperation of the Smithsonian Institution, *Early Wings for Commerce*, January 1 and 8, 1939, p. 2.

38. F. R. Bannister to Mr. Woolford, November 13, 1953.

39. J. M. Lassiter letter, April 1, 1954.

40. James M. Eaton to Gay Blair White, September 1952.
41. Rose Bryant Saunders to Edward C. Hoffman Sr., August 7, 1993.
42. United States Patent Office, Safety Device for Elevators, Patent No. 604,361, dated May 24, 1898.
43. White, *World's First Airline*, 70.
44. Saunders, "Lost Bell."
45. *Florida Aviation Historical Society Newsletter*, May 1983.
46. Mary E. Fansler to Gay Blair White, June 18, 1952.
47. Fansler, *Aero Digest*, December 1929, 263.
48. Percival Elliott Fansler to the St. Petersburg Board of Trade, February 9, 1914.
49. White, "First Airline," 5.
50. Percival Elliott Fansler to the St. Petersburg Board of Trade, March 31, 1914.
51. Jannus, "Benoist Airline Operation at St. Petersburg," 41.
52. Brown, *Florida's Aviation History*, 137.
53. *St. Petersburg Daily Times*, March 18, 1914.
54. Ibid., March 4, 1914.
55. Ibid., April 1, 1914.
56. Ibid.
57. Ibid., April 8, 1914.
58. Ibid., April 26, 1914.
59. Ibid., April 8, 1914.
60. Ibid., April 28, 1914.
61. Fansler, *Aero Digest*, December 1929, 263.
62. A. G. Threadgill, Acting Assistant Executive Director, United States Post Office Department, to Gay Blair White, September 12, 1952. According to Threadgill, there were no records of correspondence with Fansler.
63. Fansler, *Aero Digest*, December 1929, 263.
64. *Aero and Hydro*, October 31, 1914, 40.
65. *St. Petersburg Daily Times*, May 20, 1914.
66. *Aero and Hydro*, August 8, 1914, 239.

CHAPTER 14: JANNUS BROTHERS AVIATION

1. *St. Petersburg Daily Times*, April 22, 1914.
2. Associated Press Dispatch, March 3, 1914.
3. Tony Jannus to Henry Woodhouse, August 31, 1914.
4. *Aero and Hydro*, August 8, 1914, 239.
5. Clipping from *Paducah News Democrat*, J. D. Smith scrapbook.
6. *Paducah News Democrat*, July 1914.
7. James Pine, Second Lieutenant, United States Revenue-Cutter Service, to the Commanding Officer, Treasury Department, U.S. Revenue-Cutter Service, Form 2038, July 4, 1914.

8. Antony H. Jannus to the Secretary of Commerce, Washington, D.C., August 8, 1914; James Pine to the Collector of Customs, Cleveland, Ohio, July 22, 1914; Affidavit sworn by Antony H. Jannus, August 8, 1914; A. L. Thurman, Secretary of Commerce, to Antony H. Jannus, November 19, 1914.

9. Edna Dagmar Hansen to Gay Blair White, June 30, May 9, 1952.

10. Hansen to White, May 9, February 6, 1952.

11. *Aero and Hydro*, August 22, 1914, 204.

12. Hansen to White, February 6, 1952.

13. *St. Petersburg Daily Times*, December 30, 1948.

14. Reinhardt N. Ausmus to Gay Blair White, n.d.

15. *Aero and Hydro*, August 22, 1914, 264.

16. "Chalmers Convention Doings," In-House Publication, 1914.

17. Jas. V. Martin Early Bird Questionnaire, August 30, 1952.

18. *Aero and Hydro*, August 8, 1914, 239.

19. *Aeronautics*, September 1914, 91.

20. "Tony" Jannus Letterhead.

21. J. D. Smith scrapbook.

22. Ibid.

23. *Baltimore Sun*, November 1, 1914.

24. Ibid., November 6, 1914.

25. "Santa Claus Aviates," clipping from unidentified newspaper, J. D. Smith scrapbook.

26. "Jannus Building New Flying Boat," *Aeronautics*, October 15, 1914, 105.

27. Ibid.

28. Jannus Brothers Advertising Circular, Winter 1915.

29. "Belated Tars Use Aeroplane to Reach Supply Ship Glacier When Left by Liberty Boat," clipping from unidentified newspaper, J. D. Smith scrapbook.

30. "Early Airboat Mystery Unravels," *Florida Aviation Historical Society Newsletter* 3 (May 1982): 1.

31. "Aviator Smith Here on Way to Florida for Work," clipping from unidentified newspaper, J. D. Smith scrapbook.

32. *St. Petersburg Daily Times*, November 24, 1914.

33. Ibid., January 21, 1915.

34. Ibid., January 29, 1915.

35. Ibid., February 2, 1915.

36. Ibid., February 26, 1915.

37. *St. Petersburg Evening Independent*, February 26, 1915.

38. *St. Petersburg Daily Times*, February 26, 1915.

39. Tom W. Benoist to Jay D. Smith, March 9, 1915.

40. *St. Petersburg Daily Times*, February 26, 1915.

41. *St. Petersburg Times*, January 1, 1982.
42. *St. Petersburg Daily Times*, February 28, 1915.
43. Ibid., March 7, 1915.
44. L. E. McLain to Roberts Motor Co., May 15, 1915.
45. "The Jannus Flying Boat," *Flight*, June 25, 1915, 456.
46. W. H. Roberts to Tony Jannus, January 2, 1915.
47. *Baltimore Evening Sun*, April 28, 1915.
48. Mrs. Edgar Coursen to Gay Blair White, November 6, September 27, 1952.
49. Tony Jannus to Edna Hansen, April 30, 1915.

CHAPTER 15: A RUSSIAN TEST PILOT

1. Tom Benoist to W. H. Burke, the Roberts Motor Manufacturing Company, Sandusky, Ohio, June 12, 1915.
2. Casey, *Curtiss*, 2, 214.
3. "Curtiss Building Giant Aeroplanes for Allies," *Aeronautics*, July 15, 1915, 8.
4. "Curtiss Plant Rushed," *Aeronautics*, June 15, 1915, 101.
5. "Curtiss Building Giant Aeroplanes for Allies," *Aeronautics*, July 15, 1915, 8.
6. Gibbs-Smith, *Flight Through the Ages*, 110.
7. *New York Times*, September 6, 1915.
8. Ibid., September 9, 1915.
9. Tony Jannus to Edna Hansen, August 1915.
10. "Curtiss Making Air Dreadnaught," *Aeronautics*, June 30, 1915, 119.
11. Nell Coursen to Gay Blair White, September 27, 1952.
12. John P. Tarbox to Gay Blair White, September 15, 1952.
13. Andrei Alexandrov to Thomas Reilly, January 12, 1994.
14. Tom W. Benoist to Jay D. Smith, March 9, 1915.
15. Casey, *Curtiss*, 193.
16. Bowers, *Curtiss Aircraft*, 143.
17. Molson and Taylor, *Canadian Aircraft Since 1909*, 211.
18. Casey, *Curtiss*, 195.
19. Gay Blair White to Leslie E. Neville, William E. Valk, Carl Adams, Joseph S. Bennett, and Henry Kleckler, 1952.
20. John P. Tarbox to Gay Blair White, September 8, 1952.
21. Bowers, *Curtiss Aircraft*, 55.
22. Casey, *Curtiss*, 197.
23. Thomas L. Howe, of Spence, Hotchkiss, Parker & Duryee, to Jay D. Smith, March 7, 1949.
24. Stenographic Record, United States of America—v—Curtiss Aeroplane Co., et al., February 26, 1949, 4.

25. Morehouse, "The Flying Pioneers—Charles C. Witmer," 44.
26. Stenographic Record, United States of America—v—Curtiss Aeroplane Co., et al., March 5, 1949, p. 99.
27. Senior Lieutenant Ivan Ivanovich Stakhovsky to an unknown officer, October 22, 1915.
28. Senior Lieutenant A. A. Tuchkov, Commander of the Aeronautical Department of the Russian Naval General Staff to Lieutenant V. V. Utgoff.
29. Stenographic Record, United States of America—v—Curtiss Aeroplane Co., et al., March 5, 1949, p. 109.
30. "Anthony Jannus Returns from Russia," *Aerial Age Weekly*, March 27, 1916, 57.
31. *Baltimore News*, November 2, 1916.
32. Andrei Alexandrov to Edward C. Hoffman, May 21, 1993.
33. "Russian Defeats Due to Lack of Aeroplanes," *Flying*, September 1915, 671.
34. Lieutenant G. V. Piotrovsky to Senior Lieutenant I. I. Stakhovsky, January 9, 1916.
35. "Anthony Jannus Returns from Russia," *Aerial Age Weekly*, March 27, 1916, 57.
36. Ibid.
37. "Antony Jannus, Curtiss Representative in Russia," *Aerial Age Weekly*, April 10, 1916, 112.
38. *Washington Post*, April 15, 1916.
39. *Chicago Daily Tribune*, November 2, 1916.
40. "Anthony (Tony) Jannus Is Dead," *Aviation*, November 10, 1916, 263.
41. Stenographic Record, United States of America—v—Curtiss Aeroplane Co., et al., February 26, 1949, and March 5, 1949.
42. Andrei Alexandrov to Edward C. Hoffman, May 21, 1993.
43. Stenographic Record, United States of America—v—Curtiss Aeroplane Co., et al., February 26, 1949, 306.
44. Tony Jannus to Curtiss Aeroplane, July 14, 1916.
45. Lieutenant Piotrovsky to Senior Lieutenant I. I. Stakhovsky, Commander of the Black Sea Fleet Aviation, December 12, 1915.
46. Antony Jannus to Glenn Curtiss, June 23, 1916.
47. Antony Jannus to Lieutenant Commander A. A. Tuchkov, June 23, 1916.

CHAPTER 16: A MYSTERIOUS ENDING

1. Christopher Magrath to Gay Blair White, September 12, 1953.
2. Lester S. Jayson, special attorney, Department of Justice, to special agent in charge Federal Bureau of Investigation, December 1, 1949. U.S. Department of Justice, Federal Bureau of Investigation, Washington, D.C. Obtained under the Freedom of Information Act, FOIPA no. 381990, February 22, 1996.

3. Casey, *Curtiss,* 197–201.
4. Raymond V. Morris to Chauncey Brown, February 9, 1917.
5. A. V. Kolchak, Commander of the Russian Black Sea Fleet, to Russian Naval Minister, October 12, 1916.
6. Russian Naval Attaché in Washington, D.C., to Naval General Staff, Petrograd, October 22, 1916.
7. I. I. Stakhovsky, Commander of the Black Sea Fleet Aviation, to Naval General Staff, Petrograd, October 27, 1916.
8. "Podporuchik" is a Russian military rank.
9. Findings of the Russian Aviation Committee, November 1, 1916.
10. Andrei O. Alexandrov to Thomas Reilly, February 26, 1994.
11. Stenographic Record, United States of America—v—Curtiss Aeroplane Co., et al., March 9, 1949, 219.
12. Ibid., February, March, and April 1949.
13. Ibid., February 26, 1949, 21.
14. Ibid., 118–19.
15. Ibid., 125–26.

CHAPTER 17: STREETCARS AND CIGARETTES

1. Tom W. Benoist to Jay D. Smith, March 9, 1915.
2. Charles Benoist Oral History, September 2, 1952.
3. Reinhardt Ausmus Speech.
4. Fansler, *Aero Digest,* December 1929, 56.
5. Reinhardt Ausmus scrapbook.
6. *St. Louis Post-Dispatch,* August 5, 1913.
7. State of Ohio, Bureau of Vital Statistics, Certificate of Death, File No. 4541, for Thomas W. Benoist.
8. Louis A. Bernower to Manager, Chamber of Commerce, St. Petersburg, November 21, 1953.
9. Reinhardt Ausmus scrapbook.
10. Morriss, "Early Bird Remembers," 26.
11. Lincke, *Jenny Was No Lady,* 135–48.
12. Logan T. McMenemy to Gay Blair White, October 21, 1952.
13. Ibid.
14. Arthur L. Richmond to Gay Blair White, September 2, 1952.
15. Mrs. Edgar Coursen to Gay Blair White, September 27, 1952.
16. Gay Blair White to Ross Windom, City Manager, City of St. Petersburg, July 21, 1952.
17. Gay Blair White to Judge Richard A. Miller, County Court Judge, September 6, 1952.
18. *St. Petersburg Times,* March 12, 1963.
19. Friedlander and Gurney, *Higher, Faster, and Farther,* 295.

Bibliography

BOOKS

Allwood, John. *The Great Exhibition*. London: Studio Vista, 1977.

Beatty, Ken. *The Cradle of American Aviation: The National Aviation Field, College Park, MD*. Hagerstown, Md.: HPB, 1976.

Beaty, David. *The Water Jump*. New York: Harper and Row, 1976.

Bilsteen, Roger. *Flight in America, 1900–1983*. Baltimore: Johns Hopkins University Press, 1984.

Bonnalie, Alan F. *Air Transportation*. Oakland, Calif.: Boeing School of Aeronautics, 1938.

Bowers, Peter M. *Curtiss Aircraft, 1907–1947*. London: Putnam, 1979.

Boyne, Walter J. *The Smithsonian Book of Flight for Young People*. New York: Atheneum, 1982.

Brown, Warren J. *Florida's Aviation History: The First One Hundred Years*. Largo, Fla.: Aero-Medical Consultants, 1994.

Casey, Louis S. *Curtiss: The Hammondsport Era, 1907–1915*. New York: Crown, 1981.

Cooper, Jo, ed. *Pioneer Pilot*. Pasadena, Calif.: Converse, 1992.

Crouch, Tom D. *A Dream of Wings: Americans and the Airplane, 1875–1905*. New York: Norton, 1981.

Davies, R. E. G. *Airlines of the United States Since 1914*. Washington, D.C.: Smithsonian Institution Press, 1972.

———. *A History of the World's Airlines*. 2d ed. London: Oxford University Press, 1967.

———. *Lufthansa: An Airline and Its Aircraft*. New York: Orion, 1991.

Delear, Frank J. *Famous First Flights Across the Atlantic*. New York: Dodd, Mead, 1979.

Ferris, Paul. *The House of Northcliffe: A Biography of an Empire*. New York: World, 1972.

Friedlander, Mark P. Jr., and Gene Gurney. *Higher, Faster, and Farther.* New York: Morrow, 1973.

Fuller, Walter P. *St. Petersburg and Its People.* St. Petersburg, Fla.: Great Outdoors Publishing Co., 1972.

Gibbs-Smith, Charles H. *Flight Through the Ages.* New York: Thomas Y. Crowell, 1974.

Green, William. *Flying Boats.* Garden City, N.Y.: Doubleday, 1962.

Gurney, Gene. *A Chronology of World Aviation.* New York: Watts, 1965.

Harris, Sherwood. *The First to Fly: Aviation's Pioneer Days.* New York: Simon and Schuster, 1970.

Hess, Ian V. *Guns and How They Work.* New York: Everest House, 1979.

Horgan, James J. *The History of Aviation in St. Louis.* 2d ed. St. Louis: Patrice Press, 1990.

Hudson, James J. *Hostile Skies: A Combat History of the American Air Service in World War I.* Syracuse: Syracuse University Press, 1968.

Jablonski, Edward. *Man with Wings.* Garden City, N.Y.: Doubleday, 1980.

Johnson, Robert U., and Clarence C. Buel, eds. *Battles and Leaders of the Civil War.* 1884. Rpt., New York: T. Yoseloff, 1956.

Knott, Richard C. *The American Flying Boat.* Annapolis, Md.: Naval Institute Press, 1979.

Lazarus, William C. *Wings in the Sun.* Orlando: Tyn Cobb's Florida Press, 1951.

Lincke, Jack R. *Jenny Was No Lady: The Story of the JN–4D.* New York: Norton, 1970.

Lomax, Judy. *Women of the Air.* New York: Dodd, Mead, 1987.

Magoun, F. A., and E. Hodgins. *A History of Aircraft.* New York: McGraw-Hill, 1931.

Molson, K. M., and H. A. Taylor. *Canadian Aircraft Since 1909.* Toronto: Putnam, 1962.

Mondey, David, ed. *The International Encyclopedia of Aviation.* New York: Crown, 1977.

Munson, Kenneth. *Flying Boats and Seaplanes Since 1910.* New York: Macmillan, 1971.

Oakes, Claudia M. *United States Women in Aviation Through World War I.* Washington, D.C.: Smithsonian Institution Press, 1978.

Roscoe, Theodore. *On the Seas and in the Skies.* New York: Hawthorne, 1970.

Roseberry, C. R. *Glenn Curtiss, Pioneer of Flight.* Garden City, N.Y.: Doubleday, 1972.

Smith, Henry Ladd. *Airways: The History of Commercial Aviation in the United States.* New York: Knopf, 1942.

Studer, Clara. *Sky Storming Yankee: The Life of Glenn Curtiss.* New York: Stackpole Sons, 1937.

Villard, Henry Serrano. *Contact! The Story of the Early Birds.* Washington, D.C.: Smithsonian Institution Press, 1978.

White, Gay Blair. *The World's First Airline: The St. Petersburg–Tampa Airboat Line.* Largo, Fla.: Aero Medical Consultants, 1984.

Young, Andrew D., and Eugene F. Provenzo Jr. *The History of the St. Louis Car Company, Quality Shops.* Berkeley: Howell-North Books, 1978.

ARTICLES

"Another Aviator Now Has National License." *Aeronautics* (October 30, 1914), 122.

Bane, Michael. "Bringing Back the Benoist." *Sky* (August 1983), 32–34.

Beech, A. C. "In the Slip Stream." *Aero and Hydro* (February 8, 1913), 345.

Bell, Frank Merrill. "Parachute Dropping from Aeroplanes." *Aero and Hydro* (June 14, 1913), 208.

Benoist, Tom W. "European Situation Great Aero Lessons to U.S." *Aero and Hydro* (September 19, 1914), 308.

"Benoist School Operated on Mississippi." *Aero and Hydro* (November 15, 1913).

Brashear, Lee. "Early Birdman." *St. Louis Globe-Democrat* (June 15, 1952).

"Bud Morriss in Review." *Chirp* (August 17, 1935), 9.

Burritt, R. E. "Tampa Honors Pilot Tony Jannus." *Florida Municipal Record* (November 1937), 212.

Castang, Viola. "It Happened 50 Years Ago." *Air Transportation* (Mid-January 1964), 20–24.

"Curtiss JN–4 Series." *World War I Aero* (February 1982).

"Dramatic Legislation Proposed." *Aero* (January 28, 1911), 72.

Dunn, Hampton. "The Inaugural Flight: 23 Minutes." *Florida Trend* (October 1966), 23.

"Entangled Skirt Kills Two." *Aero and Hydro* (June 21, 1913), 226.

Fansler, Percival Elliott. *Aero Digest* (December 1929).

Farrant, Don. "Jack Vilas' Record Flight." *Air Classics* (October 1975).

"First Parachute Landing from an Airplane." *American Aviation Historical Society Journal* (Summer 1964), 142–43.

"Fifty Years of St. Louis Through One Man's Camera." *Bulletin of the Missouri Historical Society* (October 1956), 64–65.

"Flying Machine and Airship Competitions at St. Louis." *American Magazine of Aeronautics* (October 1907), 8.

"Flying Machines and Florida." *Florida Trend* (October 1966), 20.

Fuller, Walter P. "Early Birds of Florida." *Florida Historical Quarterly* (July 1959), 63.

Gilpatrick, J. Guy. "The Slump in Aviation," *New York Times* (October 4, 1913), 12.

Glendening, Roger II. "Tony Jannus' New Year's Flight Made History." *St. Petersburg Times* (January 1, 1994), 6.

Glines, C. V. "Number 43: On Schedule." *Frontiers* (February 1985), 42–46.

"Golden Anniversary of Powered Flight." *Florida Aviation Bulletin* (February 13, 1953), 1.

Grahame-White, A. C. "The Coming of the Air-Man." *Collier's Weekly* (October 7, 1911), 23.

———. "The World's Airmen." *Collier's Weekly* (September 30, 1911), 7.

Green, Howard E. "First Commercial Flight." *National Aeronautics* (January 1939), 8.

Hagerty, Mahlon G. "A Flying School That Made History." *Tampa Tribune* (December 31, 1980), 25.

Hardie, George Jr. "The World's First Airline." *Vintage Airplane* (March 1984), 6–9.

Hawes, Leland. "Aviator's Career Wide-Ranging." *Tampa Tribune-Times*, Bay Life Section (December 26, 1993), 4.

———. "Gasparilla Is Time to Remember." *Tampa Tribune* (February 9, 1985), 2.

Hoffman, Edward C. "Benoist Type 14." *World War I Aero* 94 (April 1983), 22–27.

Horgan, James Jr. "Aeronautics at the World's Fair of 1904." *Missouri Historical Society Bulletin* 24 (April 1968), 215–46.

Hunt, Doris. "He Has Carried Passengers Without Accident for Twenty-Three Years." *U.S. Air Services* (June 1940), 25.

Jannus, Antony. "The Aeroplane Engine." *Aeronautics* (December 1910), 190–92.

———. "Aeroplaning Unawares." *Recreation* (April 1912), 152.

———. "Benoist Airline Operation at St. Petersburg." *Aero and Hydro* (April 25, 1914), 41.

———. "The Cure for Aviation." *Aeronautics* (November 1911), 149.

———. "Dropping a Man and Parachute from an Airplane." *Aero Club of America Bulletin* (May 1912), 44.

———. "Flight Progress About the Country." *Aeronautics* (January 1911), 21–22.

———. "From Omaha to New Orleans by Hydroaeroplane." *Flying* (January 1913), 22.

———. "Learning How to Fly, Hints from a Professional Aviator." *Scientific American* (June 1911), 624.

———. "Teaching Flying Boat Operation." *Aero and Hydro* (August 2, 1913), 348.

———. "Touring with Hydroaeroplanes." *Flying* (March 1913), 23.

Jannus, Antony, and W. Wilson Southard. "Washington Aeroplane Show." *Aeronautics* (April 1911), 139.

"Jannus Flight Was Genesis of Industry." *Tampa Tribune* (March 21, 1993), 1.

"Jannus in a Benoist Makes Record." *Aero* (November 25, 1911), 160.

Key, William C. "25 Years of Scheduled Air Transport." *Pegasus* (January 1952), 1–15.

Lambert, Major Albert Bond, and Major William B. Robertson. "Early History of Aeronautics in St. Louis." *Missouri Historical Society Collections* (June 1928), 237–55.

"Latham the Hero at Baltimore Meet." *Aero* (November 12, 1910), 7.

"Lawrence and Jannus Flying Boats." *World War I Aero* (August 1990), 33–39.

Magrath, Christy C. "Wings of Old Kinloch." *Public News* (Berkeley, Mo.) (June 1955), 2.

Mitchell, John A. "News and Gossip of the Nation's Capital." *Aero* (January 1911), 51.

———. "Rex Smith Biplane Highly Favored." *Aero* (April 1, 1911), 245.

———. "To Standardize Control of Army Planes." *Aero* (April 8, 1911), 2.

Molson, K. M. "Canadians at the Wright School." *American Aviation Historical Society Journal* 8 (Spring 1963), 40.

Morehouse, Harold E. "Charles C. Witmer." *American Aviation Historical Society Journal* 8 (Spring 1963), 42–43.

———. "Flight from the Water." *American Aviation Historical Society Journal* 9 (Fall 1964), 172.

———. "The Flying Pioneers of Aviation—Max T. Lillie." *American Aviation Historical Society Journal* 4 (Fall 1959), 207.

———. "Korn Brothers." *American Aviation Historical Society Journal* 6 (Summer 1961), 104.

———. "Rexford M. Smith, Early Plane Builder-Pilot." *American Aviation Historical Society Journal* (Spring 1963), 2.

———. "Rodger W. Jannus." *American Aviation Historical Society Journal* 14 (Spring 1969), 57.

———. "Walter E. Johnson." *American Aviation Historical Society Journal* 12 (1st Quarter 1967), 28–30.

Morriss, P. G. B. "An Early Bird Remembers." *Sportsman Pilot* (May 15, 1935), 26–29.

"No Nickels for Nellie." *Tampa Magazine* (March 1981), 7.

Noel, E. Percy. "First American Convention of Aero Clubs." *Aeronautics* (March 1910), 87–88.

———. "Many Opportunities for Good Fliers." *Aero* (April 9, 1911), 40.

"A Portfolio of Early Aviation Pictures." *Bulletin of the Missouri Historical Society* 8 (July 1952), 377–79.

Provenzo, Eugene F. Jr. "Thomas W. Benoist—Early Pioneer St. Louis Aviator (1874–1917)." *Bulletin of the Missouri Historical Society* 31 (January 1975), 91–104.

"Recognition for Gardner," *Aeronautics* (October 30, 1914), 119.

Reilly, Thomas. "The Miami Curtiss Flying School." *World War I Aero* 155 (February 1997), 24–26.

———. "National Airlines: The St. Petersburg Years, 1934–1939." *Air Line Pilot* 66 (February 1997), 38–61.

———. "Roger, the Other Jannus." *American Aviation Historical Society Journal* 42 (Spring 1997), 30–33.

Roberts, E. W. "Advantages of the Two-Cycle Engine." *Aero Digest* (November 1940), 145.

Roos, Fred. "Gateway News." *American Institute of Aeronautics and Astronautics* (November 1984), 3–6.

"St. Petersburg Historical and Flight One Museum." *World War I Aero* (August 1993), 102.

"The Story of Aviation in Baltimore." *Baltimore* (November 1941), 22.

Warner, Richard Fay. "First Scheduled Air Line." *Air Line Pilot* (December 1953), 4.

"Where Are They Now." *Chirp* (March 1939), 6–7.

White, Edward J. "A Century of Transportation in Missouri." *Missouri Historical Review* 15 (October 1920), 158–62.

White, Gay. "First Airline." *Delta Digest* (January 1964), 5.

Wilkens, George. "Chalk It Up to History." *Tampa Tribune*, Bay Life Section (August 22, 1993), 1.

Woodhouse, Henry. "Growing Wings, Aviation Rises Though Aviators Fall, and Aeroplanes Steadily Become Safer." *Collier's Weekly* (November 9, 1912), 14.

PERIODICALS

Aerial Age Weekly, 1915, 1916.
Aero, 1910, 1911, 1912.
Aero and Hydro, 1912, 1913, 1914.
Aero Digest, 1929.
Aeronautics, 1910, 1911, 1912, 1913, 1914.
Aviation, 1916.
Flight, 1915, 1916.
Florida Aviation Historical Society News, 1977–94.
Florida Historical Quarterly, 1959.
Fly Magazine, 1912, 1913.
Flying, 1914, 1915.
Motor Car, 1913.

NEWSPAPERS

Baltimore Evening Sun, 1914, 1915.
Cairo Bulletin, 1912.
Chicago Daily Tribune, 1912.
Detroit Free Press, 1912.
Detroit News, 1913.
Detroit Times, 1912.
Duluth Daily News Tribune, 1913.
Grand Rapids Herald, 1913.
Houston Chronicle, 1948.
Indianapolis Star, 1914.
Kansas City Star, 1913.
Memphis Commercial Appeal, 1912.
Memphis Reveille, 1912.
Montgomery Standard, 1912.
New Orleans Times Democrat, 1913.
New York Times, 1912, 1913, 1914, 1915, 1916.
Omaha News, 1912.
Paducah News Democrat, 1913, 1914.
St. Louis Globe-Democrat, 1911, 1912, 1913, 1914, 1952.
St. Louis Post-Dispatch, 1911, 1912, 1913, 1914.
St. Louis Republic, 1911, 1912, 1913.
St. Louis Star, 1912, 1913.
St. Louis Times, 1911.
St. Petersburg Daily Times, 1912, 1913, 1914, 1915.
St. Petersburg Evening Independent, 1913, 1914.
St. Petersburg Times, 1963, 1982.
Sandusky Register, 1917.
Sandusky Register-Star-News, 1953.
Tampa Times, 1914.
Washington Post, 1908, 1910, 1911.

MISCELLANEOUS

Aero Club of America Articles of Incorporation, and Bylaws, 1911. New York: Aero
    Club of America, 1911.
Aero Club of St. Louis: Purposes-Results, 1907–1910. St. Louis: Aero Club of St.
    Louis, 1910.
American Air Mail Catalogue. Albion, Penn.: American Air Mail Society, 1947.
Ausmus, Reinhardt. Photographic album in the aviation collection of the Ru-
    therford B. Hayes Presidential Center, Fremont, Ohio.
———. Scrapbook in the aviation collection of the Rutherford B. Hayes Presi-
    dential Center, Fremont, Ohio.

———. Speech in the aviation collection of the Rutherford B. Hayes Presidential Center, Fremont, Ohio.

Benoist, Tom W. Scrapbook, Florida Aviation Historical Society Archives, St. Petersburg.

Benoist advertising catalogs, 1912, 1913, 1914, 1915, 1916, 1917. Florida Aviation Historical Society Archives, St. Petersburg, Florida.

"Chalmers Convention Doings." Chalmers in-house publication, 1914.

"Early Bird" questionnaires, 1952. Florida Aviation Historical Society Archives, St. Petersburg.

"A Guide to Aircraft at the Paul E. Garber Facility." Washington, D.C.: National Air and Space Museum.

Handbill produced by the Hefner Grocery Co., St. Petersburg Museum of History Archives, St. Petersburg.

Instructions for installing and operation, Roberts Marine Motors, no date.

"James D. Smith Story." Unpublished manuscript, Florida Aviation Historical Society Archives, St. Petersburg.

Jannus Brothers advertising circular, 1915.

Jannus, Roger W. Photographic album.

Jannus, "Tony." Letterhead.

Poster advertising Jannus's flights at St. Cloud, Minnesota, August 7, 1912. Florida Aviation Historical Society Archives, St. Petersburg.

Poster advertising the Memphis Fair, September 1912. Florida Aviation Historical Society Archives, St. Petersburg.

Poster advertising the Union City Fair, Union City, Tennessee, September 1912. Florida Aviation Historical Society Archives, St. Petersburg.

Poster advertising the Weakley County Fair, October 1912. Florida Aviation Historical Society Archives, St. Petersburg.

Roberts Aviation Motors catalog, 1916.

Roberts Aviation Motors, Roberts Mfg. Co., circular, 1911.

Roberts Aviation Motors, Roberts Motor Mfg. Co., circular, 1916.

Robinson, Hugh. Scrapbook in possession of George L. Vergara, Coral Gables, Florida.

Saunders, Rose Bryant. "The Lost Bell." Unpublished manuscript, Kemah, Texas, 1993.

Smith, James D. Diary. St. Petersburg Museum of History, St. Petersburg.

Smith, James D. Scrapbook. Florida Aviation Historical Society Archives, St. Petersburg.

White, Gay Blair. Papers. Florida Aviation Historical Society Archives, St. Petersburg.

Woodcock, Reginald D. "Benoist." Unpublished manuscript, Haverford, Penn., 1971.

GOVERNMENT DOCUMENTS

Certificate of death for Frank M. Bell. Texas Department of Health, Bureau of Vital Statistics, February 21, 1951.

Certified copy of record of death for Frank Merrill Bell. State of Mississippi, State Board of Health, Bureau of Vital Statistics, February 23, 1952.

Department of Commerce and Labor Steamboat Inspection Service license, serial no. 54578, issued to Antony H. Jannus, August 10, 1914.

Return of a birth, Office of the Health Officer, Washington, D.C. Birth certificate for Antony Habersack Jannus, 1889. Florida Aviation Historical Society Archives, St. Petersburg.

Return of a birth, Office of the Health Officer, Washington, D.C. Birth Certificate of Roger Weightman Jannus, 1886. Florida Aviation Historical Society Archives, St. Petersburg.

State of Ohio, Bureau of Vital Statistics, certificate of death, file no. 4541, for Thomas W. Benoist.

Stenographic record of the United States District Court, Southern District of New York. United States of America, Plaintiff—v—Curtiss Aeroplane Co., et al., Defendants. Civil Action, 13–450, Glenn Curtiss Museum, Hammondsport, New York.

U.S. Bureau of the Census. *Thirteenth Census of the United States: 1910, Population*. Vol. 2. Washington, D.C., 1913.

U.S. Department of the Interior, Office of Education in Washington, Radio Division, with the Cooperation of the Smithsonian Institution, *Early Wings for Commerce*, January 1 and 8, 1939, p. 2.

U.S. Patent Office, Safety Device for Elevators, Patent No. 604,361, dated May 24, 1898.

U.S. Patent Number 1,053,182, filed March 9, 1912, and patented on February 18, 1913.

United States Patent Gazette 151 (December 14, 1909): 726.

ORAL HISTORIES

Benoist, Charles. September 2, 1952, Florida Aviation Historical Society Archives, St. Petersburg.

Froelich, Russell. Interview by Christy Magrath, 1952, Florida Aviation Historical Society Archives, St. Petersburg.

Interviews with Hillery Beachey, Beckwith Havens, Matilde Moisant. Columbia University Oral History Collection.

Index

Thurman, Albert Lee, 146, 147, 162
Thurman opinion, 146, 147
Trefts Jr., William J., 48, 55, 74–78
Tuchkov, A. A., 184

United States Army Signal Corps, 13, 20, 21, 23, 53, 54, 194
United States Department of Agriculture's Weather Bureau, 153
United States Department of Interior, 154
United States of America v. Curtiss Aeroplane Co., 191, 192
United States Volunteer Aviation Corps, 160
Utgoff, Lieutenant Victor, 180, 187, 190

Védrines, Jules, 56, 57, 60
Verplanck, J. B. R., 106, 107
Verville, Alfred, 41
Vilas, Jack, 105

Waite, Henry R., 4
Walcott, Dr. Charles D., 16
Wanamaker, Rodman, 110, 111, 194
Ward, Jimmie, 35, 36
Warner, Charles, 14
Washington Monument, 14, 22
Washington Post, 15, 20, 22, 23, 26
Weddington, Harry, 152
Weightman, Major General Roger Chew, 4, 5

Weightman, Major Richard Hanson, 5
West Point, 5
Wheeler, Raymond, 51
White, Gay Blair, 6, 181, 198, 199
Whitney, H. L., 142, 144, 145, 147
Whitney, L. A., 120, 127, 130, 154
Whitney, Mrs. L. A., 147
Wigwam Hotel, 151
Williams, Dorothy, 19
Williams, Jack, 152
Wills, Nat, 20
Wilson, Julia, 152
Windom, Ross, 199
Witmer, Charles C., 183
Wood, C. Murvin, 112, 113
Wood, Colonel William T., 44
Woodcock, Reginald, 4, 29, 101, 115
Woodhouse, Henry, 120, 161
Woodlief, John, 82, 86
World War I, 1, 2, 112, 151, 161, 167, 182, 183
Wright brothers, 1, 10, 12–14, 16, 18, 30, 40, 57, 86, 90, 118, 124, 160, 188, 194, 195
Wright, Orville, 1, 30, 52, 69, 111, 112
Wright, Roderick, 188
Wright, Wilbur, 1, 30, 46, 52, 57

Yockel's Park, Maryland, 24, 166

Zahm, Dr. Alfred, 41, 181